Writing Training Materials That Work

Writing Training Materials That Work

How to Train Anyone to Do Anything

A Practical Guide for Trainers Based on Current Cognitive Psychology and ID Theory and Research

Wellesley R. Foshay
Kenneth H. Silber
Michael B. Stelnicki

JOSSEY-BASS/PFEIFFER
A Wiley Imprint
www.pfeiffer.com

Published by Jossey-Bass/Pfeiffer

A Wiley Imprint

989 Market Street, San Francisco, CA 94103-1741   www.pfeiffer.com

Jossey-Bass/Pfeiffer books and products are available through most bookstores. To contact Jossey-Bass/Pfeiffer directly call our Customer Care Department within the U.S. at 800-274-4434, outside the U.S. at 317-572-3985 or fax 317-572-4002.

Jossey-Bass/Pfeiffer also publishes its books in a variety of electronic formats. Some content that appears in print may not be available in electronic books.

Printed in the United States of America

ISBN: 0-7879-6411-5

Library of Congress Cataloging-in-Publication Data

Foshay, Rob.
Writing training materials that work : how to train anyone to do
anything / Rob Foshay, Kenneth H. Silber, Michael B. Stelnicki.
    p. cm.
    Includes bibliographical references and index.
    ISBN 0-7879-6411-5   (alk. paper)
    1. Employees—Training of. 2. Training manuals. I. Silber, Kenneth
H. II. Stelnicki, Michael B., 1939- III. Title.
HF5549.5.T7 F6677 2003
    658.3'12404—dc21
    2002014795

Acquiring Editor: Matthew Davis
Director of Development: Kathleen Dolan Davies
Editor: Rebecca Taff
Senior Production Editor: Dawn Kilgore
Manufacturing Supervisor: Becky Carreño
Cover Design: Chris Wallace

Printed in the United States of America
Printing 10 9 8 7 6 5 4 3 2

To Belinda, Miriam, and Suzanne
and, as with everything we write,
to Jim Finn, Tom Schwen,
C. Stelnicki, and Wells Foshay,
who started us on the path of
inquiry in the field.

Contents

List of Figures

Contents of the CD-ROM

Acknowledgments

We would like to thank PLATO Learning, Inc., for permission to use its instructional design knowledge base, which served as the basis of the summary tables in this book. In particular, we would like to thank Bob Mulcahy of PLATO Learning for contributing examples. In addition, we would like to thank the students at Governors' State University and Northern Illinois University, who suffered through many early drafts of each chapter and provided many valuable suggestions. We also would like to thank Paul Kasten and Steve Larson for their contributions to the case problem scenarios. We would like to thank the Association for Educational Communications and Technology and the International Association for Performance Improvement for their permission to reuse our writings from their publications. We would like to thank Suzanne Frank for her patient assistance in editing the final manuscript. We would like to thank Ruth Clark, Minjuan Wang, George Piskurich, and Janis Chan for their insightful comments during the review and editing process. Finally, and perhaps most importantly, we would like to thank Matthew C. Davies, Kathleen Dolan Davies, and Dawn Kilgore of Jossey-Bass/Pfeiffer for seeing the importance of this book and for making the book as readable and usable as it is.

Preface

We decided to write this book to provide the field of instructional design with a practical, yet theoretically based, handbook on the development of instructional materials based on cognitive psychology. We felt such a book was needed for the experienced practitioner and graduate student to provide:

- A current synthesis and summary of "best practice" ID as compared with (a) the "fad instructional techniques of the year" or (b) emerging ideas and theories that form the intellectual debates of university professors. We define this "best practice" as "specific how-to practice guidelines that (a) are research-based, (b) have been used by practitioners long enough to show they are acceptable and can be implemented in business/industry settings, and (c) produce consistently good instructional results."

- A translation of cognitive psychology research on learning and memory into useful prescriptions for the practitioner of ID. We do this translation in an eclectic, non-doctrinaire manner, drawing from multiple schools of cognitive psychology thought, while at the same time keeping the tried-and-true behaviorist ID principles that still work well.

- A focus on how to teach higher-order problem-solving skills—the skills most instructional designers need to provide in an information-age, service-oriented company. This is an area where progress on research and theory has been substantial, yet the new discoveries are not reflected in current standard ID texts. At the same time, we address the lower-level skills that you may still need to teach.

The body of knowledge of cognitive psychology is still evolving, and we are aware that there are many differing perspectives about how it should be applied to training development. Therefore, we would like to begin by presenting a set of assumptions, biases, and caveats about this book.

- The book is our synthesis of research and theory into prescriptive recommendations for daily professional practice. This is a different criterion from what would be used for a review of research or for a textbook for future researchers.

- The book is based on our assessment of what principles in the cognitive learning and instruction literature are internally consistent, prescriptive, and have been demonstrated empirically to make a worthwhile (cost-effective) difference in situations likely to be of interest to trainers. Since most current "hot topics" in the literature do not yet have that depth of research and experience, there are many current issues (most notably constructivism) which we do not include. By excluding them from discussion, we do not mean to imply that they are unimportant, only that they are not yet fully enough developed and proven to become part of the repertoire of a professional practitioner.

- We make no claim that our synthesis is the only correct one, only that it is a sound and practical one. We can say this because it is based on practice as it has evolved at PLATO Learning, Inc., over the past six years. PLATO is a major developer of computer-based multimedia training for the aviation, technical, and school markets. It's best known product is the PLATO® computer-based instructional system. In addition, we have validated the chapters teaching prescriptive principles in continuing professional training and in pre-service classes taught at Governors' State and Northern Illinois Universities.

- We have no ideological agenda; we are not attempting to displace or disparage earlier syntheses, nor do we intend to purely reflect any particular theoretical position. We have used certain theoretical frameworks (with acknowledgment, we hope), but we have combined them in ways the original authors did not—and might even disavow.

- Those seeking a simple, step-by-step "cookbook" of instructional design will be disappointed. While we have attempted to be concrete in our prescriptions and examples, our goal has been to define heuristics (principles and guidelines), not algorithms (definitive "if . . . then" rules). This approach is based on our belief that the state of the art in instructional design, particularly beyond the most introductory level, requires a heuristic approach. We will leave to others the debate over whether this is intrinsically so, or whether it is only a reflection of the current state of our knowledge.

- Our recommendations are intended to be media-neutral. This is not a book about design of platform, multimedia, or any other format for training. Although people today tend to think in terms of e-learning and computers, we have chosen to focus on instructional strategies that apply across all media and delivery strategies. In the book, we have used one example that is classroom based and one that is e-learning based to show that the strategies apply across media.

One note: Readers with a background in cognitive psychology may wonder whether we have forgotten the chapter on teaching cognitive strategies and meta-cognition. We address these topics, but indirectly. Although cognitive strategies and meta-cognition are particularly important in ill-structured problem solving, current research generally discourages attempts to teach cognitive strategies and meta-cognition—or any kind of problem solving—independent of its context. Therefore, we believe they should be addressed as part of ill-structured problem solving, rather than as independent lessons.

In our view, the recommendations for teaching ill-structured problem solving *are* the directions for teaching cognitive strategies and meta-cognition.

October 2002

Wellesley R. Foshay
Kenneth H. Silber
Michael B. Stelnicki

Introduction

*T*his book takes cognitive psychology research on learning and memory and, in a non-doctrinaire manner, converts it into useful "best practice" techniques, while at the same time retaining the tried-and-true behaviorist ID principles that still work well. This book is written to provide you with an approach to developing instructional materials that is:

- Effective
- "Best practice"
- Implementable
- Non-doctrinaire
- Fad-free
- Efficient
- Results-oriented

The approach offered in this book produces effective materials because it is based on the latest research, which measures learning outcomes in cognitive psychology. While keeping what still works from the behavioral approach to instructional design with which you are familiar, this approach will expand your repertoire of instructional strategies to include techniques based on the findings of cognitive psychologists on how people learn.

The approach identifies, synthesizes, and summarizes "best practice" ID—which we define as "specific how-to practice guidelines that (a) are research-based, (b) have been used by practitioners long enough to show they are acceptable and can be implemented in business/industry settings, and (c) produce consistently good instructional results."

Although this approach applies the latest research and theory, it is one you can implement because we have done all the work of synthesizing the complex and conflicting ideologies, theories, and issues in cognitive psychology into an approach that is correct, yet functional.

This approach provides a non-doctrinaire synthesis of principles from all schools of cognitive research. It does not require you to favor one school, author, or approach over another. If you do favor a particular one, you will still find the principles in this book congruent with those of your preference.

This approach is based on research, not on fad. It separates "research-based best practice" in ID from (a) the new "fad instructional techniques of the year" and (b) emerging "hot topics" that form the intellectual debates among university professors—none of which yet has the depth of research and experience to merit wholesale adoption.

The approach is efficient because it makes clear what instructional elements you should include in a lesson and how you should structure those elements. By following the instructionally sound templates as you design, you will build in learning effectiveness while reducing your design time.

This approach produces *results* because it is focused on teaching problem-solving skills that allow learners to generalize and transfer learning to new situations without requiring constant retraining. At the same time, it includes how to teach the lower-level skills that you might still need to teach.

SCOPE AND TREATMENT

To achieve our purpose, we included detailed discussions of the cognitive approach to instructional design, the two categories of knowledge (declarative and procedural), and instructional strategies for teaching six types of instructional objectives: facts, concepts, principles, and mental models, well-structured problem solving, troubleshooting, and ill-structured problem solving. It also contains, in Part III, more detailed discussions of the theoretical issues involved in teaching each of the types of objectives, and an overview of cognitive task analysis.

We have attempted to follow our own instructional advice in writing and designing the book, to the extent possible within the constraints of production cost, size, and the printed page. We have made extensive use of the instructional elements we recommend. One of the most common weaknesses of books in this field is a lack of examples, particularly to illustrate strategy. This book provides two examples in the initial presentation of each instructional strategy and, in Chapter 11, a fully worked lesson. Our own advice would preclude us from offering this book as a "complete training course for instructional designers." While the book contains many of the instructional elements we recommend for a sound instructional lesson, the nature of the medium and purpose of the book require us to omit some key elements, notably practice and feedback. It will require you to practice the skills on your own and to obtain feedback (as well as additional explanation and examples where appropriate) from an instructor or an exemplary instructional designer in your workplace.

In this already lengthy volume, we do *not* discuss (a) the entire instructional design process, (b) the state of cognitive learning research and theory, (c) front-end analysis of any kind, (d) evaluation, (e) cognitive task analysis, or (f) psychomotor and attitudinal learning. While these are important topics, they are beyond the scope of this book. There are other excellent books by this publisher and others that do address these areas in the detail they deserve.

INTENDED AUDIENCE

The primary audience for this book is training and instructional design practitioners in business and industry who have had at least three years' experience developing training, have taken either one of the common entry-level design workshops such as Mager, Clark, Sink, or Harless or an instructional design course at a university, and who desire to expand their skills based on the latest theory and practice in the ID field.

The secondary audience is instructional technology masters' and doctoral degree university students in an advanced instructional design course who have completed at least an introductory ID course using a textbook such as Dick and Carey (2001), Seels and Glasgow (1998), or Smith and Ragan (1999).

ORGANIZATION OF THE BOOK

This book is divided into three parts. Part I is a general introduction to the cognitive approach to instructional development and to the model for lesson development we have synthesized. Chapter 1, "The Cognitive Approach to Training Development," describes why the cognitive approach to ID/training development is important, how learning occurs according to the cognitive point of view, and the different categories of learning according to cognitive psychology. Chapter 2, "A Cognitive Training Model," is an introduction to the seventeen elements that must be in lessons readers will develop. These elements serve as the basis for "how to."

Part II is the heart, the "how to" portion, of the book, with two of its nine chapters addressing elements to include in all lessons, six explaining how to teach each of the six types of instructional objectives, and one explaining how to put it all together to create lessons that combine different types of objectives in one continuous lesson. Each chapter in this part contains a general description of the key issues in development, a set of general guidelines for development, and a set of step-by-step design prescriptions, along with examples to illustrate them.

The introduction to Part II has two purposes: it shows the structure of the nine chapters to help you navigate through them and provides information about the companies that are used for the examples.

Chapter 3, "How to Begin Any Lesson: The First Three Elements," contains an explanation of how to begin a lesson for any category of learning objective with the first three elements of a lesson: attention; what's in it for me? (WIIFM); and you can do it (YCDI). It discusses what each element is, presents a brief summary of the issues in using it, and provides a detailed "how to do it" for each lesson element.

In Chapter 4, "How to Organize and Present Information: Message Design Elements," we explain how to present and organize the information called for in the other fourteen elements of the model by focusing on the message design: chunking, text layout, and illustrations.

Chapter 5, "Teaching Facts," explains how to use the remaining fourteen elements of the model to teach fact objectives. We begin with a discussion of what facts are and a brief summary of the issues in teaching them. Then we describe the training goal and general strategies involved in teaching facts and present a detailed description of "how to do it" for each lesson element, plus examples.

Chapters 6 through 10 follow the same presentation sequence, but focus on different types of instructional objectives. Chapter 6, "Teaching Concepts," describes how to teach concepts. Chapter 7, "Teaching Principles and Mental Models," describes how to teach principles and mental models (with their supporting concepts and facts). Chapter 8, "Teaching Well-Structured Problem-Solving: Procedures," describes how to teach the simple rote procedures that form the basis of much instruction today. Chapter 9, "Teaching Ill-Structured Problem-Solving," includes the type of complex issues our learners meet in life, such as designing a new building, redesigning a work process, and introducing a new product. Chapter 10, "Teaching Troubleshooting," describes how to teach the special case of moderately structured problem solving called "troubleshooting," for example, software debugging and some kinds of medical diagnosis. Chapter 11, "Teaching Complete Lessons," explains how to create two combined continuous lessons: (1) combining facts, concepts, and principles and (2) well-structured and ill-structured problem solving. One example in this chapter uses computer-based training.

Part III is the "theory" or "why" portion of the book, where we go into some detail on the theory and research issues underlying the "how to" chapters. Chapter 12, "Issues Underlying the Cognitive Approach to Instructional Design," revisits the subject of Chapters 1 and 2 at a more theoretical level for those interested in exploring the cognitive approach with a larger theory and research base. Chapter 13, "Issues Underlying Teaching Declarative Knowledge," describes, in a more theoretical way than did Chapters 5 through 7, what declarative knowledge is, how it is different from procedural knowledge, what the types of declarative knowledge are, what the research issues in teaching declarative knowledge are, and what the research says that led to prescriptions in the earlier chapters. Chapter 14, "Issues Underlying Teaching Procedural Knowledge," follows the same pattern as Chapter 13, only addresses in more detail issues related to procedural knowledge as discussed in Chapters 8 through 10.

The "Further Reading" section contains the full references for all the citations used throughout the book and provides the interested reader with places to go to explore the topic of this book in more depth.

HOW TO USE THE BOOK

We have structured the book so that both our intended audiences can use the book most productively.

For *practitioners*, we suggest you read the book in the following sequence the first time through:

- Part I: Chapters 1 and 2
- Part II: Introduction, Chapters 3, 4, 5, 6, 7, 8, 9, 10, 11

For *graduate students and other readers interested in theory and research findings*, we suggest you read the book in this sequence the first time:

- Part I: Chapters 1 and 2
- Part III: Chapters 12, 13, 14
- Part II: Introduction, Chapters 3, 4, 5, 6, 7, 8, 9, 10, 11

You can use the "how to" chapters in Part II in different ways, depending on your purpose—learning or working. As you read Chapters 3 through 11 the first time, we suggest reading each chapter in full, and in the sequence provided:

- Overview.
- Discussion of what the objectives are and a brief summary of the issues in teaching it.
- Description of general instructional strategies involved in teaching the objective.
- Detailed description of "how to do it" for each lesson element and examples.

If you are using this book as a guide to practicing ID, we suggest you focus on the examples, detailed strategy descriptions, and design tools for whatever type of lesson you are creating. Depending on your work style, you might start with the complete examples in Chapter 11 and then move to the detailed element-by-element strategy guidelines in the appropriate chapter (5 through 10), and finally use the design tool in Chapter 2. Another approach would be to start with the design tools in Chapters 5 through 10, working through the element-by-element strategy guidelines in the appropriate chapters, and refer to the complete examples in Chapter 11 only as you put the whole lesson together.

DESIGN TOOLS

To help you do your instructional design using the cognitive approach discussed in this book, we have provided tools for you to use in your ID practice. Blank templates are on a CD-ROM and include:

- Templates for developing lessons for the following types of objectives: facts, concepts, principles and mental models, well-structured problem solving, troubleshooting, and ill-structured problem solving.

- Templates for sequencing the objectives into a coherent lesson, including a lesson with only declarative knowledge and a lesson that teaches procedural knowledge, recalling previously taught declarative knowledge.

You can find these tools both in the book (as completed examples) and on the CD that comes with the book.

We hope you will use the tools in *Writing Training Materials That Work* while using the cognitive approach to ID.

Part I

Introduction to the Cognitive Approach

*I*n this first part of the book, the basic overview of the cognitive approach and the lesson development model used throughout the book are introduced. Chapter 1 describes why the cognitive approach to instructional design is important, how learning occurs according to the cognitive point of view, and the different categories of learning according to cognitive psychology.

Chapter 2 lays out an introduction to the seventeen elements of the lesson development model in both narrative and tabular form. This model serves as the basis for the "how to" chapters in Part II. The part concludes by showing how to combine the lesson elements in the model for two types of lessons that include multiple objectives.

Think of the two chapters in this part of the book as being organized in this manner:

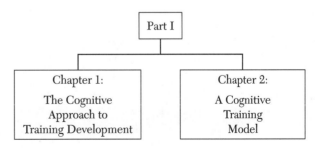

FIGURE 1.1. Chapter 1 Structure of Content

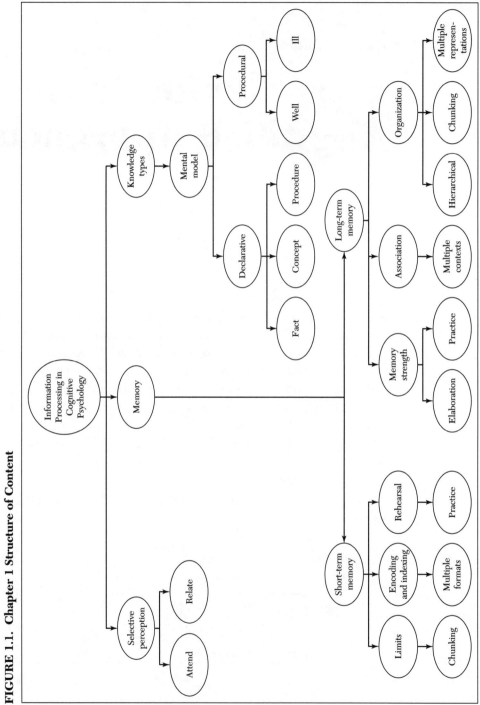

The Cognitive Approach to Training Development

LINK AND ORGANIZE

Recall

- You have already had an introductory ID workshop or course and/or have read an introductory ID textbook.

- The approach you learned there is the "traditional" behaviorally based approach to instructional design.

- You learned some categorization of different types or levels of learning (such as facts, concepts, principles, procedures, problem solving).

- You learned some set of instructional elements to include in a lesson (for example, gain attention, recall prior learning, inform of objective, present information, provide learning guidance, practice, feedback, test, transfer).

Relate to What You Already Know

- The cognitive approach is one that you can add to your existing ID skills; you do *not* need to forget everything you already know.

- The cognitive view of how learning takes place is different from the behavioral one. It is based on how new information is processed, stored, and retrieved in the mind, rather than on how behavior changes.

- The cognitive approach you are going to learn in this book builds on what you know, but adds some new elements:
    - It adds to the types or levels of learning you already know.
    - It adds to or changes the instructional elements you already know.

Structure of Content
- See Figure 1.1.

Objectives
- To describe why the cognitive approach to ID/training development is important.
- To describe how learning occurs according to the cognitive point of view.
- To describe the different categories of learning according to cognitive psychology.

THE COGNITIVE APPROACH TO INSTRUCTIONAL DESIGN

The cognitive approach to instructional design (ID) has become popular recently for two reasons, one based in the theory of learning and instructional design, the other based in business.

From the perspective of theory, the cognitive approach was developed to overcome a number of limitations of the behavioral approach currently used. These are listed below:

- Learners sometimes have trouble transferring what they have learned from training to the job.

- Learners can have trouble attaining expert-level performance in troubleshooting and problem solving on the job.

- Learners often have trouble generalizing their training from one situation to another, leading to skill gaps every time the job, content, or technology changes and creating the need for retraining.

- Learners may have difficulty with divergent reasoning (many right answers or many ways to get to the answer), as opposed to convergent reasoning (one right answer and one way to get it).

- Designers do not have adequate prescriptions for designing the kinds of training we are now being asked to design—problem solving, troubleshooting (especially in settings where content volatility is high), heuristic-based thinking (using guidelines versus algorithmic thinking, which uses formulas with 100 percent predictable outcomes), strategic thinking, and the like.

From the perspective of business, the current behavioral approach to ID sometimes leads to excessive development and delivery costs because it requires:

- Longer training sessions to cover all the specific algorithms or other content variations.

- More retraining time, to address lack of transfer to new situations.

- More development time, since there are no guidelines for creating training for higher order thinking and developers must either guess or treat problem solving as a large number of low-level procedures and concepts.

The cognitive approach to ID offers remedies to these problems. It provides designers with another way to design training that works well in situations where higher-order thinking, problem solving, and transfer to new situations are training goals.

THE COGNITIVE POINT OF VIEW ON HOW LEARNING OCCURS

There are many theoretical models in cognitive psychology about how learning occurs. According to these models, there are several components of the mind, and each is involved in the learning process in certain ways. Further, how each component of the mind works has implications for how we design instruction. The components are:

- Perception and sensory stores.
- Short-term memory.
- Long-term memory.

Perception and Sensory Stores

Perception Is Selective. There is more stimulation in the environment than we are capable of attending to and then encoding (internally translating) for storage in memory. Therefore, we only attend to certain things. We attend to and see/hear what we expect to see in a given situation. We attend to those things that interest us because they are either (a) related to what we already know or (b) so novel they force us to attend to them.

Limits of the Sensory Stores. Our sensory stores, also called sensory memories or "buffers," are capable of storing almost complete records of what we attend to. The catch is that they hold those records *very briefly.* During that very brief time before the record decays, we do one of two things: (1) we note the relationships among the elements in the record and encode it into a more permanent memory or (2) we lose the record forever.

IMPLICATIONS FOR ID

- Get the learner to *attend to* the parts of the environment you want learned (hence the emphasis on capturing the learner's attention and on motivational statements).
- Help the learner note *relationships* among the bits of information quickly (hence the importance of organizing the information you are presenting and of clearly relating the new information to existing familiar or important contexts and knowledge).

Short-Term or Working Memory

Controversy. There is disagreement among cognitive psychologists about whether short-term memory is "separate and different" from long-term memory—whether the two types of memory are physically different or whether they are just conceptually different constructs. There is also discussion about how information is encoded, how it is stored, and so on. Regardless of the theoretical differences, most psychologists agree on the following points.

Rehearsal. When information is passed from the sensory stores to memory, we mentally rehearse it. Examples include repeating phone numbers several times or creating associations to names (*Ted* with the *red* hair) to help memorize them. The former, simply repeating the information over and over, is called *passive rehearsal.* It does not seem to improve memory as well as rehearsing the information in a *deep and meaningful* way, such as by creating associations.

Limited Capacity. There seems to be a limit on the amount of information we can rehearse at one time. A classic study by Bell Labs in (Miller, 1956) showed we can remember 7 ± 2 bits of information at most, and that to remember more we have to "chunk" (or group) information in manageable sizes; that's why your phone number has seven digits and why people in the United States remember phone numbers in three chunks (1aaa-bbb-cccc).

Format. At this point in the learning process, the information being rehearsed is not yet organized and encoded as it will be when it is later stored in memory. Also, there is some evidence that there are separate spaces for storing and rehearsing verbal information and visual/spatial information, and possibly separate spaces for other types of memories as well.

IMPLICATIONS FOR ID

- Help learners use meaningful ways of rehearsing the information, as opposed to simply repeating it (through the use of analogies, by relating new information to existing knowledge or situations, and so on).
- Present the information in meaningful "chunks" of appropriate size for the learner population (knowing what your learners already know about the subject they are learning is critical to determining "appropriate size").
- Present the information in multiple formats (verbal, auditory, visual), which can help learners rehearse, and therefore remember, better.
- Present the information in a way that allows the learner to move quickly from rehearsing the information to encoding it and integrating (indexing) it with other information in long-term memory.

Long-Term Memory

In general, theorists believe that long-term memory is organized based on context and experience. That means we encode, store, and retrieve information in the way we have used knowledge in the past and expect to use it again in the future. Psychologists note several phenomena that strengthen the memory process.

Memory Strength. Information in memory has a characteristic called *strength,* which increases with practice. A *power law of learning* governs the relationship between amount of practice and response time or error rates (strength = practice to power X). In simple terms, this means that practice increases the strength of learning exponentially (double the practice at least squares the strength of the learned information in memory; triple the practice increases the strength by a factor of nine).

Elaboration. Elaboration means adding information to the information being learned. The more we elaborate on what we learn through processing, the better we remember it. This is because, as we tie the new information to existing information or we create other information related to the new information, we create more pathways to get to the new information as we try to remember it.

Chunking. Memories are stored not as individual bits or as long strings of information, but in "chunks," with each chunk containing about seven elements. As explained earlier, how large an "element" and a "chunk" are differs based on the learner's existing knowledge.

Verbal and Visual Information. It seems we encode verbal and visual information differently in memory. We use a linear code for verbal information and a spatial code for visual information. We remember visual information very well, especially if we can place a meaningful interpretation on the visuals. In addition, it has been shown in Gestalt psychology that we remember incomplete and strange images better than complete, standard ones. With verbal information, we remember the meaning of the information, not the exact words.

Associations and Hierarchy. Information is organized in memory, grouped in a set of relationships or structures (for example, hierarchically). Using such a structure makes it easier for us to remember, because more related pieces of information are activated when we search for information. While you may not remember one specific piece of information in the structure, you may remember the overall structure and some pieces in it, and from that you can remember or create the missing piece of information. For example, you may not remember all the numbers in the 12×12 multiplication tables, but if you remember some key ones (1, 2, 3, and 5 times a number) you can construct the rest.

By comparison with computers, humans can remember far fewer separate pieces of data, but are much better equipped for pattern recognition skills, such as analogical reasoning, inference, and comprehension of visual and verbal languages.

IMPLICATIONS FOR ID

- Build a lot of meaningful practice into training to increase the probability of retention (for example, the PQ4R method = preview, question, read, reflect, review, recite).
- Provide learners with information or allow them to create information that elaborates on the information to be learned.
- Present the information in meaningful "chunks" of appropriate size for the learner population (knowing your learners is critical).
- Present the information so it uses the learners' abilities to remember both verbal and visual information.
- Organize the information being presented hierarchically (to approximate the way information is stored in memory) to increase retention.
- Provide many associations to the information being learned to increase the chances the information will be retrieved when called for.
- Teach learners to organize/index their memories so they have many associations, many retrieval paths, and appropriate structures.
- Use authentic (real-world) contexts for explanations, examples, and practice to help the learners relate what they learn to situations in which they will need to use the knowledge.

DECLARATIVE AND PROCEDURAL KNOWLEDGE AND THEIR SUBTYPES

Cognitive psychologists often draw distinctions between different categories of knowledge. When you design training, you will probably find it helpful to use these distinctions. The biggest distinction is between *declarative* and *procedural* knowledge: *Declarative* knowledge is knowing *that*, whereas *procedural* knowledge is knowing *how*.

Examples of Declarative Knowledge

- Remembering your telephone number.
- Being able to tell the difference between a table and a tray.
- Stating that for a car engine to run, it must have air, fuel, and electrical current for the ignition.

Examples of Procedural Knowledge

- Following a recipe to bake a cake.
- Building a spreadsheet "from scratch" using a software package for spreadsheets.
- Fixing the copier so it will stop jamming.
- Designing a copier that can't jam.

The basic difference between the two types of knowledge is that declarative knowledge tells you *how the world is*, while procedural knowledge tells you *how to do things in the world*.

Trainers who don't understand this distinction often confuse *knowing* and *doing*, and thus make the following kinds of mistakes when designing training:

- They try to teach (and test) procedural knowledge using strategies suited for declarative knowledge.
- They teach declarative knowledge and stop, assuming that the procedural knowledge will naturally follow on its own.
- They try to teach the procedural knowledge without teaching the associated declarative knowledge.

It's important to understand the different types of declarative and procedural knowledge so that, when you plan your instruction, you can use instructional strategies appropriate to each type. If you're good at making these distinctions, you may be able to save considerable time and expense in developing and delivering your training, while improving its effectiveness. The different types are discussed briefly below and described in detail in later chapters devoted to how to teach each type.

Types of Declarative Knowledge

There are three types of declarative knowledge: *facts, concepts,* and *principles and mental models.* The discussion of these types below is a synthesis of much that is already familiar and commonly accepted. The reader will note that these types of declarative knowledge are very similar to the types of learning proposed by Gagne (1985) and taught in most basic ID texts (for example, Dick & Carey, 2001). However, the notion of mental models is ours and we have described the characteristics of all in slightly different terms.

Facts. A fact is a simple association among a set of verbal and/or visual propositions. Some examples of facts are:

- On a traffic light, red means stop, green means go, and yellow means prepare to stop.
- In 1492 Christopher Columbus sailed from Spain and landed in the Caribbean; he was not the first to do so, nor did he discover America.
- Miller's (1956) study for Bell Labs said the largest number of digits a person could remember easily was seven.
- The five steps to create a table in MS Word 6.0 for Windows 95 are (1) select tables, (2) select number of rows, (3) select number of columns, (4) select line appearance, (5) click OK.

When you know a fact, you have placed it in a structure so you can recall it from memory. Learning facts as part of a structure that will help you recall them in the way you need them is much more efficient than trying to memorize each fact by itself. Simply knowing a fact does *not* mean you can generalize it to new situations, explain what it means, identify its relationship to other facts, or apply it to do anything.

Concepts. A concept is a category of objects, actions, or abstract ideas you group together with a single name because they share characteristics in common. Some examples of concepts are:

- Cars (vs. trucks, campers, or utility vehicles)
- Jogging (vs. running, walking)
- Beautiful sunrises (vs. beautiful sunsets, ugly sunrises)
- Justice (vs. injustice)
- Performance improvement (vs. training)

When you know a concept, you can classify new objects, actions, or ideas as either in the category or not. People typically learn concepts by remembering the best example of the category they've seen (or imagined). They may or may not be able to state the concept verbally. Concepts do not exist in isolation; all concepts have related concepts (parts or kinds, more general, more specific). Items in a given category that do not belong to one concept in the category do belong to another concept in the category.

Principles. A principle is a cause-effect relationship. When you understand a principle, you know how something works. Principles are frequently stated as "if . . . then . . ." statements. You can demonstrate your understanding of a principle by explaining why something happens or predicting what will happen. For example, you know that:

- If you see lightening nearby, you will hear thunder.
- If you turn the ignition key in a car, the engine will probably start.
- If you rob a bank, you may go to jail.
- If you write test items to match instructional objectives, the test will have certain types of validity.

Mental Models. The three types of declarative knowledge we've talked about so far fit together into structures called mental models or networks of principles, along with their supporting concepts and facts, stored in a meaningful structure based on (a) the context for which it was created and (b) the past learning and experiences of the learner. For cognitive psychologists, mental models are the key to learning and using knowledge because:

- They tie together all the declarative knowledge in memory.
- They are the structures into which you organize information, put it into memory, retrieve it from memory when needed, and learn by expanding and restructuring existing structures.
- They provide the most meaningful application of declarative knowledge (as adults we rarely spout networks of facts or run around finding new instances of concepts, but we do frequently try to explain how or why things happen or work).
- They form a bridge between declarative knowledge (knowledge about) and procedural knowledge (knowing how); before you can do procedures (other than rote ones), you have to "know how the system works," that is, have a mental model of the system.

Therefore, most would argue that, for training of adults, the instructional design must not only teach isolated facts, concepts, and principles, but must also help the learner create the appropriate mental models for optimum structuring of the information learned for storage, retrieval, and application.

Types of Procedural Knowledge

Procedural knowledge is the ability to string together a series of mental and physical actions to achieve a goal. Procedural knowledge is used to solve problems.

The way "problem" is used in this book may be a new concept for many readers. In the behavioral approach, instructional designers think about "procedures" and "problem solving" as two different things—two different levels in a hierarchy such as Gagne's. In the cognitive approach used in this book, the tendency is to use "procedural knowledge" and "problem solving" interchangeably, which many might find confusing initially. But our reasoning is that, since procedural knowledge is used to solve problems, the type of problem the knowledge is used to solve is what leads to the name of the procedural knowledge. See Figure 1.2 for problem characteristics.

FIGURE 1.2. Problem Characteristics

Definition	Example
a. There is an *initial state*, or the elements of the problem the learner is presented with.	You want to record five different TV programs broadcast on five different nights, each at a different time.
b. There is a *goal state*, or a description of the situation that would be a solution to the problem.	You need to program the VCR correctly to record the programs.
c. There is a *set of operations*, or things the learner can do to get from the initial state to the goal state.	You need to follow the step-by-step programming procedure furnished by your VCR and TV set manufacturers.
d. There is a *set of constraints*, or conditions which must not be violated by the learner in solving the problem (Glass, 1985). Anderson (1995) uses "Search" instead, as the mechanism of chaining together operations to get from initial to end state.	You must input the correct day, time, and channel for each program in the correct sequence. You must make sure there are no fund drives, presidential press conferences, "special" programs, or any other scheduling changes that would throw off the original times. You also have to make sure you're correctly specifying a.m. and p.m., correctly associated network name and channel number, and so on.

As you can see, problems always have a starting or *initial state* (car not running), an end or *goal state* (running car), a sequence of actions or *set of operations* (open door, get in, apply brake, insert key in ignition switch, turn key), and *set of constraints* (works only if you have the right key).

If the types of procedural knowledge and problem solving are placed on a continuum, at the most precise end are well-structured problems; at the least precise end are ill-structured problems; and in the middle are moderately structured problems.

Well-Structured Problem Solving. A term you may sometimes hear for well-defined procedural knowledge is *rote procedure.* We consider performing rote procedures to be well-structured problem solving. All elements of the problem situation are known. The initial state, goal state, and constraints are clearly defined. The operations are also clearly defined, although they may include a choice of alternatives (branches). The learner knows when to start the procedure and when to stop it. Examples of well-structured problem solving include:

- Ringing up a sale in a department stores.
- Calculating heating and air conditioning requirements for a building.
- Implementing a design for a database.
- Printing marketing pieces.

Well-structured problems are usually performed simply by recalling procedures and performing them exactly as taught. It's not even necessary to understand why the procedure works. Thus, in many situations it is optional to understand underlying *principles* that explain the *why* of a well-structured procedure.

Moderately Structured Problem Solving. In moderately structured problems, which include troubleshooting, the goal state is clear, and the learners might know the initial state and constraints. However, the learners probably have to recall and assemble in a novel way the operations that will take them from the initial state to the goal state, given the constraints. Examples of moderately structured problems include:

- Troubleshooting a "mis-ring" on a sale item in a department store.
- Developing a floor plan for a building.
- Planning how to implement a redesigned work process.
- Planning a marketing focus group.

Other examples are deciding on the most advantageous retirement package, deciding whether or not to fire an employee, determining whether to repair your old DVD player or buy a new one, determining whether or not to recommend that an employee seek company-provided counseling.

For moderately structured problems, it is important to understand the principles that underlie them. For example, a manager who wants to figure out how to motivate an employee needs to understand a few basic principles of motivation, if only at the common sense level.

Troubleshooting is a special "compound" case, in which an expert treats unfamiliar and/or complex problems as moderately structured and generates the operations. Some examples include determining the cause/source of a food poisoning outbreak, finding the source of a scraping noise when your car starts, determining why a metal stamping machine damages its stampings on a random basis, and figuring out why your refrigerator defrosts continually or your coffee maker doesn't work.

Ill-Structured Problem Solving. In ill-structured problems, which include most of the complex problems our learners encounter, three or all four of the elements of a problem are either missing completely or are present but not clear. Examples of ill-structured problems include:

- Deciding on the sale price for an item in a department store.
- Designing a new building.
- Redesigning a work process.
- Introducing a new product.

Other examples are holding a press conference on a highly controversial issue, conducting a workshop with learners who are highly resistant to learning the content, designing an artificial pancreas or an acceptable human blood substitute or an automobile that never wears out.

You've probably heard the old saw that "defining a problem is most of solving it." That refers especially to these ill-structured problems.

In Our View. For purposes of instructional design, in most circumstances there is little difference between moderately and ill-structured problems. Therefore, we will consider only two classes of problems: well-structured and ill-structured. We will consider moderately structured problems only in their special case— troubleshooting.

SUMMARY

In this chapter we have briefly described the key theoretical elements of *cognitive psychology* that underlie the ID strategies we will describe in this book.

We began by discussing the advantages of the cognitive approach, from both an instructional and a business perspective.

Then we discussed the cognitive view of the learning process: *perception and memory stores, short-term memory,* and *long-term memory.* For each element, we explained how the element works, some issues that impact learning, and some implications for instructional design.

Then we explained the different types of knowledge and gave brief descriptions and examples of each: declarative knowledge (*facts, concepts,* and *principles and mental models*).

We then briefly discussed the three types of procedural knowledge along a continuum from *well-structured* problems (at the most precise end of the continuum) to *moderately structured* problems (in the middle) to *ill-structured* problems (at the least precise end of the continuum).

FIGURE 2.1. Chapter 2 Structure of Content

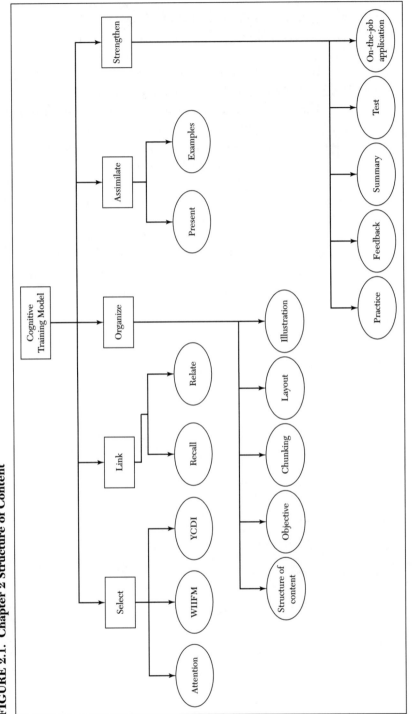

Chapter 2

A Cognitive Training Model

Recall (from Chapter 1)

- Research in the field of cognitive psychology into how perceptions and memories are stored and how short-term and long-term memory work has implications for how we design instruction.

- The cognitive approach to instructional design offers ways to design training content in the areas of problem solving, troubleshooting, and heuristic-based and strategic-based thinking.

- There are three types of declarative knowledge: facts, concepts, and principles/mental models.

- There are three types of procedural knowledge: well-structured, moderately structured, and ill-structured problem solving.

Relate to What You Already Know

- As an experienced instructional designer, you are probably already familiar with other teaching-learning models such as Gagne's "events of instruction" and Dick and Carey's "systematic design of instruction." These and others, like the cognitive training model presented in this chapter, consider what learners have to do to learn and what the instructional designer has to do to help them learn.

Structure of Content

- See Figure 2.1.

Objectives

- To describe the elements of a cognitive training model.
- To describe what is unique about the model.
- To describe how to apply the model.

A NEW COGNITIVE MODEL

Our summary of cognitive psychology presented in Chapter 1 described what we now understand about how people learn. We even showed, in general, how this new way of thinking about learning might affect instructional design. But thus far we did not tell you specifically how to apply these insights to design instruction differently.

The purpose of this book is to do just that, and this chapter serves as the beginning of the process. It is what you will learn to call a *structure of content* for the book and for each chapter. It describes at a high level what to include in cognitively based lessons you design.

This chapter presents a model that takes into account the five learning tasks cognitive psychologists have identified. For each learning task, we describe the two to five lesson elements trainers must use to help learners accomplish the learning task. We provide the blueprint for the lessons you will learn to develop in this book.

The model allows us:

- To synthesize and summarize the components of a well-designed lesson.
- To relate what learners have to do to learn to what we have to do as designers to help them.
- To present a general framework for instructional design up-front (each subsequent chapter will show how to apply this framework to teaching a certain type of knowledge).
- To provide a job aid that you can use as you design training.

We will present the model in two formats, first as a narrative description and then in tabular form.

LEARNER TASKS AND LESSON ELEMENTS

Learner Task 1: Select the Information to Attend To

The first task learners have is to select the information to attend to. The three lesson elements you will use to help learners accomplish this task are *attention, WIIFM* (What's in It for Me), and *YCDI* (You Can Do It).

In a training situation, stimuli related to what we want students to learn and extraneous stimuli are both present. You need to provide cues and signals to help learners select the appropriate stimuli in a form that can remain permanently in their minds, while they ignore unimportant but potentially distracting stimuli.

The first lesson element is *attention.* This element focuses the learners at the beginning of the lesson and keeps them focused throughout. One way to apply this lesson element is to introduce the new knowledge in a way that creates novelty or unpredictability. Another is to direct the learners' attention to specific verbal and visual parts of the lesson.

The second lesson element that helps learners select the information to attend to is *WIIFM,* or "What's in It for Me." This lesson element helps learners decide what to do with the new knowledge. For example, you might suggest how the material is relevant to their lives, can meet some specific needs, or can make their lives or jobs more productive or enjoyable. To apply the WIIFM, you will relate the training goals to the skills and knowledge the learners need, their personal goals, the needs of their organization, their job satisfaction, and the like.

The third lesson element that focuses and maintains the learners' attention is *YCDI,* or "You Can Do It." Lack of confidence is common among adult learners, and training designers often neglect to create confidence. People are more likely to learn when they feel that they are capable of mastering the new knowledge. To build confidence, relate the ways in which other learners have succeeded or explain how the people who are taking this training have already acquired knowledge related to the present content.

Learner Task 2: Link the New Information with Existing Knowledge

Next, learners need to link the new information with their existing knowledge. The two lesson elements you will use to help the learners do this are *recall* and *relate.*

When a learner says, "I didn't have a clue as to what the instructor was talking about!" the trainer has failed in helping the person relate the new information to what he or she already knew. Learners' memories need to be refreshed with prior or "old" content before they start processing the new material. That is, they need a review of previously learned facts, concepts, mental models, and procedures that they will need to learn the new material. In addition, they need to connect this prior learning to the new material and understand how it fits in with what they already know.

The first lesson element used to help learners link old and new information is *recall*. An effective recall covers all the prerequisite knowledge needed. Recall sessions should be interesting enough to hold the learners' attention. They might be in the form of a question-and-answer session, a quiz, an applied exercise, a brief lecture, or a discussion. A recall session could also be a combination of one or more of these forms.

The second lesson element in linking old and new information is *relate*. This involves tying the new knowledge to the old. In other words, you need to build a bridge from what the learners already know to what they are learning. Another way of picturing relating is showing the learner how one edge of a major jigsaw puzzle piece (what is to be learned) fits into an already partially constructed puzzle. Another way of thinking about relating is that you have to show the similarities and differences between the new knowledge and the already known in order to prepare the way for the integration of the new knowledge into existing structures of knowledge in the learners' minds.

Learner Task 3: Organize the Information

Third, learners have to organize the new information so that it fits into some pattern they already have in their minds for related knowledge. Doing this makes it easier for them to learn, integrate, and retrieve the new knowledge.

The first lesson element for organizing the new information is *structure of content*. This presents the boundaries and structure of the new knowledge. The format should best represent the way the new knowledge is structured. For example, the structure of content for a concept lesson should present a diagram showing the relationship between the concepts. In teaching the structure and operation of a piece of machinery, the structure of content would be a diagram of the parts and how they are related.

The second lesson element for this task is to provide a standard three-part performance *objective* that lets learners know what the knowledge to be learned is, the conditions under which the new knowledge will be used, and how well they will be expected to perform.

Chunking is the third lesson element for organizing the new information. Essentially, you "chunk" large units of information by breaking them down into smaller, simpler pieces that are easier to process and giving these smaller "chunks" labels that suggest their content.

The fourth way to help the learners process new knowledge more effectively and efficiently is by using *text layout* strategies. The way information is presented on the page or screen affects learners' processing, encoding, storing, and retrieving operations. For example, you can create an obvious organization by using headings and subheadings, perhaps with icons or shading to call out different kinds of material (Overview of Content, Summary of Content, Objective[s], Body of Content, Questions, Applied Exercise, Feedback, Summary). Once a pattern has been established, learners will quickly recognize the different types of sections as they are repeated throughout the training materials.

The fifth organizational strategy is the use of *illustrations*. When appropriate illustrations are used as part of a lesson, learners assign two meanings to them—verbal representations and visual images—and store the two meanings in different memories in the brain. So once the knowledge is encoded, the learners can retrieve the information from either visual or verbal memory. This dual coding enhances the ability to recall knowledge. One illustration technique is to use line drawings to highlight details of the subject matter. These make it easier to direct attention to the pertinent parts of the visual.

Learner Task 4: Assimilate the New Knowledge into Existing Knowledge

The fourth task for the learners is to assimilate the new knowledge into their existing store of knowledge, integrating the new content with the old to produce a new unified, expanded, and reorganized piece of knowledge.

The first lesson element for this task is *present new knowledge*. To apply this element, you will need to use a different approach for each type of knowledge: fact, concept, principle and mental model, and well-moderately, and ill-structured problem solving learning. You will learn different strategies for each of these types of knowledge later in the book.

Once you have presented the new knowledge, you will help learners assimilate the new knowledge into the existing knowledge by using the second lesson element, *present examples.* The number and type of examples you need also depends on the type of knowledge being taught.

Learner Task 5: Strengthen the New Knowledge in Memory

The learners' fifth and final task is to strengthen the new knowledge by internalizing it so they can remember, recall, and apply it as needed. This task includes five lesson elements: *practice, feedback, summary, test,* and *on-the-job application.*

Every instructional designer is familiar with the first element, *practice,* which consists of having learners do something with the new knowledge. The kind of practice activities you design will be determined by the kind of knowledge you are teaching. For example, when people are learning *concepts,* practice generally consists of having them classify concepts that were not used in the present examples phase and/or construct additional examples. For a lesson on *principles,* one practice strategy would be to ask questions that require learners to apply the principles to new situations.

The next lesson element, *feedback,* follows logically from practice. Feedback lets learners know how well they've done in applying the new knowledge, what problems they're having, and why they are having those problems.

The next lesson element used to help the learner strengthen the new knowledge is *summary.* For this element, you will repeat the structure of content that was first presented as part of the third task, organizing the information.

The lesson element *test* then helps the learners strengthen new knowledge by asking them to use it again in new and novel situations. This element also gives learners the opportunity to prove to themselves, to the instructor, and to their employers that they met the objectives of the lesson.

The final element in this phase—and in the lesson you are designing— is *on-the-job application.* To help learners strengthen the new knowledge and to ensure that they do not forget it, have them apply what they have learned on the job. For example, by prior arrangement with the learners' supervisors, you can set up projects in the workplace that require the learners to apply a procedure they learned in the training session. Both the learners and the supervisors are encouraged to relay performance feedback results to the instructor.

HOW TO READ THE COGNITIVE TRAINING MODEL

The Cognitive Training Model, shown in Figure 2.2, has two columns and five rows. The left column lists the five tasks learners have to do in learning, one in each row:

1. Select the information to attend to.

2. Link the new information with existing knowledge.

3. Organize the information.

4. Assimilate the new knowledge into existing knowledge.

5. Strengthen the new knowledge in memory.

A brief description of these five learning processes also appears in the left-hand column.

The right column in the figure lists the seventeen elements of a training lesson that you design to help learners accomplish those five learning tasks. In each row, the lesson elements that relate to each of the five learning tasks are described briefly. Eight of the seventeen elements are the same for all categories of knowledge and appear in boldface in the table. The other nine elements vary by type of knowledge and appear in boldface italics in the table.

FIGURE 2.2. The Cognitive Training Model

Learners Must Do This to Learn	Trainers Put These Elements in Lessons to Help Learners
1. Select the Information to Attend To. Heighten their attention and focus it on the new knowledge being taught because that new knowledge is seen as important and capable of being learned.	**Attention.** Gain and focus learners' attention on the new knowledge. **WIIFM.** Answer What's in It for Me? for the learners. **YCDI.** Tell the learners You Can Do It regarding learning the new knowledge.
2. Link the New Information with Existing Knowledge. Put the new knowledge in an existing framework by recalling existing/old knowledge related to the new knowledge and linking the new knowledge to the old.	*Recall.* Bring to the forefront the pre-requisite existing (old) knowledge that forms the base on which the new knowledge is built *Relate.* Show similarities or differences between the new knowledge and old knowledge, so that the new knowledge is tied to the old.
3. Organize the Information. Organize new knowledge in a way that matches the organization already in mind for related existing knowledge to make it easier to learn, cut mental processing time, minimize confusion, and stress only relevant information.	**Structure of Content.** Present the boundaries and structure of the new knowledge in a format that best represents the way the new knowledge itself is structured. *Objectives.* Specify both the desired behavior and the knowledge to be learned. **Chunking.** Organize and limit the amount of new knowledge presented to match human information processing capacity. **Text Layout.** Organize text presentation to help learners organize new knowledge. **Illustrations.** Use well-designed illustrations to assist learners' organization and assimilation of new knowledge.
4. Assimilate the New Knowledge into Existing Knowledge. Integrate the new knowledge into the old knowledge so they combine to produce a new unified, expanded, and reorganized set of knowledge.	*Present New Knowledge.* Using a different approach for each type of knowledge, present the new knowledge in a way that makes it easiest to understand. *Present Examples.* Demonstrate real-life examples of how the new knowledge works when it is applied.
5. Strengthen the New Knowledge in Memory. Strengthen the new knowledge so that it will be remembered and can be brought to bear in future job and learning situations.	*Practice.* Involve learners by having them do something with the new knowledge. *Feedback.* Let learners know how well they've done in using the new knowledge, what problems they're having, and why. **Summary.** Present the structure of content again, including the entire structure of knowledge. *Test.* Have learners use the new knowledge again, this time to prove to themselves, you, and their employer that they have met the objectives of the training. *On-the-Job Application.* Have learners use new knowledge in a structured way on the job to ensure they "use it, not lose it."

The elements on the right side of the model are intentionally *not numbered* because, within any row, you can manipulate the sequence of the elements depending on what the situation calls for. To accomplish the learning task, it is crucial that all elements listed in any row be included. However, it is not crucial that they be done in a particular order. For example, you could begin a lesson with any of these sequences:

Attention	→	WIIFM	→	YCDI
Attention	→	YCDI	→	WIIFM
YCDI	→	WIIFM	→	Attention
YCDI	→	Attention	→	WIIFM
WIIFM	→	Attention	→	YCDI
WIIFM	→	YCDI	→	Attention

DIFFERENTIATING OUR MODEL FROM GAGNE'S

At first glance, the model might seem to some a mere restatement of Gagne's nine events of instruction. However, while we certainly owe a great debt to that groundbreaking work, our model is different in both content and emphasis. The major differences are:

- The five stages of our model are sequential, but the elements within each stage are *not* necessarily done in the same sequence as listed in the model.

- Our model is more concerned with *linking* and *organizing* the new information, based on the principles of cognitive psychology described above.

- Our model integrates the work of Keller (1987) on the importance of *relevance* (What's In It For Me) and *confidence* (You Can Do It) to learning.

- In addition to learners *recalling* existing knowledge, our model is focused on *relating* the new knowledge to the existing knowledge.

- In addition to using *objectives* to help the learner organize knowledge, our model uses a *structure of content,* plus what we know about *chunking, text layout, and illustrations.*

- The *present new knowledge* and *present examples* elements of our model are structured very differently for each type of declarative and procedural knowledge (while the details are too lengthy for this treatment, some examples are (1) use of prototypical examples and coordinate concept structures rather than critical attributes as the basis for concept teaching; (2) use of mental models and heuristics rather than algorithms for troubleshooting teaching; and (3) specific teaching of mental models to consolidate all declarative knowledge components).

- The *practice* element of our model, for both declarative and procedural knowledge, involves a great deal more explanation and application that demonstrates the existence of a desired mental model and the ability to articulate as well as perform problem-solving strategies.

Thus, for this model we have taken the best of what we know works from the existing ID approach and built on it—adding those new emphases and elements that cognitive theory provides to make a more robust and effective ID approach.

HOW TO USE THE MODEL

Because Chapters 3 through 11 provide you with the details of how to design lessons for each type of knowledge you might want to teach, the guidelines below provide only a brief overview of how to use the model.

You use this model to develop all training, regardless of purpose or medium. For each piece of knowledge you want to teach in a given lesson:

1. Decide what type of knowledge it is: declarative (fact, concept, principle/ mental model) or procedural (well-structured, moderately structured, or ill-structured problem solving). It's common for a given lesson to include many pieces of different types.

2. Do the appropriate analysis to identify knowledge, examples, and relationships to other knowledge.

3. Write the design prescriptions for the generic elements of the lesson based on the outline of the model given here (and the additional detail in later chapters). *Note:* Remember, as long as you begin the lesson with and include all the elements, their exact sequence does not matter.

4. Based on the type of knowledge you are teaching, write design prescriptions for how the other lesson elements should look for that type of knowledge using the model in Figure 2.2 to guide you and applying the specific information for that type of knowledge from Chapters 5 through 10.

Including all seventeen lesson elements for each piece of knowledge may seem excessive, but in most cases it is necessary for learners to accomplish their learning tasks. After you attain some level of expertise in cognitive instructional design, you will probably identify those situations in which you can omit some elements without negatively affecting the learning or can use a single lesson element for more than one piece of knowledge. For example, it's common to design Attention, WIIFM, YCDI, Structure of Content, and Objectives the first three lesson elements so they apply to an entire lesson, rather than to each individual piece of knowledge in the lesson. With experience, you'll be able to identify these situations and use the efficiencies to save development cost and time, as well as making the lesson flow more easily. It is common to reduce the number of lesson elements by teaching more than one objective in one lesson. We will explain how to do this in Chapter 11.

SUMMARY

In this chapter we presented a cognitive training model that serves as a structure for the chapter and for the book.

We explained the five learner tasks and, for each of these tasks, two to five lesson elements trainers must use to help learners achieve the learning tasks. The learner tasks and their lesson elements are:

1. Select the Information to Attend To (Attention, WIIFM, and YCDI).

2. Link the New Information with Existing Knowledge (Recall and Relate).

3. Organize the Information (Structure of Content, Objectives, Chunking, Text Layout, and Illustrations).

4. Assimilate the New Knowledge into Existing Knowledge (Present New Knowledge and Present Examples).

5. Strengthen the New Knowledge in Memory (Practice, Feedback, Summary, Test, and On-the-Job-Application).

We then discussed, in detail, how to read the model, what is new and different about the model, and finally, how to apply the model to designing lessons.

Part II

How to Design Lessons Using the Cognitive Approach

*T*his introduction to the longest and most complex portion of the book serves two purposes. First, it provides a visual overview of the structure (what you will learn in Chapter 4 to call a "structure of content"). Second, we provide information about the companies we will be using throughout the book as the basis for the examples.

OVERVIEW OF THE STRUCTURE OF PART II

In Part II we explain how to use the Cognitive Training Model to teach facts, concepts, principles and mental models, well-structured problem-solving procedures, ill-structured problem-solving procedures, troubleshooting, and complete lessons. In each chapter we give two examples. You can think of the nine chapters in this part of the book as being organized in this manner:

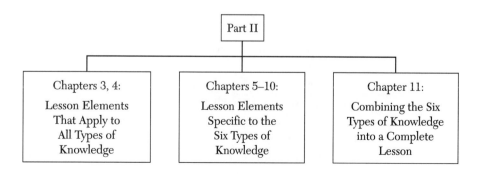

Part II

Chapters 3, 4:	Chapters 5–10:	Chapter 11:
Lesson Elements That Apply to All Types of Knowledge	Lesson Elements Specific to the Six Types of Knowledge	Combining the Six Types of Knowledge into a Complete Lesson

EXAMPLES

Before describing the companies on which our examples are based, we want to be clear about why we have created the examples in the way we have. Our goal was to create for you an "example rich" book (since, as you will learn shortly, people learn more from examples than from explanations). To do so, we have provided twenty-two extensive examples.

There are three examples in Chapter 3, six examples in Chapter 4, and two examples in each of Chapters 5 through 10, and one example in Chapter 11. Although based on the same two companies, the examples used in Chapters 5 through 10 are not all components of the same course or subject matter; the examples are chosen to best illustrate the knowledge types in each chapter rather than to slavishly force-fit them into an artificial sequence or course.

To show how complete lessons combining different types of knowledge would look, we have provided a brand new complete example lesson in Chapter 11. This example is based on one of the companies and does follow the same subject matter all the way through.

Aside from Chapter 11, all the examples are based on a classroom, instructor-led, instructional strategy. This is not because we are unaware of e-learning and the use of technology in training. It is because instructor-led examples make it easier to focus on the concepts being addressed in this book, and to not get sidetracked with issues that are particular to technology-based training, such as screen design, interactivity types and frequency, and so forth. These are important topics, but are the province of books other than this one (for example, Clark & Mayer, 2002). Addressing them here would muddy the waters for those trying to focus on the cognitive ID principles. In Chapter 11, we do show what a computer-based-training lesson using these cognitive principles would look like.

This section presents the profiles of the two companies used in the book. The solutions to one company's training needs are used as examples in the narrative portion of each chapter. The solutions to the other company's training needs are used as the job-aid example at the end of each chapter. Each chapter includes company descriptions and learning objectives.

The company we use for our illustrative examples in the body of the chapter is a service firm that rents automobiles. It is called AutoRent. A performance analysis has been done, and AutoRent has many training problems we can solve through application of the techniques in the book. The training topics here are directed at managers, customer service representatives, and vehicle service specialists.

The company we use in the job aid example at the end of each chapter is a general merchandise discount chain. It is called YourMart. Again, a thorough performance analysis has been done, and YourMart also has lots of training problems we can solve through application of the techniques in the book. The examples we use here are training new employees on word processing techniques and other technical subjects.

The Company

AutoRent is a thirty-five-year-old company with headquarters in the Chicago area and branch offices in one hundred large U.S. cities. They rent cars to businesspeople traveling by train. The company began with one location, in downtown Chicago, with one manager, one mechanic, and five cars. Their size and revenue increased each year for twenty-seven years, but over the last three years the company has begun to lose revenue, market share, and employees. Today they have $600M in revenue, ten thousand cars, and 15 percent of the rental car market. They employ 6,700 people and are downsizing at the rate of two hundred people per month.

The People

Headquarters Management

The three hundred employees in headquarters management positions have an average of fifteen years' management experience. All are male, with an average age of 50 and average length of service of ten years. Fifty percent have advanced degrees. They tend to be conservative and live the suburban lifestyle.

Field Management

The one thousand people in field management positions have an average of one year of management experience. Seventy-five percent are male, and they range in age from 18 to 25, with an average of two years of field experience. Fifty percent have bachelor's degrees. The other 50 percent were hired "off the street." Being younger, they tend to enjoy the single lifestyle.

Headquarters Staff

The seven hundred staff at headquarters consist of 85 percent males with an average of four years of field experience. The average age is 30. They live the Yuppie lifestyle and have disdain for the field, wishing to become managers.

CSRs and Others in the Field

There are 4,300 CSRs, vehicle service specialists, reservation takers, car jockeys, and clerical people, with an average age of 22. Seventy-five percent have held one other job before joining AutoRent—almost all clerical or telemarketing—for a maximum of one year. Half are male, half female. The ethnic composition reflects all races and national origins. Because only a few see any chance of promotion, there is little job satisfaction, given their quotas of "number of customers per hour." Most do not like their jobs, their managers, headquarters, nor the "obnoxious" customers they must deal with. Most tend to be "couch potatoes," with few interests outside of television, pizza, and beer.

Mechanics

The four hundred mechanics are similar to the CSR group except that all are male and they have had at one year of technical training and at least one year of experience before joining AutoRent.

The Problem

Market share is plummeting as customers move to the competition in droves. When asked why, the indicate that (1) it's inconvenient to go to the rental locations; (2) the reservation phone lines are always busy, and when they do get through their reservations are usually messed up; (3) there is always a long line to pick up and return cars; (4) the people behind the counter seem surly and complain about other customers and about the mistakes their managers make; and (5) the cars are ugly, dirty, old, or don't work.

(Continued)

Performance Improvement Interventions

To solve the problem, AutoRent has hired Performance Improvement People, Inc. (PIP). PIP has conducted a complete performance analysis, including (but not limited to) organization mapping, performance engineering, behavior engineering, front-end analysis, strategic planning analysis, and value and corporate analysis. They have made the following recommendations:

- Moving the rental locations from downtown to the airports
- Promoting CSRs and phone reservationists to management, rather than hiring "green" managers
- Increasing the troubleshooting skills of the vehicle service specialists in order to take some pressure off mechanics
- Getting rid of the "elite headquarters" notion and moving from a traditional organizational structure to self-directed teams
- Reducing the number of managers and increasing the number of CSRs, vehicle service specialists, mechanics, car jockeys, and phone reservationists
- Evaluating, paying, and promoting CSRs and phone reservationists based on customer satisfaction rather than on number per hour
- Instilling the "provide superior customer service" attitude in everyone—and in every customer transaction

Fact Training Objective. Given specific questions about AutoRent's car sizes, features, accessory and safety packages, passenger capacities and rental rates, CSRs will respond with the correct facts.

Concept Training Objective. Given examples of different kinds of organizations, AutoRent employees will correctly label those that are examples of self-directed team organizations.

Principle Training Objective. Given a series of "unavailability of rental cars" simulations and AutoRent's customer satisfaction and unavailability of rental car principles, predict the situational outcomes when these principles are and are not applied and use the principles to resolve the situations and, when resolved, explain why.

Procedure Training Objective. Given a returned vehicle and proper tools, supplies, and equipment, service the vehicle by applying AutoRent's eight-step servicing procedure.

Troubleshooting Training Objective. Given AutoRent vehicles that don't start either by not cranking at all (dead silence) or cranking but not catching, determine (troubleshoot) the cause and either correct the problem or refer it to a mechanic.

Ill-Structured Problem Training Objective. An AutoRent task force must determine why the company's profits are going down and suggest solutions.

The Company

YourMart is a ninety-year-old company headquartered in suburban Atlanta. The company has over two thousand retail stores in the forty-eight continental states. Stores are located in urban areas, suburbs, small towns, and rural areas.

YourMart started as K & M Variety Stores. The original stores were located in major cities and small towns and sold everything from aspirin to zippers. In the mid-1900s, as America began to move from the inner cities, so did K & M. Management found that the original seven hundred stores were too few and too small to keep up with the growing population and that the population's tastes were changing.

Therefore, K & M launched its YourMart division in 1966, with one hundred discount department stores, averaging twenty thousand square feet of space and selling at 25 percent off list. YourMart was very successful, growing to seventeen hundred stores by 1980. In the early 1980s, another retailer, More Merchandise, Less Cost, began opening stores around the country, which cut into the YourMart customer base with clean, attractive stores; helpful, courteous staff; an incredible selection of up-to-date goods; and up to 35 percent discounts.

YourMart revenues in 1997 were $23 billion with a profit of just under $1 billion. The company has 250,000 employees, including headquarters and stores.

Work Processes

All merchandise is bought by headquarters and shipped to stores from regional warehouses.

People

Headquarters

YourMart headquarters employs three thousand people, who handle all types of support functions. Seventy-five percent of buyers are male, with an average age of 49 and an average of twenty-five years' experience with YourMart. Only 30 percent have a college education. Most are married, conservative, dress in dark suits, have little sense of humor, play golf, and think ahead to their next vacation.

IS Department

The corporate IS department has one executive vice president, three vice presidents, twenty-eight directors, seventy-five managers, five hundred nonexempt analysts/programmers, and three hundred clerical people. Analysts/programmers are college-educated (90 percent), have an average of four years with the company, and average 32 years of age. Most would be considered "yuppies" in lifestyle and spending habits. Management has the same profile as the buyers.

Stores

Managers

Stores are managed by college-educated (60 percent), male (70 percent), relatively young (37) individuals with an average of fourteen years with the company. Each store has one general manager and three assistant managers.

Staff

Within each store, there are thirty different position and pay levels. Store employees are mostly female (75 percent), high school graduates (95 percent), young (average 27), with an average of seven years with the company. Store employees tend to reflect the ethnic

(Continued)

groups of the areas in which they serve. Most (70 percent) are second wage earners who view their jobs as a means to make additional money and have neither a positive nor negative attitude toward the job.

Freight

Each store has a six- or seven-member freight processing center team that consists of the processing center manager, an assistant manager, two or three "markers," an unloader, and a shipping clerk. Everyone reports to the processing store manager, who reports to one of the assistant store managers. These employee demographics are the same as the other store staff.

Processing

Processing of freight takes place in the stockroom, which can be hot or cold, depending on the weather, as the loading dock doors are left open to receive incoming freight. The rooms are poorly lit, dirty, and noisy.

The Problem

In order to compete with More Merchandise, Less Cost, YourMart senior management decided to increase their in-stock position by automating the freight receiving process. A new software/hardware system was put in place. The new system required "markers," the use of scanning wands, and "can" of an item's UPC code as it is received.

In 1997, the IS department, in consultation with buyers, selected the computer hardware and software, tested the system in two stores near headquarters. Once the bugs were worked out, the system was installed in all stores over a period of three years. Use of the system requires the ability to use MS Word, an ability no user has.

Performance Improvement Interventions

To solve this problem, YourMart has hired the Performance Improvement People, Inc. (PIP). PIP has conducted a complete performance analysis, including (but not limited to) organization mapping, performance engineering, behavior engineering, front-end analysis, strategic planning analysis, and value and corporate analysis. PIP has recommended the following:

- Increasing the efficiency and effectiveness of store and departmental meetings
- Getting rid of the "elite headquarters" notion and putting the experienced people into high-ranking and high-paid jobs in the field
- Reducing the number of managers and increasing the number of staff, creating career paths for staff
- Instilling a quality attitude in all personnel
- Training people on the prerequisite skills for using MS Word
- Training people on using the computer hardware and repairing it when necessary

Fact Training Objective. Given a font with any combination of attributes set, use keystroke shortcuts in Word.

Concept Training Objective. Given a formatted paragraph, identify the format attributes used to format the paragraph.

(Continued)

Principle Training Objective. Predict the operation of a simple AC circuit with a half-wave rectifier.

Procedure Training Objective. Apply the procedure for creating a mail merge.

Troubleshooting Training Objective. Given a malfunctioning modem, determine the cause and fix it.

Ill-Structured Problem Training Objective. Apply the general strategy for mail merges to unusual jobs, such as the "quarterly fax."

FIGURE 3.1. Chapter 3 Structure of Content

Learners Have to Do This to Learn	Trainers Put These Elements in Lessons to Help Learners
1. *Select the information to attend to.* Heighten learners' attention and focus it on the new knowledge being taught because that new knowledge is seen as important and capable of being learned.	*Attention.* Gain and focus learners' attention on the new knowledge. *WIIFM.* Help learners see "What's in it for me?" in the new knowledge. *YCDI.* Tell the learners "You can do it" in learning the new knowledge.

Chapter 3

How to Begin Any Lesson

The First Three Lesson Elements

LINK AND ORGANIZE

Recall (from Chapter 1)

- We attend to those things that interest us, either because they are related to what we already know or because they are so novel they force us to attend to them. Therefore, getting the learner to attend to the parts of the environment you want learned is crucial.

Recall (from Chapter 2)

- In our Cognitive Training Model, the first learner task is to *select the information to attend to.* The lesson elements you apply to help the learner do this are attention, WIIFM (What's in it for me), and YCDI (You can do it).

Relate to What You Already Know

- When you look up from your newspaper to watch a TV commercial, something caused you to refocus your attention from the newspaper to the TV. It might have been loud music or quick motion or somebody saying something that caught your ear. Whatever it was, the TV ad producer succeeded in gaining your attention.

- If you've ever decided to change jobs, you probably sat down and wrote down the pluses and minuses of doing so. You were performing a "What's in it for me?"—figuring out how important the change would be to your career, your self-worth, your earning power, and so on.

- Motivational speakers are always applying the "you can do it" lesson element. Along with whatever skills they're talking about, they wrap them in motivating statements that tell you that you can achieve them.

Structure of Content

- See Figure 3.1.

Objectives

- To be able to describe what the first three lesson elements—attention, WIIFM (What's in it for me), and YCDI (You can do it)—are.
- To apply general strategies for applying the lessons.
- To design a lesson incorporating the three elements.

At AutoRent, new customer service representative trainees in a class on basic rental car features and other rental facts are focusing on the effects of the new tax laws on their just-received paychecks; don't know why they need to know all these facts; and think that because there are so many facts they'll never be able to memorize all of them.

Because it is Friday afternoon, YourMart word processing trainees aren't attending well to the unit on performing keyboard shortcuts for formatting fonts; think that learning shortcuts to formatting fonts is just busy work; and aren't sure they can learn one more method in this session.

ABOUT USING THE LESSON ELEMENTS ATTENTION, WIIFM, AND YCDI TO BEGIN A LESSON

This chapter explains how to begin designing a lesson for any category of procedural or declarative knowledge learning objective with the first three elements of a lesson—those that help the learner *select the information to attend to*:

- Attention.
- What's in it for me (WIIFM).
- You can do it (YCDI).

You carry out these three elements of a lesson the same way, regardless of the type of procedural or declarative knowledge you are teaching. Therefore, we will discuss them here. We will not present them again in every chapter, but will refer you back to this chapter.

We present here a more detailed discussion of what each of the three elements is and a brief summary of the issues in teaching each. We then present the training goal, a detailed description of "how to" for each lesson element, and an example from an AutoRent training segment to illustrate each lesson element. We conclude the chapter with a job aid summarizing "what to do," combined with a complete example.

Attention

As we discussed in the presentation of the model in Chapter 2, the first thing learners have to do is *select the information to attend to*. They must heighten their attention, focus on the new knowledge being taught, and establish their expectations of how to interpret the new knowledge they will encounter.

We are constantly bombarded by environmental stimuli—sights, sounds, and odors. In a training situation, these stimuli include those related to what we want students to learn, as well as many extraneous stimuli we do not want students to learn about—or even pay attention to.

We have the capacity to take in a lot of this stimulation, both relevant and extraneous. But just taking it in is not enough: All those stimuli disappear from our minds rather quickly, as we take in more than we can process in the short time before they disappear. So our first task as trainers is to provide appropriate cues and signals to our learners to help them retain the stimuli related to the relevant new knowledge by selecting, focusing on, and interpreting the relevant stimuli before they are lost and by converting those selected relevant stimuli into some other form that can remain more permanently in the mind, while the other stimuli rapidly disappear.

How to Develop the Lesson Element

You can attract the learners' attention and focus it on the new knowledge by using one or more of the following strategies. Whether you use all or only a few of these strategies rests on your analysis of the learners' prior knowledge, motivation, and physical state.

- Introduce the new knowledge in a way that creates novelty, unpredictability, and uncertainty (perhaps in the form of a story, game, or problem scenario).

- Introduce the new knowledge by presenting contradictory or conflicting opinions or ideas (perhaps a debate by two experts).

- Use verbal and visual cues to tell the learners where to direct their attention.

- Present a situation (context) that is interesting and/or familiar to the learner and that is related to the new learning.

- Present an interesting scenario that involves the new learning and requires a response on the learner's part (perhaps a problem or question that invites inquiry about the new knowledge or requires the new knowledge for its solution).

- Vary the stimuli throughout the presentation by manipulating lecture, media, and classroom activities.

WIIFM

Have your learners ever asked you (or each other in the hallway during breaks), "Why are we learning this? What does this have to do with my job or me? How is this going to help me?" These kinds of "What's in it for me?" (WIIFM) questions are the questions learners most frequently ask when learning something new. To help them remain attentive to the lesson and decide what to do with the new knowledge once it has been presented, learners have to know how what they are learning is relevant to their lives and jobs; meets their needs and wants; and will make their lives or jobs easier or more enjoyable.

Establishing the right WIIFM is important for all types of learners. It's especially important for adults, because they decide how much time and effort they will put into the training (instead of all the other tasks competing for their time and energy) based on the answer. When learners get into the hard work of learning something new, it's the WIIFM that will keep them going. Without a strong WIIFM, they'll drop out mentally—and physically, if they have the chance.

Keep in mind that, while we're discussing the WIIFM as an important element of the beginning of a lesson, it's important throughout the lesson. What you do at the beginning establishes a motivational theme that you must carry throughout the lesson. A common mistake in training design is to treat the WIIFM as a "motivational pill" you give the learner at the beginning and then forget about as you grimly slog through the presentation. To help avoid this error, think of the WIIFM as a learning objective in its own right, which gives the lesson its depth and humanity.

How to Develop the Lesson Element

You can let the learners know what's in it for them by using two or more of the following strategies:

- Relate the new knowledge to learners' personal needs, values, and concerns.
- Explain how the new knowledge relates to the learners' on-the-job skills, job satisfaction, professional achievement, or income.
- Explain how the new knowledge will make the learners' jobs easier, better, faster, more productive, more pleasant, more interesting, or more important.
- Relate the new knowledge to needs, values, and concerns of the organization and the job.

You Can Do It (YCDI)

Learners are more likely to learn new knowledge they believe they are capable of mastering than knowledge they believe they will never comprehend. They are more likely to use the knowledge after the training if they have confidence in the skills they have learned. One of the important characteristics of experts is that they persist longer in solving problems than novices do, because they believe there is a solution to their problem and that they can find it.

Unfortunately, a lack of this confidence is common among adult learners. Yet most trainers do not spend time giving learners confidence that the new knowledge is something they can learn and succeed at applying on the job, nor do they help the learners confirm that their freshly acquired knowledge really will work in the "real world," even if they can use it in training.

To instill this confidence, trainers need to give learners a sense of "you can do it" or YCDI.

How to Develop the Lesson Element

You help learners gain a sense that they can do it by using two or more of the following strategies:

- Use research results or testimonials from role models or other learners to explain how people like themselves have succeeded in learning this new knowledge.

- Point out that they have already succeeded at learning something similar to what you are teaching.

- Emphasize the support resources in the organization (people, money, facilities, equipment) that are available to help them.

- Be honest about the initial difficulty of learning the new information and skills.

- Separate their ability to learn the new knowledge (danger of task failure) from their worth as a person and work (danger of personal failure).

- Have learners compete with themselves rather than with others.

- Make sure your training ends with practice in realistic contexts with realistic difficulty levels, distractions, stresses, and so forth.

- Be sure to tell the learner in a believable way what is "reality" and that they succeeded.

Do these things throughout the lesson, not just at the beginning. Like the WIIFM, the YCDI is a theme, not a single event. You can think in the same way as the WIIFM, which adds depth and humanity to your training.

USING THE LESSON ELEMENTS ATTENTION, WIIFM, AND YCDI TO BEGIN A LESSON

Example Scenario

As part of their basic training, all AutoRent customer service representatives (CSRs) need to learn a large amount of fact level knowledge concerning vehicle characteristics, rental rates, and rental packages. The three examples below illustrate the application of the first three lesson elements for one of these sessions.

Lesson Element: Attention

Description. Get learners to focus on the new facts.

> AutoRent Example: "This session is all about the types of cars we rent, their features, and their rental costs. Let's take a look at how knowing or not knowing these facts can affect a customer transaction." [*Show a two-part video. The first part shows a customer asking questions about car makes and models, number of passengers they can carry comfortably, gas mileage, and so forth. The customer service representative (CSR) pauses to ask another CSR for some of the information, calls someone on the phone to find out additional information, and generally fumbles around. The customer grows increasingly frustrated. The line grows longer. Suddenly all of the customers start shouting and throwing things at the CSR. The second part shows a CSR in command of the facts fielding questions easily. The transaction is short; the customer is happy; people in a short line cheer the CSR.*] "In this session you'll learn facts that will help you to answer most questions customers ask about our car makes and models, passenger capacity, gas mileage, rental cost, safety features, and accessory packages."

Lesson Element: WIIFM

Description. Tell them how the new facts will help them.

> AutoRent Example: "Although the scenario you just saw was a bit exaggerated, learning these facts will help you to help customers make up their minds quickly and efficiently with less misunderstanding and fewer errors. You'll be able to speed customer transactions, save time, and avoid mistakes. Your customer contracts will be error-free. You'll contribute greatly to customers' satisfaction from the very beginning of their contact with AR."

Lesson Element: YCDI

Description. Reassure the learners that they will be able to master the facts.

> AutoRent Example: "The best way to learn these facts is through repetitive use. It may seem like a lot of things to remember at first, but this is a natural reaction. You'll practice with a role play in this session with a fact sheet. This chart [*refer to job aid fact sheet*] will also help you back on the job. After a while you won't even need it. All the facts will be committed to your memory. Just ask a CSR who has been on the job for a while."

Figure 3.2 gives the information to attend to for teaching YourMart new hires using this segment of the model. Recall that the trainer wants to convince people of the value of performing keyboard shortcuts to format fonts (characters). The training session is taking place on a Friday afternoon.

FIGURE 3.2. Job Aid for Learner Task 1

Lesson Element	Example
1. Select the Information to Attend To *Attention.* Get learners to focus on the new facts.	"OK, everybody, in the next few minutes you're going to learn a few shortcuts! Hold off on your mental plans for the weekend a bit longer because you're going to learn how the pros get their documents done so fast. In honor of the coming weekend, the first words we'll practice changing fonts on will be 'Friday,' 'Saturday,' and 'Sunday.'"
WIIFM. Tell them how the new facts will help them.	"These shortcuts in word processing will, I guarantee, save you a great deal of time as you become proficient in using the system."
YCDI. Reassure the learners that they will be able to master these facts.	"This formatting may seem confusing at first, but that happens to everybody. We'll practice nice and slowly until you feel confident in using these shortcuts."

SUMMARY

In this chapter we discussed both what learners must do at the beginning of a lesson and how you can help them do it. For any category of declarative and/or procedural knowledge lessons, learners must select the information to attend to. The three lesson elements that you should use to help them do this are:

- *Attention*—Provide appropriate cues and signals to learners to help them focus and retain the stimuli related to the relevant new knowledge.
- *WIIFM (What's in it for me)*—Show learners how the learning is important to them personally and/or for their jobs and/or to their careers.
- *YCDI (You can do it)*—Instill a sense of confidence in learners that they can learn the lesson content and use it on the job.

For each of these lesson elements we presented:

- A detailed discussion of what the elements are.
- A brief summary of the issues involved in using them.
- A "how-to-develop them" section with examples.
- A final example in job aid format.

FIGURE 4.1. Chapter 4 Structure of Content

Learners Have to Do This to Learn	Trainers Put These Elements in Lessons to Help Learners
3. *Organize the information.* Organize new knowledge in a way that matches the organization of what learners already know in order to make it easier to learn, cut mental processing time, minimize confusion, and stress only relevant information.	*Structure of content.* Present the boundaries and structure of the new knowledge in a format that best represents the way the new knowledge itself is structured. *Objectives.* Specify both the desired behavior and the knowledge to be learned. *Chunking.* Organize and limit the amount of new knowledge presented to match human information processing capacity. *Text Layout.* Organize text presentation to help learners organize new knowledge. *Illustrations.* Use well-designed illustrations to assist learners' organization and assimilation of new knowledge.

Chapter 4

How to Organize and Present Information

Message Design Principles

LINK AND ORGANIZE

Recall (from Chapter 1)

- Because our sensory memories can briefly store almost complete records of what we attend to, it is critical that we help the learners note relationships among the learning content so that they are able to encode it in a more permanent memory.

- Because working memory has limited capacity, we need to present the learning content in meaningful "chunks" of appropriate size.

- Presenting learning content in a way that enables learners to use their abilities to remember both verbal and visual learning content can increase memory and retrieval.

Recall (from Chapter 2)

- In the overview of the Cognitive Training Model, you learned that the third learner task is *to organize the information.* The lesson elements you apply to help the learner do this are Structure of Content, Objectives, Chunking, Text Layout, and Illustrations.

Relate to What You Already Know

- Many of the "knock-down" bookshelves, end tables, and entertainment centers that you buy and have to assemble yourself come with good directions. A structure of content is like the page in the directions that shows all the parts "exploded" but in relation to each other. This lesson element displays the parts of the learning content and their relationships to each other.

- Many tasks we do every day can be put into performance objectives, for example, if the boss says, "Take these two sets of data and do a comparison," the task translated into a performance objective would go something like, "Given data ABC and data XYZ, create a spreadsheet that accurately compares the two sets."

- Some of the better-organized cookbooks these days use the chunking lesson element in their presentation of recipes. Instead of running all the steps for preparing a dish together, they organize the steps into groups or chunks with specific purposes like preparing the dough, preparing the filling, preparing the topping, preparing the baking dish, and so on.

- If you've ever tried to make sense out of a document you've received that is single-spaced with narrow margins and that looks like one giant paragraph on a page, you know how hard it is to extract information from poorly designed text. Conversely, if you read a page of text that tells you what it is all about—with a title in the upper left-hand corner, short sentences in short paragraphs, spaced out paragraphs, and labels for content in the left margin—you're more likely to comprehend the subject matter.

- There are few things as annoying as reading text loaded with illustrations where the references to them are not on the same page or where the illustrations are so detailed that it is hard to pick out the specific detail being discussed in the text. These are examples of how not to use illustrations. Good examples of the lesson element "illustrations" are found in texts where the graphics are "integrated" with the text, that is, on the same page, and where illustrations emphasize only what that text describes.

Structure of Content
- See Figure 4.1.

Objectives
- To describe what the third set of Lesson Elements—Structure of Content, Objectives, Chunking, Text Layout, and Illustrations—are.
- To apply general strategies for applying them.
- To design a lesson incorporating them.

At AutoRent the new vehicle service specialist trainees need to learn the company's four-unit vehicle servicing procedures.

At YourMart new word processing trainees need to learn the procedure for setting up a mail merge.

*T*he third task that learners have to accomplish is to organize the new information in some way that fits with what they have in their minds for the related existing knowledge. This organization makes it easier for them to learn, as well as to retrieve the new knowledge when they need it. It reduces the amount of mental processing of the new knowledge they must do, minimizes confusion in understanding, and focuses them on only the parts of the new knowledge that are relevant to them.

ABOUT USING THE LESSON ELEMENTS TO HELP LEARNERS ORGANIZE THE INFORMATION

This chapter focuses on the lesson elements that help learners perform their third learning task, Organizing the Information. These lesson elements are the same for all types of knowledge. To help learners organize, provide two sets of lesson elements. The first set should deal with how we prepare the learner to organize the information. These lesson elements include structure of content, objectives, and summary.

The second set of lesson elements deal with how much information we present at a time and how we group it. These also deal with how we lay out pages of text and compose illustrations. They are discussed here at a very general level, because detailed discussions of text layout and illustration design vary by medium and are addressed in other books focusing on this subject exclusively.

Example Scenario

A major part of an AutoRent's vehicle service specialist's (VSS) job consists of refueling, servicing, inspecting, and cleaning or "prepping" returned cars for re-rental. New VSS hires are taught these procedures in a four-unit sequence. They've just completed training on Unit 1, refueling procedure. In Unit 2, they learn the procedure for servicing the car. In Unit 3 they learn what and how to inspect the car. The four-unit training objective and parts of Units 2 and 3 are used below to illustrate the lesson elements.

Structure of Content

What your English teacher told you about good writing ("Tell 'em what you're gonna tell 'em, tell 'em, and tell 'em what you told 'em") is still good advice. Ausubel (1968) talked about the importance of advance organizers in an early cognitive view of instruction, and the idea resurfaced again in elaboration theory as the "epitome." We refer to "tell 'em what you're going to tell 'em" as the "structure of content" lesson element.

Structure of content is a way of keeping the learner oriented to "the big picture." Cognitively, it helps the learner create an empty framework of knowledge on which to "hang" the details as the lesson progresses. The process is known as "encoding."

You present the structure of content as part of the overview, at the beginning of your lesson. The "content" portion of "structure of content" refers to the highest-level, or most essential, knowledge components to be taught. But content alone is not enough. You must also show how the content parts relate to each other. The "structure" portion refers to the relationships among the content points. For example, if you are teaching the parts of a car, the *content* taught might be the names of major subsystems (body, engine, drive train, electrical system). You might say "a car has five major subsystems. . . ." The *structure* would then be a verbal or diagrammatic representation that shows how those five subsystems relate to one another. In that way, you help learners begin to create a schema or *mental model* that aids encoding, storage, and retrieval.

During the lesson, when you make a transition from one content part to another (for example, from engine to drive train), you will re-orient the learner by referring back to the structure of content and pointing out the change.

We refer to the "tell 'em what you told 'em" portion of the lesson as the *summary lesson element.* At the end of a lesson, you restate the entire structure of content to help the learner encode the knowledge into his or her knowledge structure. The summary cannot add new content. The summary must merely repeat the structure of content, although its format may be different from that of the structure of content (for example, one can be a diagram, and one can be a narrative).

How to Develop This Lesson Element

Here are some strategies for providing the structure of content that helps learners prepare to encode and retrieve the new knowledge:

Description	*Example*
Create an "empty framework" the learner can fill in as the lesson progresses. [Always]	*Example:* "This is a five-step procedure." *Example:* Show a master graphic based on the concept structure you developed in cognitive task analysis.
Keep the learner oriented to where he/she is in the lesson. Whenever the lesson has more than three to five subtopics OR has more than seven to nine presentation/practice components.	*Example:* "First we'll talk about [topic 1], then we'll talk about [topic 2]" *Example:* Show a master graphic based on the concept structure or procedure structure, then zoom in on the first point. Say, "Let's start our discussion here." *Example:* Item counters and progress indicators (such as "Item 1 of 9")

Lesson Element:
Structure of Content

Description. Present the boundaries and structure of the new knowledge in a format that best represents the way the new knowledge itself is structured.

> AutoRent Example: In Unit 2 VSSs learn the servicing procedures, namely checking fluid levels and tire pressures. For teaching procedure-level knowledge, the lesson element structure of content is the steps of the procedure. In this example the steps in Figure 4.2 are presented at the beginning of the Unit 2 lesson. These steps are the structure of content for the servicing lesson.

FIGURE 4.2. Servicing Procedure

Servicing Procedures

Check and, if necessary, correct these fluid levels in the following order:

1. Window washer fluid reservoir (white cover).
2. Engine oil (wipe stick and reinsert for correct reading).
3. Transmission fluid (same as oil).
4. Power steering fluid (to marked line).
5. Battery (check indicator—if green, OK; if red—open, check, and fill).
6. Radiator reservoir (red cover) to marked level
7. Tires. Find correct tire pressure. Tire inflation information is found on the manufacturer's label. The label may be located in any one of these places: on the driver's side door jam, inside the gas filler door, inside glove compartment door. Check pressure. Correct if needed.
8. Fill out Part 2 of Vehicle Service Record found in glove compartment.

Objectives

Since Mager wrote the original version of *Preparing Instructional Objectives* in 1963, instructional designers have known about the importance of objectives that clearly state what learners will be able to do when training is completed, the conditions under which they will be expected to do it, and the standards or criteria by which their performance will be evaluated. Objectives remain an important part of training design for the cognitive approach.

How to Develop This Lesson Element

With this cognitive approach, the verbs used to state the objectives are less related to lists of behaviors—as in behavioral instructional design—and more related to the cognitive processes called for by a particular type of knowledge. For example, in a principle lesson, the objective is likely to be "predict." Also, when using the cognitive approach, it is important to state the objective in terms that the learner will understand, rather than a formally stated objective. (Chapters 5 through 10 will provide you with detailed examples of stating objectives for each of the six types of knowledge.)

Lesson Element:
Objectives

Description. Specify both the desired behavior and the knowledge to be learned.

> AutoRent Example: "Given a returned rental vehicle, work orders, and proper equipment, refuel, service, inspect and clean the vehicle according to the AutoRent manual of procedures."

Chunking

When people receive new knowledge, they have to store it temporarily while they work on encoding it into a more useful and lasting format. This short-term storage is like a workshop where new material is integrated into existing material to construct meaning and to prepare it for long-term storage and retrieval.

But people's short-term storage capacity is limited. In normal situations, an adult's maximum short-term storage capacity is generally considered to be about seven items, plus or minus two "items," with an "item" being something the learner must make sense of and relate to other items. Each group of approximately seven "items" is called a "chunk," and grouping items together for further processing is called "chunking." Chunking is a way to overcome the limited size of short-term storage. The mind processes a chunk of as many as nine items as one "item" for purposes of short-term storage, leaving room for six other "chunks" to be held there as well.

Chunking, however, is not a simple process. Psychologists do not all agree on what a "chunk" actually consists of nor how large it is, nor what the processes for encoding knowledge into long-term memory are. What they do know is that, for people who are experts in something, a chunk can be larger and consist of different elements than for someone who is new to the topic or process. For training designers, the importance of this discovery is that the way you group together or chunk information for a novice should be different from the way you would chunk the same information for someone who already knows a lot about the subject. Also, how you chunk the information depends on what the learners already know and how they will use their new knowledge.

Chunking is one of the things that makes training specific to a given target population. A successful chunking strategy increases the amount of new knowledge the learner can store in short-term memory. But if you group items together the wrong way—for example, if you put too many items into a single chunk or make the chunks too small—learners may feel that the lesson is too difficult or too elementary, too fast or too slow, too boring, or "over their heads."

How to Teach This Lesson Element

The training task for chunking is two-fold:

1. To help learners perceive and "work on" the most efficient number of items at a time, by grouping and labeling the items as a single unit.

2. To organize and present units of information grouped by a familiar rule or pattern.

Below are the steps for grouping (chunking) large amounts of information into "bite size" pieces:

1. Divide the items of information (facts, ideas, or steps) you have to present into logical chunks of about seven items each, using a rule (organizing pattern) that is likely to match the learners' existing knowledge structures and the way the learners need to retrieve the knowledge. If the learners are likely to find the information difficult to grasp, limit the chunks to five items. If the information is likely to be relatively easy, you can include up to nine items in a chunk.

2. Label each chunk with a name that suggests its contents and that is meaningful for the learner.

3. In the lesson, first present the listing of chunk names. This acts as a structure of content.

4. Then, for each chunk, present the knowledge in it until all chunks have been presented.

Lesson Element:
Chunking

Description. Organize and limit the amount of new knowledge presented to match human information processing capacity.

AutoRent Example: In Unit 3 AutoRent's VSSs learned how to inspect the vehicles' equipment. For purposes of instruction and learner application, the instructional designer chunked the equipment to be inspected by location within the vehicle and the lights by their location inside and outside the vehicle.

Chunked by Location Within the Vehicle

- At the steering wheel.
  - Washers.
  - Wipers.
  - Tilt wheel (if equipped).
  - Horn.

- On the dashboard.
  - Stereo/CD/cassette.
  - Lighter (if equipped).
  - Glove compartment.

Chunked by Location Inside and Outside the Vehicle

- Lights—exterior: headlights, brake lights, hazard lights, turn signals.
- Lights—interior: dash light, dome light, turn signal indicators, warning light indicator, high beam indicator.

Text Layout

How the written words are laid out on the page (or screen) affects how easily learners can process, understand (encode), store, and later retrieve what they have learned. There is a good deal of research on ways to organize text on a page to help learners process new knowledge more effectively and efficiently. Comparable research on design of text on computer screens is underway. Consequently, we suggest using the principles for text design for both print and computer screens. You may already be familiar with text design systems that apply this research, such as Structured Writing and Information Mapping™. In general, these systems emphasize practices such as:

- Blank space on the page or screen.
- Blocks of information related to chunks of knowledge.
- Bulleted lists of characteristics.
- Page and column size layouts that facilitate scanning.

To comprehend new textual material, learners use a five-step process that is something like the one shown below, in which proper text design helps at every step:

1. First, learners must decide on their purpose for reading. A good text layout makes the purpose of the text clear.

2. Second, learners have to select the information they will attend to. Good text layout helps them quickly find and focus on the relevant information and process it into new knowledge.

3. Third, learners must link the new knowledge with existing knowledge. Text layout techniques that use the chunking principles and cues that learners already know make it easier for them to retrieve existing knowledge and link the new knowledge with the old.

4. Fourth, learners have to organize the new knowledge. Text layout techniques that visually present the organization or structure of the information help learners build their own new knowledge structures.

5. Finally, learners have to assimilate the new knowledge into the existing knowledge. Text layout techniques that make clear the relationships of new and old knowledge and show what the new expanded set of knowledge "looks like" help learners accomplish this assimilation.

How to Develop This Lesson Element

The training task for text layout (whether in print or on a computer screen) involves the following:

- Using chunking to create an obvious organization to the content.
- Blocking and separating the different components of the organization.
- Emphasizing what is important by directing attention to key points.
- Making it easy for learners to scan the material quickly and retrieve it easily.

Here are several techniques for text layout:

1. Create an obvious organizational pattern and block and separate the different components of the organization:

   - Use subheadings, single or multiple word labels that call out or summarize the information in the text. The subheadings can be placed at the beginning of a subsection or along the right margin, directly opposite the text they describe. Use short (one-chunk) lists separated by subheadings.

   - Use bullets instead of numerals unless the items in a list must be completed in a specific order or unless they are shown in order of priority (most important to least important, for example).

   - Use numerals for lists of procedural steps, to indicate that the items must be done in order, or to show the order of priority.

2. Emphasize items and direct the learners' attention to specific items:

   - Use contrasting font attributes (boldface, italics, or underlining) for points to be emphasized.

   - Use different fonts and sizes to differentiate chapter, topic, subtopic, and smaller units of information. Make sure each font and font attribute has a consistent meaning throughout the text. Be sure not to overdo using different fonts; too many can make the document look cluttered.

- Use matrices, tables, and flowcharts to highlight attributes of one concept or compare attributes of two or more related concepts.

- Show sequential steps in a procedure.

- Emphasize decision points and appropriate actions to take.

3. To facilitate rapid scanning:

- Write short sentences.

- Organize sentences into short paragraphs.

- Use blank space to reduce text density.

- Put boxes around text portions of special interest or importance.

- Place explanations next to, above, or below the illustrations they describe.

AutoRent Example: Figure 4.3 is a sample text page from the AutoRent training manual used for Unit 2. It uses chunking, white space, typographical lines, a matrix, blocked and separated pieces of information, and labels, and consists of short sentences organized into short paragraphs.

Illustrations

The old adage, "One picture is worth a thousand words," is actually supported by cognitive psychology principles. In "getting" pictures into long-term memory, people actually encode them twice. First, they assign a meaning to the picture, and then they interpret the visual image. We call this "dual coding," compared with the single coding that occurs for purely verbal information. Dual coding makes it easier to retrieve information learned from illustrations because the content can be retrieved from either verbal memory or visual memory.

How to Develop This Lesson Element

To make the following types of information more concrete and memorable, use as many illustrations as possible:

- Representations of ideas, concepts, things.

- Relative sizes of objects.

- Steps in a process or procedure.

- Specific details of objects.

FIGURE 4.3. AutoRent Procedure

Unit 2—How To Service a Vehicle	
Introduction	In Unit 1, Refueling, you learned the first of several operations to prepare our vehicles for re-rental. In this second unit you'll learn how to apply the eight-step procedure that deals with checking the vehicle's fluid levels and tire pressures and correcting them when necessary. The parts you'll be servicing are the tires, the battery, transmission, engine, brakes, power steering, and radiator reservoir.
When to Perform This Procedure	You perform this procedure upon getting a service work order for a specific vehicle from the service manager. The work order tells you the vehicle data and its location.
Where to Perform This Procedure	The service manager will provide you with the vehicle's keys along with the work order. Park it in any open service bay in the garage.
Equipment You Need to Perform This Procedure	On the workbench at the end of your bay, you'll find clearly marked containers with the fluids you'll need for replacement. Also, every two bays share an air hose and gauges for checking tire air pressures and filling the tires when necessary.
Servicing Procedure	Check and, if necessary, correct these fluid levels in the following six steps in order.

Step	Action
1.	Window Washer Fluid Reservoir (white cover—fill to line).
2.	Engine Oil (wipe stick and reinsert for correct reading).
3.	Transmission Fluid (wipe stick and reinsert with engine running).
4.	Power Steering Fluid (fill to line).
5.	Battery (check indicator—if red, fill; if green, re-cover.
6.	Radiator Reservoir (red cover—fill to line).
7.	Check Tires Pressures—fill to correct pressure, if needed.
8.	Fill out Part 2 of Vehicle Service Record found in the glove compartment.

- Parts of objects.
- Generalized shapes.
- Relative distances.
- Spatial relationships.

Follow these guidelines when designing and using illustrations to present new knowledge:

- Use a style that is attractive to the learner.
- Use captions, questions, or explanations with the illustrations to
    - Help learners relate the content to what they already know.
    - Tell learners what to look for in the illustration.
    - Help learners remember the illustration.
- Use line drawings rather than pictures or photos to highlight the details of the subject matter.
- Begin with less detailed graphics to convey an overview of the concept or object and use detailed "inset" or "pullout" graphics to show specific examples or portions of the subject matter.
- Use lines, arrows, color, and highlighting to
    - Emphasize items.
    - Separate items.
    - Indicate movement.
    - Show hierarchical or procedural relationships.
- Follow the chunking principle in using parts of an illustration. Emphasize a maximum of seven parts per picture.
- When sequencing illustrations, keep learners oriented by repeating the overall view as you present the detailed views.

AutoRent Example: The AutoRent organization makes extensive use of a UPCL scanner system for tracking parts inventory and parts flow. Because the scanners malfunction at times, the parts managers go through a brief training session on the major causes of malfunctions in the system. Figure 4.4 is taken from a training manual used by AutoRent parts managers for this session. It is from the section in the manual that explains how UPCL labels can cause a malfunction.

The illustration separates each cause and labels it; reproduces the image in actual size; doesn't exceed the chunking principle; and uses line drawings instead of photos.

**FIGURE 4.4. UPCL
Code Failure Modes**

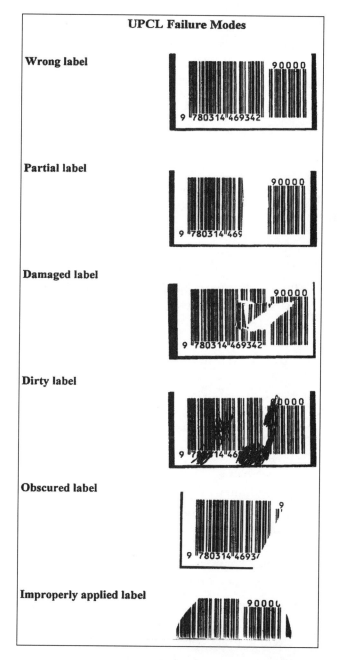

A lesson segment for YourMart is shown below in tabular form (Figure 4.5). It illustrates two lesson elements, structure of content and objectives, that help the learner with the third task, organize the information. The segment is part of a lesson that teaches YourMart new hire word processors the three-step procedure for doing a mail merge. Because it is a summary version, it does not include examples of the lesson elements of chunking, text layout, or illustrations.

FIGURE 4.5. Job Aid for Learner Task 3

Learner Task and Lesson Element	Example
3. *Organize the Information.* Organize the new knowledge so that it matches the organization of existing knowledge. *Structure of Content.* Name the number of steps in the procedure and highlight any branches.	"When you click on 'Tools . . . Mail Merge,' the mail merge helper dialog box first asks you what kind of merge you want to do. Then it shows you the three basic steps of the process: 1. Create (or edit) the main document 2. Find (or create) the data source document 3. Merge the data with the document."
Objectives. Specify both the desired behavior and the knowledge to be learned.	"If you follow the instructions as they appear on the screen, you'll be able to do the three-step procedure."

SUMMARY

In this chapter, we expanded on the third learner task in the Cognitive Training Model introduced in Chapter 2. This third task for the learner is to Organize the Information. We discussed both what learners must do to organize the information and how you can help them do it. The five lesson elements that you use to help them do this are

- *Structure of Content*—This lesson element displays the major learning components of the content and the relationship among the components. It is presented at the beginning of the lesson to help learners begin to create a schema or mental model that aids encoding, storage, and retrieval.

- *Objectives*—This lesson element states what learners will be able to do when training is completed; the conditions under which they will be expected to do it; and the standards or criteria by which their performance will be evaluated. The verbs used to state objectives are less related to lists of behaviors in this approach than they are in behavioral instructional design and more related to the cognitive processes called for by a particular type of knowledge.

- *Chunking*—This lesson element groups and labels large bodies of learning information into smaller labeled units to help learners process the content to short-term memory and beyond.

- *Text Layout*—This lesson element organizes text to help learners process new knowledge more effectively and efficiently.

- *Illustrations*—This lesson element makes it easier for learners to retrieve information learned from illustrations because the content can be retrieved from either verbal memory or visual memory.

For each of these lesson elements we presented:

- A detailed discussion of what the elements are.
- A brief summary of the issues involved in using them.
- A "how to develop and apply them" section with examples.
- A final example in job aid format.

FIGURE 5.1. Chapter 5 Structure of Content

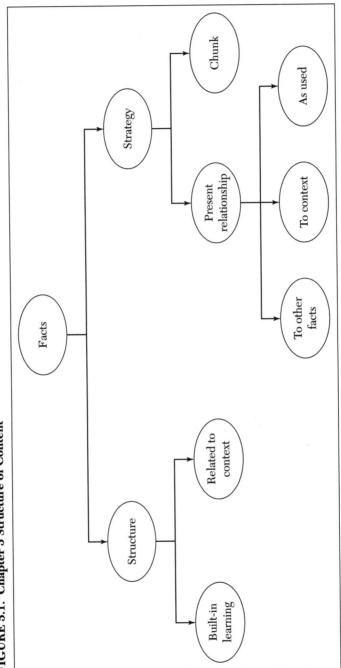

Chapter 5

Teaching Facts

LINK AND ORGANIZE

Recall (from Chapter 1)

- Facts are one type of declarative knowledge
- A fact is a simple association among a set of verbal and/or visual propositions.

Relate to What You Already Know

- Facts as we refer to them are exactly the same as facts in the Gagne categorization (and all others derived from Gagne, such as Dick & Carey).
- Examples of facts you already know are:
    - On a traffic light, red means stop, green means go, and yellow means prepare to stop.
    - In 1492 Christopher Columbus sailed from Spain and landed in the Caribbean; he was not the first to do so, nor did he discover America.

Structure of Content

- See Figure 5.1.

Objectives

- To describe what facts are.
- To apply general strategies for teaching facts.
- To design a lesson to teach facts including all lesson elements.

ABOUT FACTS

At AutoRent customer service representatives need to know vehicle names, models, and features, rental cost, and rental package features to inform customers of options.

At YourMart new secretaries need to learn keyboard shortcuts to add to their word processing skills.

A fact is the simplest form of declarative knowledge. It consists of a statement that expresses a relationship between two or more objects or events. Cognitive psychologists call these statements "meaningful propositions" because they express a simple but complete thought. They are basic to everyday life and are needed for use in further learning.

As you recall from Chapter 1, declarative knowledge is stored in long-term memory in what cognitive psychologists call "propositional networks" or "schemata." This notion tells us a lot about facts and has many implications for how we teach them.

Facts Do Not Exist in Isolation

Facts are not isolated bits of information. They are related to one another and to other kinds of knowledge. They are stored in long-term memory in networks that are based on those relationships and retrieved through those networks. You can visualize these networks, as shown in Figure 5.2.

FIGURE 5.2. Possible Network of Facts for a Telephone Number

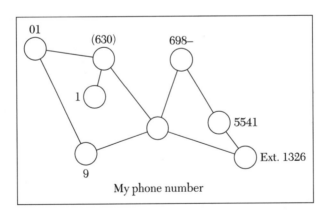

For example, we might have a structure of facts that relate to the location of a city we visit frequently. Our structure might include best hotel, our favorite restaurants, the record and schedule of our favorite sports team or program of the symphony orchestra, the names and addresses of local friends, the route from the hotel to each of three clients, and so forth. In our network, each of those bits of information is related to all the other bits as facts.

Networks Are Created Based on Context

The networks in which these facts are stored are created, and are related to one another, based on the context in which the facts are learned and used. Different theorists have different terms for this ("schema" or "script"); all you need to remember is the idea that they are in some kind of structure. For example, the context for the set of facts in the example above could be "business trip to City X." That context would determine:

- Which bits of information we put in the network.
- How we relate or connect the bits of information in the network.

Of course, the residents of the town in the example would also have structures of bits of information about the town in their own networks. But the bits they stored would be different, and they would organize them differently because they would use the information differently—for living in the city, not for making a business trip to it. They might store and relate facts focused on shopping (best stores and hours), movies, school locations and hours, and traffic routes, and so on.

Facts Are Best Retrieved in the Same Context in Which They Are Learned

All of us have had the experience of "I know I know that, but I can't seem to remember it." Frequently, that's because we learned a fact (including the face of a person we can't place) in one context, such as work, and are trying to recall it in another context, such as a social gathering.

Since the networks in which facts are stored are determined by the context in which they are learned and used, it makes sense that they would be easiest to remember in the same context and most difficult to remember in a totally different context. That's because in a different context we have no clue about what facts we have stored where. And we have far too many networks of facts in memory to go through them all.

We Learn Facts by Building On Existing Networks of Facts

We don't start from scratch. We learn facts by building on (psychologists call it "elaborating") existing networks of facts. When presented with a fact to learn in a context, we immediately search our memory for a network of facts that fit that context and seem to be related to it. Then we add the new fact onto the existing network, or completely restructure the existing network to better fit the new fact. Then we store away the new structure until we need it again.

GENERAL STRATEGIES FOR TEACHING FACTS

Based on what facts are and on how they are stored and retrieved, we suggest the following general strategies for teaching facts:

- Relate new facts to existing declarative knowledge structures so that learners will be able to make the associations needed to remember and recall them when, where, and how they are needed.

- Present both the learners' existing knowledge structure and the new facts, and show how the facts and knowledge structure relate in the context of a meaningful use of the facts.

- Teach facts in a context—preferably the context in which you expect them to be used; in the case of training, this is usually the job setting and tasks.

- When asking people to recall facts, have them do so in the same context in which they learned them.

- Give learners a hint about which existing networks to recall and add to.

- Provide suggestions about how the new fact fits into the existing structure or requires a restructuring of the network.

- When writing objectives for fact-level teaching, use verbs such as state, define, recite, or list.

- Depending on how the facts are used, consider giving learners a job aid so they can look up facts as needed, rather than requiring them to memorize large amounts of information. Their performance may be slow at first while they look things up, but they will soon have memorized the facts they frequently use. If that slow initial performance is acceptable, keep fact teaching to a minimum.

- If the number of facts to be taught at once is limited to a very few (perhaps just one or two) chunks, consider embedding fact teaching within the teaching of other kinds of learning.

- If the number of facts is larger than a few chunks, construct a separate instructional event to teach facts, using the strategy described below.

USING THE LESSON ELEMENTS TO TEACH FACTS

Example Scenario

As part of their basic training, all AutoRent customer service representatives need to learn a large amount of fact-level knowledge concerning vehicle characteristics, rental rates, and rental packages. The example below describes a fact-level segment from one of these sessions. To avoid redundancy, Learner Task 1, Select the Information to Attend To, and its corresponding lesson elements, Attention, WIIFM, and YCDI, are not shown. (For descriptions see Chapter 3.) The lesson segment begins with Learner Task 2, Link the New Information with Existing Knowledge.

Learner Task 2: Link the New Information with Existing Knowledge

Lesson Element: Recall

Description. You should stimulate recall by the learner of all those appropriate knowledge networks (structures) that will include the facts to be learned. Be clear about which networks are specific to the context and which will be of more general use. One portion of the "advance organizer" we've all heard about is to recall previously learned knowledge on which the new knowledge is based.

> AutoRent Example: "Most of you own a car. If it wasn't given to you, you went through some process of determining what kind of a car you wanted before you went shopping for it. You decided on a make, a size, what kind of gas mileage you wanted, what accessories you wanted, such as air conditioning or a tape deck, and what safety features were important to you."

Lesson Element: Relate

Description. Relate the new facts to what the learner already knows (the knowledge structures you just helped the learner to recall). If we can cleverly use a setting (context) that is the same or similar to the one the learner will be in when the facts will be needed, then we will increase the likelihood that the learner will recall the facts then. Again, a portion of the advance organizer model emphasizes bridging or linking the new knowledge to the old by emphasizing the similarities and differences between them.

You do this by using various cues, including verbal statements, images, tables, and so forth to point out the relationships you want the learner to form. What is important is that the relationships be meaningful to the learner within the structure of the task. We recommend minimizing the use of "memory tricks" (mnemonic strategies) that are purely arbitrary (such as associating each fact with a location on your desk), because the relationships they provide are not related to how the facts will be used. The memory tricks may help you as you initially learn the facts, but they may abandon you when the context changes to one in which the facts are used.

> AutoRent Example: "Our customers are no different. They look for these same things in a rental car. So you need to know all these facts about AutoRent's fleet of rental vehicles to help the customer make a satisfactory rental decision."

Learner Task 3: Organize the Information

Lesson Element:
Structure of Content

Description. You should state how you have structured the facts for easy learning. This helps the learner prepare to receive the new facts and relate them to appropriate existing networks of facts in memory. This is the place in the lesson where you present the structure of the facts to the learner. Remember that it's best if the structure is directly related to how the facts will be used.

> AutoRent Example: "All these facts are displayed in the chart found in your training manual. Vehicle sizes and types are across the top, and the facts for each are under each of the vehicle types and sizes." (This fact chart is shown in Figure 5.3).

FIGURE 5.3. Rental Car Fact Sheet

Size	Small	Medium	Large	Luxury	Minivan	SUV	Sporty
Vehicle Make	Chevy Cavalier	Chevy Lumina	Buick LeSabre	Cadillac Fleetwood	Chevy Astro	Chevy Blazer	Chevy Corvette
Number of Doors	2	4	4	4	3 plus rear	4	2
Passenger Capacity	2/3	3/3	3/3	3/3	2/3/3	3/3	2
Accessory Package	All models come equipped with power steering, power brakes, power windows, power locks, AM/FM radio, tape deck, AC, and automatic transmission.						
Safety Package	All models equipped with driver and passenger air bags and anti-lock brakes.						
Gas Mileage/ Fuel Grade	26/reg	22/reg	20/reg	na/prem	15/reg	17/reg	na/prem
Luggage Capacity (cubic feet)	14	16	17	14	—	—	—
Engine Size	120 hp 2.2 L	160 hp 3.1 L	205 hp V6 3.8 L	275 hp V8 4.6 L	190 hp V6 4.3 L	190 hp V6 4.3 L	345 hp V8 5.7 L
Drive	Front	Front	Front	Front	Rear	4WD	Rear
Per Day Rental							
Per Week Rental							
Per Weekend Rental							

Lesson Element:
Objectives

Description. State both the desired content and behavior.

> AutoRent Example: "At the end of this training session, you'll be able to answer, from memory and by using the chart, customer inquires about our vehicle makes and models and facts about each: number of passengers, gas mileage, accessory packages, safety features, and rental cost."

Learner Task 4: Assimilate the New Knowledge into Existing Knowledge

Lesson Element: Present
New Knowledge

Description. We discussed above how facts should be presented within structures. You do this by providing cues that signal the structure. These cues need to be distinctive, meaningful, and related to the learner's existing networks of facts. Where appropriate, use visual images of the facts, maps, diagrams, colors, tables, typography, and even sounds to provide additional cues to the learner about the structure of the facts.

Follow these guidelines for what cues to include and the sequence in which to include them:

Step 1. Show the Facts

a. Use the structure you presented above.

b. Establish links to what the learners already know.

c. Reinforce the way the structure will be used.

Step 2. Explain the Structure

a. Include an explanation of the structure you presented.

b. If possible, retain the display of the facts during the explanation to help support encoding and storage (memorization).

> AutoRent Example: Step 1. [*Show the chart on slide. Trainees have individual copies of the chart.*] "You can see this chart contains much, if not all, of the type of information you needed when you were buying a car. The chart displays all the important facts for each of AutoRent's vehicles. Each of our seven sizes and makes go across the top, from smallest to biggest. Underneath each are number of doors, passenger capacity, accessory package, safety package, gas mileage luggage capacity, engine size, front- or rear-wheel drive, any additional features, and the per day, per week, and per weekend rental rates. The chart is simple to use. Locate the vehicle size requested across the top and read down for all the information. Let's work an example."
>
> [*Show isolated Chevy Cavalier column on overhead.*] "Let's say your customer asked you about renting a small car. Your reply—either from

memory or with help from the chart—would be something like this, 'Our small car is a Chevy Cavalier. It's a two-door, seats two in front and three in back, and comes with our standard accessory package—power steering, brakes, power windows and locks, AM/FM radio, tape deck, and air conditioning. The safety package includes both passenger and driver air bags and anti-lock brakes.'" [*Explain that it isn't necessary to state gas mileage, luggage capacity, engine size, or whether the car has front- or rear-wheel drive unless the customer asks.*] "How many days were you planning on renting the car?"

"Once you find out how long the customer wants the car, you can again refer to the chart or your memory for the correct information."

Step 2. "Most customers will first ask about the availability of car sizes, so we've arranged the chart with the car sizes and makes in the top rows, followed by passenger capacity and then, continuing down, accessory package, safety package, gas mileage, luggage capacity, engine size, front- or rear-wheel drive, any additional features, and finally, the three primary rental rates. The columns are arranged from the smallest car to the largest. So to repeat, the chart is organized by car size and make at the tops of the columns, with all pertinent facts following underneath. This order follows the most frequently asked questions about rentals."

Learner Task 5: Strengthen the Knowledge in Memory

Lesson Element: Practice

Description. Practice is more critical in learning facts than for most other types of learning. It is crucial to aid the learner both in building the new fact network and in retrieving it at the appropriate time. Follow these guidelines in building practice into the lesson:

- Use only questions that present the cues the learner will use on the job.
- For wrong-answer feedback, restate the structure rule the learner violated, if possible, as well as the factual association.
- Practice first within the structure you presented (even if it's only a list); then intermix items from different parts of the structure.
- At the beginning, keep the total number of facts being practiced at one time to one structure or list of nine or fewer facts; then broaden out until the entire structure of facts is being practiced in a sequence that reinforces the rule structure.
- Late in practice, vary the sequence of questions randomly, unless the facts are to be recalled only in a particular order (such as a lock's combination or a phone number).
- To build proficiency, when a learner consistently and rapidly provides the right answer, drop the fact from the practice list and add "new" facts to

the list of facts being practiced. *Hint*: Learners often find proficiency-building practice tedious. This is a great opportunity to build in a game to add interest, but be sure to build a game that applies the rules above and will be interesting and fun for the learners (just because you like the latest version of *Asteroid Blasters* doesn't necessarily mean your learners will, or that it will help them recall the facts on the job).

AutoRent Example: "All right. Now you get the chance to help a customer. Suzanne, I come up to your counter and tell you I'm interested in renting a midsize car. What's your response?" [*Continue asking practice questions about different sized cars until there are few or no errors. Next introduce practice questions requiring the trainee to access the chart from points other than the top. After this exercise, divide trainees into pairs and have them role play customer and CSR until some facts are remembered rather than retrieved from the chart.*]

Lesson Element: Feedback

Description. Let learners know how well they've done in using the new knowledge, what problems they're having, and why.

AutoRent Example: "Frank, you seem to be having some trouble with some of the larger model car facts. Are they clear to you? Is there anything on the chart you don't understand?" [*Continue in this manner until you're satisfied that major difficulties are cleared up.*]

Lesson Element: Summary

Description. Present the structure of content again, including the entire structure of facts. But you don't need to list each individual fact.

AutoRent Example: "See how easy it is to use the fact chart to answer questions? Many of you at the end of the role-playing game could reply to inquiries without looking at the chart. Through practice you're beginning automatically to commit many of the facts to memory. By the time you begin working the reservation counter, you won't need the chart, right?! Just kidding. Remember to bring your chart with you and refer to it when you have to. Most of these facts will get into your memory whether you like it or not!"

Lesson Element: Test

Description. Have learners use the new knowledge again, this time to prove to themselves, you, and their managers that they have met the training objectives.

AutoRent Example: [*The test in this training session consists of a fact chart that has only the names of the vehicles. The trainees' task is to fill in as many of the facts as they can recall for each of the models in the chart. This will give you and the trainees a good idea of how many facts about each of the vehicles they can immediately recall. Reassure them that while on the job they will still be able to use their fact charts.*]

Lesson Element:
On-the-Job Application

Description. Have the learners use new knowledge in a structured way on the job to ensure they "use it, not lose it."

AutoRent Example: [*Give the learners' managers copies of the fact chart. Tell them what they learned and what the trainees should be capable of doing. If you can, make up a "contest" type game that the manager can use to reinforce the factual learning.*]

A second fact-level lesson sample is shown below in tabular form (Figure 5.4). It illustrates the design for teaching YourMart secretaries how to perform keyboard shortcuts.

FIGURE 5.4. Job Aid for Teaching Facts

Lesson Element	Example
1. Select the Information to Attend To *Attention.* Get learners to focus on the new facts.	"OK, everybody, in the next few minutes you're going to learn a few shortcuts!"
WIIFM. Tell them how the new facts will help them.	"These shortcuts in word processing will, I guarantee, save you a great deal of time as you become proficient in using the system."
YCDI. Reassure the learners that they will be able to master these facts.	"This formatting may seem confusing at first but that happens to everybody. We'll practice nice and slowly until you feel confident in using these shortcuts."
2. Link the New Information with Existing Knowledge *Recall* related fact structures.	"For example, you already know about many of the basic font formats, such as **bold**, *italic*, underlines, ALL CAPS, subscript, and superscript".
Relate to what the learner already knows about when or how the facts are used.	"And you already know how to apply these formats using the mouse, just by clicking on an icon or menus and dialog box choices."
3. Organize the Information *Structure of Content.* State how you have structured the content for easy learning.	"Most of the keyboard shortcuts for formatting use keys that remind you of the term Word uses to describe them."
Objectives	"In this lesson, you'll learn about the keyboard shortcuts to format fonts (characters). You'll learn what they are and practice formatting a paragraph using them."

FIGURE 5.4. (Continued)

Lesson Element	Example
4. Assimilate the New Knowledge into Existing Knowledge *Present New Knowledge.* Show the facts using the structure you presented above; establish links to what the learners already know; and reinforce the way the structure will be used.	[*This is an example of rule-governed association.*] "Here are the most common ones for the font formats you already know: Bold CTRL B Underline CTRL U Italic CTRL I Subscript CTRL = Superscript CTRL Shift =
Present Examples. Include an explanation of the structure you selected in analysis. Retain the display of the facts, if possible.	"Notice that these keyboard shortcuts are easy to remember because: • In each case, you hold down the CTRL key (and Shift key) while pressing the key shown. • The bold, italic, and underline use the first letter of each word. • Superscript is like an 'uppercase subscript.' • They all toggle on and off: for example, to return to normal text from any of these character formats, simply press the keyboard shortcut again."
5. Strengthen the New Knowledge in Memory *Practice* • Use only questions that present the cues the learner will use "on the job." • Use only questions that ask the learner to remember the association from cue to response (never from response to cue, unless the job requires the learner to remember the association bi-directionally). • For wrong-answer feedback, restate the structure rule the learner violated, if possible, as well as the factual association.	[*Step 1:*] "Now, you try it. Type these letters: t, **t**, r, **r**, w, *w*, $_a$, a, ^{e}, e." [*Continue similar practice until there are few errors. Step 2:*] "Now, try typing this sentence: Remember, keyboard shortcuts will save you time, where $(t_m - t^k) * n$ = total time saved in typing a document." [*Continue practice with additional sentences until there are few errors.*]

(Continued)

FIGURE 5.4. Job Aid for Teaching Facts (*Continued*)

Lesson Element	Example
• Practice first within the lists or other structure you presented, then intermix items from different parts of the structure. At the beginning, keep the total number of facts being practiced at one time to one structure or list, then broaden out until the entire body of facts is being practiced in a sequence that reinforces the rule structure. • Vary the sequence of questions randomly. • To build proficiency, when a learner consistently and rapidly provides the right answer, drop the fact from the practice list and add "new" facts to the list being practiced.	[*Step 3: Present another list of keyboard shortcuts using an appropriate strategy you selected in your analysis.*] [*Step 4: Present practice like Step 1 above, but using elements from all lists presented so far. Be sure to randomize sequence and eliminate items from practice as the learner gets them consistently right.*] [*Step 5: Present practice like Step 2 above, but using elements from all lists presented so far.*] [*Step 6: Continue adding lists and practicing like Steps 1 and 2 until all keyboard shortcuts have been presented and proficiency is at the desired level of accuracy and response time (fluency).*]
Feedback. Let learners know how well they've done, what problems they're having and why.	[*During and after the practice provide encouragement and corrective reinforcement.*]
Summary. The structure of content is the entire structure of facts.	"As you have seen, knowing just a few points about the keyboard shortcuts make them easy to remember." [*Show the entire list of keyboard shortcuts in the fact structures by which you first presented them. Show the relevant structure rules next to each fact structure.*]
Test. Have learners use the new knowledge. Give them application exercises that measure their ability to apply this factual knowledge.	[*Test them on their ability to recall the keyboard shortcuts and these fact structures.*]
On-the-Job Application. Have learners use the new knowledge on their jobs to reinforce the learning.	[*Give the learners a job aid containing the new knowledge along with a series of typical application problems. Suggest that they apply what they learned to these typical situations.*]

SUMMARY

In this chapter, we described the cognitive aspects of fact-level learning and the general strategies for teaching facts and provided an example of how to teach a fact-level lesson segment using the lesson elements.

We began the chapter with an explanation of fact learning from a cognitive psychology point of view, explaining that:

- Facts do not exist in isolation.

- Facts are embedded in networks based on learning and "how they are reused contexts."

- Facts are retrieved best in the same context as learned.

- Facts are learned by building on existing fact networks.

Next we discussed general strategies for teaching facts, including:

- The importance of content and recall of existing networks.

- The use of specific action verbs for fact-level objectives.

- The use of job aids.

- Chunking of appropriate amounts of related information.

In the final part of the chapter, we focused on how to teach a fact-level lesson segment using the lesson elements. The segment dealt with teaching AutoRent's new customer service representatives rental car characteristics and other rental facts they need to function as rental car agents.

We concluded the chapter with an example in job-aid format that illustrates the design for teaching YourMart secretaries how to perform keyboard shortcuts.

FIGURE 6.1. Chapter 6 Structure of Content

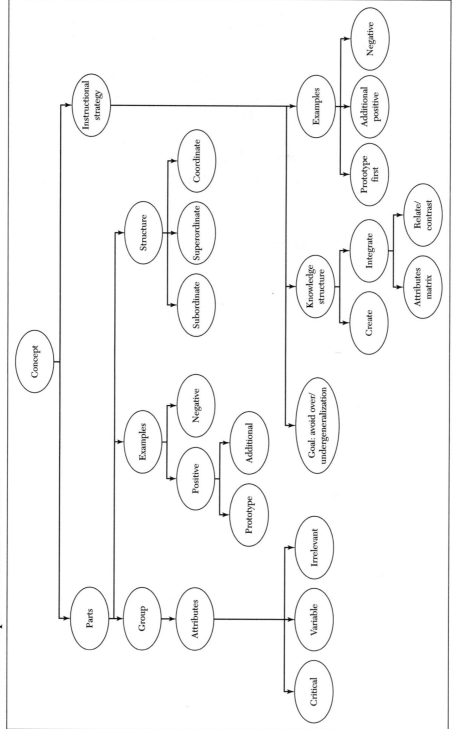

Chapter 6
Teaching Concepts

Recall (from Chapter 1)

- Concepts are one type of declarative knowledge.
- A concept is a category of objects, actions, or abstract ideas that are grouped together with a single name because they share characteristics in common.

Relate to What You Already Know

- Concepts as we refer to them are exactly the same as concepts in the Gagne categorization (and all others derived from his, such as Dick & Carey).
- Examples of concepts you already know are:
  - Sail boats, exercise, bridges, mammals, mountains, love, square.
  - Sailboat is the name given to a category of objects (boats) having common characteristics such as mast, sail, keel, rudder.

Structure of Content

- See Figure 6.1.

Objectives

- To describe what concepts are.
- To apply general strategies for teaching concepts.
- To design a lesson to teach facts, including all lesson elements.

ABOUT CONCEPTS

At AutoRent because of upcoming large-scale organizational changes, employees need to be able to recognize examples of self-directed team organization's and traditional organization's structures.

At YourMart the new word processors need to recognize examples of character formatting.

These training problems involve *concepts*—understanding what something is. These concepts are the basic building blocks of all knowledge, so if your learners are having trouble here, they will have troubles with everything else they learn. So teaching concepts well is critical to the success of all training.

Just what are concepts? When we use the word concept here, we do not use it in the usual conversational way: "I've got the concept"—meaning the idea. We mean something very specific. A concept is a group of objects, actions, or abstract ideas that have something in common and usually are referred to by a common name.

There are five key elements that make a concept a concept:

1. It is a group of things (objects, events, or abstract ideas).

2. The objects, events, or ideas in the group have some features in common that cause us to think of them as being related to one another, including features they must have to be in the group. However, the things in the group are not identical, and they therefore also have some features that are different. But these differences do not exclude them from the group.

3. The concept has a prototypical example.

4. The concept is related to other concepts in one of several ways: coordinate, subordinate, or superordinate.

5. The concept (along with related concepts, a name for the group of concepts, the attributes of each concept, and a prototypical example of each concept) fits together into a knowledge structure.

Let's look at these five parts of what a concept means in more detail. We will discuss them in the above sequence, but please note that this sequence is not necessarily the sequence a learner follows in learning concepts. Figure 6.2 contains a summary and examples of points 2, 3, and 4.

1. Group of Things

First, a concept is a group of things (objects, events, ideas). Some common concepts include: table, building, party, dine, democracy, and friendship. Each

FIGURE 6.2. Superordinate, Subordinate, and Coordinate Concepts with Examples

	Paper Only		Electronic & Paper		Electronic Only	
	Snail Mail	Overnight Mail	Fax	Fax File Transfer	Modem File Transfer	E-Mail
How It Works	document in envelope; post office truck/plane/truck; carrier delivers	document in envelope; post office truck/plane/truck; carrier delivers	feed document into fax machine; dial phone # of receiving fax machine; machine sends document over phone lines; receiving fax machine prints document	fax software on computer dials phone number of receiving fax machine; fax software sends electronic file to receiving fax machine; receiving fax machine prints document	software on computer dials phone number of receiving computer; software sends electronic file to receiving computer; receiving computer can print or use document	e-mail software on computer sends message to ID of receiving computer; e-mail software sends electronic file to host computer; host computer receives electronic file; when receiver logs on, document is available
Cost	$.37 + $.23 additional oz. over 1	$13.65 for 8 oz. for next day delivery	$.50 per page	$.25 per page	<$.01 per page	<$.01 per page
Speed	4 to 7 days	1 day	15 sec per page	2 sec per page	5–30 sec per document, depending on size & modem speed	5–30 sec per document, depending on size & modem speed
Advantages	cheap, familiar	fast, cost-effective for larger documents	fast, cost-effective for small documents	can do from laptop PC from anywhere	can do from laptop PC from anywhere, easy to respond to and comment on	can do from laptop PC from anywhere, easy to respond to and comment on
Problems	slow, frequent loss of documents	expensive	receiving machine may be busy, slow for long documents, not secure	software cumbersome to set up, same disadvantages as fax	software cumbersome to set up, receiver must be available	recipient must have e-mail address
Prototypical Examples	Birthday cards from relatives	Report (printed in color)	Letter or memo	Letter or memo	Report to be edited by receiver	Report to be edited by receiver

of these concepts is made up of a group of things: There are many different types and examples of tables, buildings, parties, dining establishments, democracies, and friendships. The technical concepts mentioned in the brief examples above are compact cars, subcompact cars, just-in-time inventory, regular inventory, and format.

2. Critical, Variable, and Irrelevant Attributes

Second, the things in the group have some features in common that cause us to think of them as being related to one another—and which things must have to be in the group. For example, a table must have some kind of raised, flat top and must be used to place things on for various purposes in order for us to think of it as a table; if the top is not raised, we call it a tray. The features a thing must have are *critical* to its being included in a group because they must always be present in a single way, and are cleverly named *critical features* or *critical attributes*.

The things in the group are not identical and therefore have some features that are different. There are two types of differences. The first is differences that help define what's in the group and what's not. For example, a table must have a base for us to think of it as a table (if it has none, we think of it as a tray), but the type of base on the tables in the group can vary (legs, pedestal, and so on). And yet all things with one of these bases are tables—still all in the group. Since some form of these features must be present, although the form can vary among members of the group, they are called *variable features* or *variable attributes*.

The second kind of differences is differences that have no effect on what's in the group and what's not. They may or may not be present, but their presence or absence does not affect group membership. For example, tables can vary in shape (circle, square, triangle, rectangle), material (wood, plastic, glass, combo), and size, but still be tables. Since presence, absence, or form of these features is irrelevant to whether things are in the group or not, they are cleverly called *irrelevant features* or *irrelevant attributes*.

As instructional designers, it is important for us to know the attributes for concepts we are trying to teach. However, as you will see later in this chapter, we do not always state these attributes to learners.

3. Examples and Concepts

In the behaviorist days of instructional design, we believed that the most important part of learning concepts was learning the critical and variable *attributes.* Cognitivists, however, place a greater value and role on the *examples.* Many believe that what many learners really remember is the prototype (idealized) example of a concept they encounter, not the definition or attributes of the concepts. Examples, then, are critical in learning, storing, and retrieving concepts.

Learners probably store in memory the idealized example they see as a prototype. Some theorists believe the prototype example often bears a close resemblance to the first example of a concept the learner encounters. Concepts are stored and related to each other according to how they will be used, as well as their attributes. This makes it very important to pick a first example based not only on its possession of critical and variable attributes, but also on the context in which the concept will be used. This way, the prototypical example relates directly to the context knowledge structure the learner already has, and it can be retrieved from memory in the appropriate context on the job.

One example is not enough, however. Learners usually need additional examples to understand a concept. The examples that would seem to make the concept clearest to learners are the "bulls-eye" examples. These are examples that are closest to the "prototypical" example and have all the critical and variable attributes. For the concept "tables," for example, we might use an antique oak table with a pedestal base or a modern metal/plastic table with four iron legs.

We do need those kinds of examples, but they're not enough. We also need some examples that show all the different ways the variable attributes can change. And we need examples that vary the irrelevant attributes. We also need some examples that are barely examples of the concept, and some that are barely not examples of this concept but are examples of a coordinate concept.

4. Coordinate and Subordinate/Superordinate Concepts

Third, if we just change one or more critical attributes in a concept, we have a different, but related concept: subcompact versus compact cars; just in time versus regular inventory; effective versus ineffective meetings. These are called *coordinate* concepts. Something that is not a member of one of the concept groups is a member of the other.

In addition, most concepts are part of other concepts—and have concepts that are part of them. A concept is called *subordinate* to another concept if it refers only to some of the members of the class of the larger concept. Subcompact cars are a concept that is subordinate to the concept cars. The concept "cars" is, in turn, subordinate to the concept four-wheel land-based transportation vehicles, which is, in turn subordinate to . . . well, you get the idea.

A concept is called *superordinate* to others if it includes many other concepts. The concept "transportation vehicles" is *superordinate* to the concepts land-based transportation vehicles, water-based transportation vehicles, and air-based transportation vehicles. In turn, the concept land-based transportation vehicles is superordinate to the concepts two-wheeled land-based transportation vehicles and four-wheeled land-based transportation vehicles. The concept four-wheeled land-based transportation vehicles is superordinate to the concept cars.

Figure 6.2 illustrates the ideas of superordinate, subordinate, and coordinate concepts and of concept attributes for a different subject matter: methods of document transfer.

5. Knowledge Structures

Fifth and finally, we create a knowledge structure and name for the group. Since there are so many things in the group, we make it easy for ourselves to deal with the concept by putting all the things that fit in the concept in a knowledge structure that relates them to one another and to other concepts, and we learn or create a name that describes the concept—the knowledge structure and all the things in it.

GENERAL STRATEGIES FOR TEACHING CONCEPTS

Based on the five components of a concept and on what the research says about teaching concepts, we suggest the following general strategies for teaching concepts:

- Help the learner avoid overgeneralization, under-generalization, and misconception.

- Help the learner create a correct knowledge structure that allows for the correct application of the prototypical example or critical and variable attributes so that new examples can be easily categorized.

- Make sure the learner integrates the concepts into an appropriate structure, so they will be retrieved and used when needed.

- Don't just present one concept and its critical and variable attributes, but rather teach, relate, and differentiate several new concepts at the same time.

- Develop and integrate the knowledge structure surrounding the concept, including: a prototypical example of the concepts; the critical and variable attributes of the concepts (which the learner may or may not be able to articulate); and relationships to other concepts.

- Relate the new concepts to the appropriate superordinate and subordinate concepts in the knowledge structure.

- Relate the prototypical example (and, if appropriate, critical and variable attributes) of each concept to those of the others, so generalization and discrimination occur.

- Write the first draft of the instruction "lean," then try out the instruction on some actual learners.

- Add definitions and examples only where the learners make errors which show misconceptions.

- Begin presenting a concept, NOT with the definition, but rather with the prototypical example; then present the attributes of the concept if appropriate; finally, if needed, present additional example/non-examples.

- Do NOT present a narrative definition, but rather present a bulleted list of attributes of a single concept or an attribute matrix for all the related concepts.

USING THE LESSON ELEMENTS TO TEACH CONCEPTS

Example Scenario

Customers have to wait long periods of time to get an assigned vehicle after completing the rental contract at all of AutoRent's major market car rental centers (thirty-five across the country). This is directly caused by the time it takes to "turn the vehicle around" after the last customer use. The longer the time, the more delays, backups, and waiting time by new customers. Customer complaints are on the increase, and AutoRent's competitors are guaranteeing customers that "If you have to wait, we pay."

A company task force consisting of center managers, customer service representatives, vehicle service specialists, and an organization development consultant determined the following:

- Center employees at all the levels compartmentalized their tasks, that is, they performed only tasks in their job descriptions.

- Center managers tightly controlled the centers' operations.

- Little information about center operations was available to the employees.

- Any incentive to improve job performance was up to the individual and, therefore, very difficult to obtain.

- Managers were solely responsible for the centers' operational plans. There was no other input.

The task force concluded that the chronic problem of long turnaround times (along with a number of other company problems) was the result of a tightly controlled, rigid, management philosophy and style.

After examining several companies that had experienced similar operating problems and the solutions they attempted, the task force recommended that the company gradually change its current management style to one of empowerment and self-directed teams. The task force concluded that these major interventions would have a number of benefits, among them faster vehicle turnaround time at the centers.

The performance goal of the resultant course was to train center employees how to work in self-directed teams. Among the first things the trainees had to learn in the course was the concept of "self-directed team organizations" and how they differed from traditional organizations.

The following example describes a concept-level segment from one of these sessions. To avoid redundancy, Learner Task 1, Select the Information to Attend To, and its corresponding lesson elements, Attention, WIIFM, and YCDI, are not shown. (For descriptions see Chapter 3.) The lesson segment begins with Learner Task 2, Link the New Information with Existing Knowledge.

Learner Task 2: Link the New Information with Existing Knowledge

Lesson Element: Recall

Description. Recall existing concept structures that the learner needs to understand the new concept knowledge you are teaching.

> AutoRent Example: "Most, if not all of you, have been in situations where you had to do a job by yourself with little or no help from anyone. This works out if we're talking about a hobby or a simple task where you don't need to rely on other people to get the job done. Everything was under your control, it was up to you, and you got the job done. On the other hand, many of you have been in situations where it was impossible for you to complete a job or large task alone. Playing on a team is a good example. Everybody working together accomplished more than one person could. These experiences will help you understand how the team approach can be applied to everybody in a company."

Lesson Element: Relate

Description. Relate the concepts you are teaching to their place in concept structures the learner already knows.

> AutoRent Example: "Before we get into the specific procedures and techniques you need to know to work on a self-directed team, I want to start with a wider view of the subject. Let's begin with a look at the concept of the self-directed team organization and how it differs from a traditional organization."

Learner Task 3: Organize the Information

Lesson Element: Structure of Content

Description. The structure of content should show the relationships among from five to nine new concepts. If the concept structure is larger than that, show those that are at the "high level."

AutoRent Example: "We'll do this by pointing out the differences between the two organizations." [*Direct their attention to the partially filled out comparison chart in their training manuals. Show chart on the slide (Figure 6.3).*] "Across the top of the chart are the two organization types (traditional and self-directed). Down the side are seven key elements of comparison—organizational structure, job design, management role, leadership, information flow, rewards, and job process. We'll go through these individually."

FIGURE 6.3. Differences Between Traditional and Empowered Organizations

Element	Traditional Organizations	Self-Directed Teams
How Companies Organize		
What People Do		
What Management Does		
Who Leads and How		
How Everyone Communicates		
How People Are Rewarded		
How People Do Their Jobs		

From R.C. Wellins, W.C. Byham, & J.M. Wilson, *Empowered Teams* (San Francisco, CA: Jossey-Bass, 1991).

Lesson Element: Objectives

Description. The objectives should describe both the behaviors to be learned and the knowledge to be understood.

AutoRent Example: [*Display objective on slide.*] "After this part of the workshop, you'll be able to recognize examples of the two types of organizations and make up some examples of your own."

Learner Task 4: Assimilate the New Knowledge into Existing Knowledge

Lesson Elements: Present New Knowledge and Present Examples

Description. Follow these guidelines for what to include and the sequence in which to include them:

Step 1. Show the concepts, using a sequence which includes prototype examples, followed as needed by definitions and contrasts and additional examples. People probably remember the prototype (first or idealized) example, not the definition. Therefore, focus on presenting the prototype example. Use abstract diagrams or definitions when needed to highlight key attributes. Otherwise, use realistic videos, photos, or illustrations.

Step 2. If learners need more help in understanding the concepts, then:

• Compare and contrast and/or show the logical relationships between the concepts.

- Use a hierarchy or a contrast table to make the comparisons visible and easy to see.

- Reinforce the knowledge structure and related concepts (declarative knowledge).

- Demonstrate the concept and suggest the procedural knowledge needed to set the attributes.

Step 3. Present as many additional examples as needed to assure appropriate generalization, while avoiding errors of misconception, overgeneralization, and under-generalization. Use these principles to select and construct the examples:

Strategy

- Include initial practice by having learners label and classify the examples.

- Contrast examples of one concept with those of others you are teaching or those the learner already knows.

- Keep all examples in view, if possible, or present them in close succession.

Sequencing

- Start with "close in" examples similar to the prototype example, then include more "far out" ones.

- After presenting some positive examples, mix positive and negative examples.

Range

- Use a range of examples to emphasize the variability of positive examples.

- Remember that in a coordinate concept set, any positive example of one concept is a negative example of all the others.

- Be sure to use examples across the whole concept structure at once, not just isolated concepts.

AutoRent Example: [*Display previous chart (Figure 6.3) on slide.*] "As we consider each of these elements, we'll write the specific characteristics in the appropriate blank square. So, for example, as I begin the discussion on the structure of the traditional organization you would write that particular characteristic in the appropriate space in your own charts." [*Present the elements*

of each organization here (The completed chart is shown in Figure 6.4),
comparing and contrasting the seven elements. Develop the presentation by
pointing out the differences between the two concepts element by element until
the entire chart is filled out. Keep the filled out chart in full view.] "We'll use
two real companies to illustrate these two different organizational patterns.
In fact we'll use AutoRent as the example of a traditional organization and
our competitor, YourCar, as the example of an empowered team organization.
YourCar began changing to the team concept two years ago. Currently, their
average auto in/out time is roughly half of ours. Also, average processing time
from customer at counter to customer in car is half that of ours. These figures
are based on the same number of employees involved in the operations, with
the same computer support. Let's begin with the first element, 'How Companies Organize.'

"For both companies I'm going to start from the individual rental
location up to international headquarters. Typically, at each AutoRent
location there are three shifts of CSRs, mechanics, and ASRs. These people report to their shift managers. Each of the shift managers reports to a
location manager. The location managers report to the territory managers.
The territory managers report to regional managers. The regional managers
report to the vice president of operations, and that position reports to the
CEO.

"At YourCar, the empowered team organization, the picture looks like
this. At each location there are teams (the number depends on location size)
made up of two CSRs, a mechanic, and two ASRs. These teams report to their
individual shift managers, who report to the location owners/managers. The
location owners/managers report to an owners/managers council. The council and what are called 'regional consultants' report to the vice president of
operations. That position reports to the CEO.

"So the major differences in how the companies are organized are:
AutoRent has seven layers of management with individuals reporting to individuals, whereas YourCar is flatter with five layers and teams, councils,
and individuals reporting to each other." [*Continue until the chart is completed. After discussion, present another example of self-directed team
organizations in the form of company profiles. The profiles contain the seven
key elements as they appear on the comparison chart. Process each example by either pointing out each of the elements or asking the learners to
do so.*]

[*Next, present additional examples with the seven elements appearing in
the same order as on the chart. Then present company profiles with the seven
elements in random order. Either point them out or ask trainees to do so.
Get them to recognize the self-directed team organization, even though the
elements are scrambled. Finally, introduce company profiles that are non-
examples (that is, examples made up of the seven elements of the traditional*

organization), company profiles that are examples, and company profiles that are non-examples but contain mixed elements of both organizations. Turn the projector off.]

FIGURE 6.4. Differences Between Traditional and Empowered Organizations

Element	Traditional Organizations	Self-Directed Teams
How Companies Organize	Layered/Individual	Flat/Team
What People Do	Narrow single task	Whole process/Multiple task
What Management Does	Direct/Control	Coach/Facilitate
Who Leads and How	Top-down	Shared with team
How Everyone Communicates	Controlled/Limited	Open/Shared
How People Are Rewarded	Individual/Seniority	Team-based/Skills-based
How People Do Their Jobs	Managers plan, controlled, improve	Teams plan, controlled, improve

From R.C. Wellins, W.C. Byham, & J.M. Wilson, *Empowered Teams* (San Francisco, CA: Jossey-Bass, 1991).

Learner Task 5: Strengthen the New Knowledge in Memory

Lesson Element: Practice

Description. Practice with additional examples. Use these principles to build the practice:

- Begin by having the learner classify or construct additional examples. Use the same practice formats as you used earlier.
- Use practice examples that are new to the learner.
- Use realistic contexts, preferably using simulations or scenario-based exercises.
- Include context and irrelevant information so the learner is required to select only the relevant information.

  AutoRent Example: [*Give the learners a case study. Ask them to describe it in terms of either a traditional or team organization; then ask them to describe how that organization might change.*]

Lesson Element: Feedback

Description. Let the learners know how well they've done in using the new concept knowledge, what problems they're having, and why.

- Include prompts and cues not found in the real world only when essential or for wrong-answer feedback.

- In wrong-answer feedback, include an explanation of the attribute missed.

AutoRent Example: [*Process the case study exercise. Look for over- or under-generalization. Reemphasize critical and variable attributes where necessary. Reinforce correct descriptions.*]

Lesson Element: Summary

Description. Present the structure of content, showing the critical and variable attributes and/or the prototypical example.

AutoRent Example: [*Show slide of the filled out comparison chart (Figure 6.4).*] "You now can describe what a self-directed team organization is and, given a fairly complete description of a company, decide whether it is a self-directed type of organization or a traditional one. Next we'll go into the specific dynamics of self-directed teams."

Lesson Element: Test

Description. Have learners use the new knowledge again to prove to themselves and upper management that they can perform the training objective.

AutoRent Example: [*Include a number of descriptions of different types of organizations and their attributes. The learners' task is to recognize examples of traditional organizations and self-directed team organizations. They should be able to give the reasons why they are examples of these two organizations. They should also be able to give reasons why those that are not, are not. Also ask them to generate a few examples of both organizations.*]

Lesson Element: On-the-Job Application

Description. Have learners use the new knowledge in a structured way on the job to ensure they won't "lose it."

AutoRent Example: [*This is the beginning of a series of training workshops for AutoRent center employees that will result in a transition from a relatively tightly controlled organization to one of self-directed teams. Learners will be applying this basic knowledge as they participate in the organizational change. Make sure those subsequent workshops start with a review of these concepts and that the participants are able to continue to recognize examples of these two major types of organizational models.*]

A second concept-level lesson segment is shown in tabular form (Figure 6.5). It illustrates the design for teaching YourMart word processors how to recognize examples of "character formatting."

FIGURE 6.5. Job Aid for Teaching Concepts

Lesson Elements	Example
1. Select the Information to Attend To *Attention.* Gain and focus learners' attention on the new knowledge.	"Being able to change the size of type and its font or underline a word or change it to bold or italic with a few keystrokes is something that the inventors of printing could not even dream of."
WIIFM. Tell learners "What's in it for me?"	"Being able to quickly change words or strings of words to boldface or headline size or underlined and more launches you on your way to professional level word processing skills."
YCDI. Encourage the learners by telling them: "You can do it."	"Although it may seem that lots of information is coming at you fast and furious and you may feel that you'll never remember any of this, don't worry. Through practice and repetition you'll begin to absorb this stuff like sponges."
2. Link the New Information with Existing Knowledge *Recall* concept structures that the learner needs to understand what you are teaching.	"You probably already know some formatting concepts from experience with typewriters and other word processors. For example, you probably know character-formatting concepts such as fonts (as from pica to elite to italic). And you know about subscript and superscript. In paragraph formatting, you know about indenting, centering, right justification, left justification, as well as full justification, when each line is stretched to reach the right and left margins."
Relate the concepts you are teaching to their place in concept structures the learner already knows.	"We'll show some additional examples of some of these concepts, and you'll see some additional formatting concepts. Some will be for character formatting, and some will be for paragraph formatting."
3. Organize the Information *Structure of Content.* Show the relationship between up to five to nine concepts. If the concept structure is larger than that, show those that are at the "high level."	"Word makes a distinction between character formatting and paragraph formatting. In this lesson, we'll look at character formatting. This includes font and point size, modified fonts such as italic, the case of characters, spacing between characters, color, and hidden text. The concepts we'll be looking at are related like this" [*Show diagram*].
Objectives.	"In this lesson, you'll see some sample documents and see how Word describes the character formatting in them. Later, you'll learn how to do the formatting you've learned about."

FIGURE 6.5. (*Continued*)

Lesson Elements	Example

4. Assimilate the New Knowledge into Existing Knowledge
Present New Knowledge and Present Examples. Show the concepts, using a sequence which includes prototype examples.
	[*Show an example of a well-composed finished printed page; highlight and label attributes; group and explain like this:*
	Fonts
	  Times New Roman, 12 point
	  Arial, 10 point
	  Arial, 14 point
	Font Modifications
	  Bold vs. Normal
	  Italic vs. Normal
	  Word Underline
	  Continuous Underline
	  Strike Through
	  Double Underline
	  Superscript vs. Subscript
	  Hidden Text (not visible—show and explain where it will appear on screen, but not in print.)
	  Color
	Case
	  All caps
	  Small caps
	Spacing
	  Wide character spacing
	  Condensed character spacing]

If learners need more help in understanding the concepts, then: present the definition (rule); facilitate comparison/contrast, between the concepts; use a hierarchy or a contrast table. Practice with the hierarchy reinforces the knowledge structure, which relates concepts (declarative knowledge); practice with the actual screen gives further practice with the concept attributes in their context, and also suggests the procedural knowledge needed to set the attributes.	"Now let's look at the document you just saw, from inside Word. You'll be able to see what settings of toolbar buttons and pull-down menu choices created each feature. To see how the combinations of features go together, find them on the structure chart. To see how the system defines them, open the document and highlight each feature. Then compare the settings you see with the screen prints I'm giving you and find them all on your system." [*Distribute Word screen prints which show and have highlighted the buttons and menu choices which created each text attribute.*]
Present additional examples as needed: *Strategy:* have learners label and classify examples; contrast examples of the concepts; keep all examples in view.	"Here are three additional examples that combine the character attributes you've just learned. Look at them on paper and try to predict the Word button and menu settings which created each format. Then check your prediction by opening the document in Word and looking at the settings."

(*Continued*)

FIGURE 6.5. Job Aid for Teaching Concepts (*Continued*)

Lesson Elements	Example
Sequencing: move from "close in" examples to more "far out" ones; after presenting some positive examples, mix positive and negative examples. *Range:* use a range of examples which emphasize the variability of variable attributes; pair examples of coordinate concepts to get non-examples for each concept; use examples across the whole concept structure	[*Distribute the sample documents and the online file containing them. Examples should show combinations of attributes, such as: Arial Bold 18 Point Continuous Underlined; Times Roman 12 pt. Italic Small Caps Strike Through; Courier 12 pt. Italic Word Underlined wide spacing and so on.*]
5. Strengthen the New Knowledge in Memory *Practice.* Have the learner classify or construct additional examples. Use only examples new to the learner. Use realistic contexts. Include irrelevant information. Include prompts and cues not found in the real world only when essential.	"Here is a draft printout of a file called pract1. All character formatting is set to Times Roman 12 point. Here is a finished printed page of the document with the character formatting set as in the final copy. Use the hierarchy as an aid, and mark up the draft printout with the character formatting attributes required to make it look like the final version. If you get stuck, refer to the procedure reference in Word Help or the printed documentation, or ask me." [*Pract1 should have formatting combinations comparable in complexity to the examples used above. It should also include some paragraph formatting which has not yet been taught, but which is needed now for coordinate concept practice.*]
Feedback. Let the learners know how well they've done in using the knowledge, what problems they're having and why. In wrong-answer feedback, include the attribute missed.	[*Reinforce the learners for correct responses. For those having difficulty, point out their errors and the probable reasons why they answered the way they did.*]
Summary. Show and summarize the "structure of content" material.	[*Show the diagram illustrating the relationship of five to nine concepts of character formatting displayed first in the structure of content section.*]
Test. Have learners use the new knowledge again to offer evidence that they have met the objectives of the training.	[*Give the learners another draft printout of a file with a different type font and size. Their task is to mark up the draft printout with the character formatting attributes required to look like the final version. This test exercise is what they did for the practice section.*]

FIGURE 6.5. *(Continued)*

Lesson Elements	Example
On-the-Job Application. Have learners use new knowledge in a structured way on the job to ensure they "use it, not lose it."	[*Inform the group that when they get back to their desks they will have a small word processing project to complete involving the character formatting they just learned. These projects consist of creating charts for use at the counters and garage. Also, tell them that their supervisors have a copy of the training manual so they are informed as to what the trainees will be capable of doing after the training sessions.*]

SUMMARY

In this chapter, we explained the nature of concepts, general strategies for teaching concepts, and how to teach a concept lesson using the lesson elements.

The chapter began with a definition of a "concept":

A group of things having features in common, having a prototypical example, related to other concepts in one of several ways, with elements that fit together in knowledge structures.

Then we discussed general strategies for teaching concepts. These included helping the learner:

- To avoid overgeneralization and under-generalization and misconceptions by creating correct knowledge structures.

- To integrate concepts into an appropriate structure by teaching several new concepts at once.

- To integrate the surrounding knowledge structures by relating new concepts to other concepts in the knowledge structure.

  - By relating prototypical examples of each concept to those of others.

  - By trying out a "lean" version of the lesson on learners and adjusting definitions and examples as needed.

  - By presenting a prototypical example first, then attributes and additional examples if necessary.

  - By presenting the concept definition in the form of a bulleted list of attributes or in an attribute matrix.

In the final part of the chapter we integrated these strategies into a concept-level lesson segment using the lesson elements. This segment demonstrates how to apply the lesson elements to teach AutoRent's employees how to recognize differences between the concepts of a "self-directed" team or organization and a "traditional" team or organization.

We concluded the chapter with an example in job-aid format that illustrates the design for teaching YourMart word processors how to recognize examples of "chapter formatting."

FIGURE 7.1. Chapter 7 Structure of Content

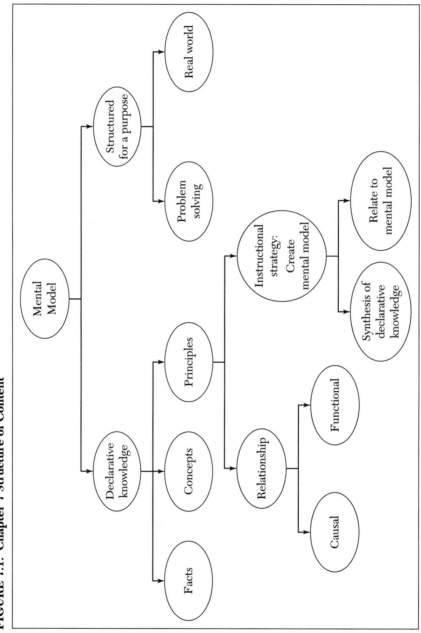

Chapter 7

Teaching Principles and Mental Models

Recall (from Chapter 1)

- Principles and mental models are types of declarative knowledge.

- A principle is a cause-effect relationship. When you understand a principle it will help you to know how something works. Principles are frequently stated as "if . . . then" statements.

- A mental model is a network of principles with supporting concepts and facts. Mental models tie together all the declarative knowledge in memory. Information is organized within them. Mental models are the structures that go into memory.

Relate to What You Already Know

- Examples of principles you already know are: If you over-inflate an inner tube, it will burst. If you put a flame into a can of kerosene, it will ignite. If you stick a metal handled screwdriver into a live electrical socket, you'll get a shock.

- An example of a mental model you already know is "restaurant." When you think of "restaurant" you think of name, reservations, tables, chairs, waiters, seating, atmosphere, types of food, level of service, themes, and so on. All of these make up your mental model for "restaurant."

Structure of Content

- See Figure 7.1.

Objectives

- To describe what principles and mental models are.
- To apply general strategies for teaching principles and mental models.
- To design a lesson to teach principles and mental models including all lesson elements.

ABOUT PRINCIPLES AND MENTAL MODELS

At AutoRent customer service representatives are calling their managers to settle problems generated by reserved vehicles not being available when customers come to the counter to rent them, because guidelines are nonexistent.

At YourMart warehouse technicians need to be able to predict what will happen when electrical components are connected in a variety of ways as part of their "install and maintain robots" training course.

These types of training problems involve *principles* and *mental models*—causal relationships about how the world works. Mental models are a key part of the bridge between declarative and procedural knowledge, so if your learners are having trouble here, they will have trouble solving problems using knowledge. So teaching principles and mental models well is critical to training being applied back on the job.

Principles

A principle is a statement of a cause-effect relationship that explains why or how something works as it does. For example, you know that by pressing the accelerator, a car's engine will speed up (and the principle works in both directions unless the accelerator is stuck!). Understanding that principle about how a car works helps you figure out how to drive a car. It also helps you predict what would happen, even if you're not now doing the action (for example, "I know that if I step on the accelerator in that car, it will go faster, even though I'm not now driving it").

It's sometimes hard to tell the difference between a principle and a concept. A simple test is to try to express the idea as an if . . . then statement or mathematical equation. If you can do so, it's a principle. For example, a basic principle of electricity is Ohm's law: voltage = current $\times$ resistance ($E = IR$). In words, Ohm's law means that if current stays constant, and if resistance is increased, then voltage goes up. The concepts involved are voltage, resistance, and current (as well as increase and decrease (and the facts are the units of measure for each concept).

Principles often are stated as assertions (rules) rather than if . . . then statements, so you may need to rewrite them in an unfamiliar form. For example, you know that "you can add numbers together in any order." It would be awkward, but you could rewrite the statement as an if . . . then: "If the numbers are in any order, then the total does not change."

Learners need to know principles when:

- Learning goals require the learner to be able to explain (why) or give a reason (because) for a decision, event, operation, or procedure.

- Learning goals require the learner to predict or model the operation of a system.

- The learner must solve problems that are *moderately structured* or *ill-structured.*

- Generalization to new situations is a major goal of training.

- You cannot precisely predict what problems the learner will have to solve.

- Details of knowledge are likely to go out-of-date quickly, and the learners are expected to learn new details on their own, without further formal training.

- Learners already know part of the problem space, or many details of it, and need to see the "big picture."

Like facts and concepts, principles fit together in structures, and they underlie procedures. Some analysts like to draw single structures that incorporate all the relationships among the facts, concepts, and principles in a given domain of knowledge.

Mental Models

A mental model is (1) a network of facts, concepts, and principles constructed by the learner; (2) who weaves them together into a functional network of knowledge for some purpose; (3) the "behavior" of which mirrors some known or expected aspect of the "real world"; and (4) which serves as the basis for procedural knowledge.

A sample mental model is shown in Figure 7.2. Let's look at the four parts of a mental model in more detail.

1. Network of Facts, Concepts, and Principles. Learners construct mental models by synthesizing their knowledge of facts, concepts, and principles into a model (often hierarchical) with causal relationships. A complete mental

FIGURE 7.2. Sample of a Mental Model

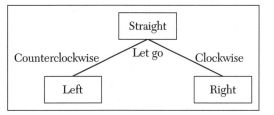

model of a problem space (for example, "conducting large group meetings") includes:

- Principles describing how the system works when it works correctly.
- Principles describing how the system works when it does not work.
- All the concepts referred to by the principles (and represented in the concept analysis.
- The prototypical examples ("great meetings I have known" and "failed meetings I have known"), stored as war stories ("First, George did this, then he did that, then Frank did this, then . . .").

2. Functional for a Purpose. The mental model is constructed for the purpose of explaining or predicting some chunk of observable "real world" behavior. Thus, mental models are constructed for a particular purpose and are very context-bound. Knowledge learned and organized in one context may not all be recalled or transferable to other contexts. The same knowledge would be organized very differently by two different people who were going to apply it in two different contexts. For example, a mechanic's mental model of an engine would be different from that of the engineer who designed it, even though both mental models would include the same engine component parts.

3. Behavior Mirrors the "Real World." Since mental models are created for a purpose, to operate in a context, mental models are not necessarily a full, detailed, or accurate picture of "reality." Nor do they match other people's mental models of the same "reality." For example, mental models of trees and how they function will differ by whether the creator is a forester, an ecologist, a tree surgeon, or a tree worshipper; if your mental model of a tree includes a tree spirit, that's OK as long as it predicts and explains whatever tree properties and behavior you want.

4. Basis for Procedural Knowledge. The mental model is the basis of procedural knowledge. In effect, synthesis of (passive/descriptive) declarative knowledge into a mental model builds the basis of (active/predictive) procedural knowledge. It is the key step in learning to do problem solving, which is why problem solving is so much a context-bound skill. Solving problems involves constructing (or modifying or otherwise manipulating) a mental model of the problem.

When you start to solve a problem, you build a specific mental model for the specific situation (for example, of the meeting you're trying to plan/fix) as an instantiation of the generalized mental model, and you manipulate that instantiation according to the rules of the general model you have (in this case, of meetings) and predict or explain how it will or has behaved. That tells you what you need to change in order to get the desired behavior of the "real" meeting.

GENERAL STRATEGIES FOR TEACHING PRINCIPLES AND MENTAL MODELS

The key in teaching principles and mental models is to:

- Relate the principles to one another and to existing knowledge in mental models.

- Get the learner to predict or explain the behavior of the model by using the principles.

- Learn and/or create mental models that are related to the context in which they will be using the knowledge.

- Synthesize the declarative knowledge (facts, concepts, and principles) well enough to use it as the basis for the problem-solving tasks the learners will be learning to do next.

USING THE LESSON ELEMENTS TO TEACH PRINCIPLES AND MENTAL MODELS

Example Scenario

A recent AutoRent customer survey showed an unacceptable number of customer complaints concerning both the unavailability of the type of car they reserved at the time of rental (a non-training problem here) and the lackluster efforts of the customer service agents (CSRs) to remedy the situation. The company decided to empower CSRs in this particular situation ("unavailability of rental car") by giving them a short training segment on the principles they should use to arrive at a rental solution acceptable to the customer.

The performance objective became: Given a series of "unavailability of rental car" simulations and AutoRent's "customer satisfaction principles," use the principles to predict or bring about a rental decision acceptable to the customer. To avoid redundancy, Learner Task 1, Select the Information to Attend To, and its corresponding lesson elements, Attention, WIIFM, and YCDI, are not shown. (For descriptions see Chapter 3.) The lesson segment begins with Learner Task 2, Link the New Information with Existing Knowledge.

Learner Task 2: Link the New Information with Existing Knowledge

Lesson Element: Recall

Description. Recall existing declarative knowledge structures (facts, concepts, principles, and mental models) that the learner needs to understand the new principles and mental model knowledge you are teaching.

> AutoRent Example: "Recall what you've learned in the previous 'Customer Satisfaction Course.' In these units you've learned to apply your knowledge about the types of vehicles in AutoRent's fleet, along with rental rates and costs, AutoRent's major customer satisfaction guidelines, and interpersonal principles used when dealing with dissatisfied customers." [*Before continuing, refresh trainees' mental models of these structures by presenting them with a variety of situations requiring them both to predict outcomes when using the content and to apply the content.*]

The knowledge structures to be recalled here are in Chapter 5, Figure 5.3. The major customer satisfaction and problem resolution guidelines are shown in Figures 7.3 and 7.4.

FIGURE 7.3. Principles of AutoRent's Customer Satisfaction Course

Unit 1—Major Customer Satisfaction Guidelines

Principles

- Maximize customer convenience.
- Minimize customer time.
- If you cannot give the customer the value purchased, give him/her one step more, but never less.
- Keep the customer's business if it can be done without violating our first two principles.
- Always remember that customer convenience and time, as well as giving the customer value purchased and keeping the customer's business take precedence over company profitability.
- Maximize company revenue if and when you can.

Lesson Element: Relate

Description. Relate the principles and mental model you are teaching to existing knowledge structures (facts, concepts, principles, and mental models) the learner already has and the context in which the new mental model will be used.

> AutoRent Example: [*Explain that what the group is about to learn will be used in situations in which the customer at the counter has reserved a specific vehicle and that vehicle is not available (Figure 7.3). After establishing this context, continue explaining how their knowledge of AutoRent's price and package structures and vehicle classifications will be used to resolve each*

FIGURE 7.4. AutoRent's Problem Resolution Model

Unit 2—Resolving Customer Problems
Part 1—Active Listening
Facts, Concepts, Principles, Mental Model(s), and Procedures

Facts/Concepts

listening	critical listening	paraphrase
empathic listening	eye contact	retaining
apology	hearing	open-ended questions
listening circle	active listening	evaluating
neutral listening	feedback	closed questions
focus	nodding	answering
receiving	understanding	nonverbals

Principles

- If the CSA states in his/her own words what he/she thinks the customer idea of the problem is, then it will increase the likelihood of understanding because the customer can correct the restatement if necessary.
- If the CSA restates the feelings he/she felt the customer was expressing about the problem, then it allows the CSA to check on his/her perception of those feelings and the customer to see his/her feelings more objectively and gives the customer the chance to elaborate on those feelings.
- If the CSA asks questions to obtain additional understanding of the customer's thoughts and feelings regarding the problem, then the customer is more likely to feel that the CSA is interested and concerned.

Procedures

1. State in your own words what you think the customer said about the problem.
2. State or restate in your own words the feelings the customer is expressing.
3. Ask open-ended questions to make sure you understand the customer's feelings, the problem, and any additional information you may need.

situation. Also relate how the skills they learned for how to treat upset customers (Figure 7.4) need to be applied in many of these situations. Show them a video clip of an "unavailability of rental car" transaction. Before viewing the segment, tell them to watch closely and answer the discussion questions: "What is the CSR using in this situation that you already know?" "Why is it being used?" and "How is the CSR resolving the problem?" Process the questions after viewing the video segment. If the learners state some or all of the principles (both to deal specifically with the vehicle situation and the interpersonal interaction), then list them and reinforce them and lead into the "Structure of Content" section.]

Learner Task 3: Organize the Information

Lesson Element:
Structure of Content

Description. The structure of content should show the complete new mental model, including context, principles, and structure, and incorporate existing mental model(s), concept structures, and facts.

AutoRent Example: "We have observed one of our CSRs dealing with an 'unavailability of rental car' situation. The principles she used are the ones you're going to learn and practice in just a few minutes. The first and most important one that she used is 'If the vehicle the customer reserved isn't available, upgrade to the next vehicle but charge the rate of the original reservation.' She also used some active listening skills and her ability to put herself in the place of the customer, stuff you already know. What I want to

FIGURE 7.5. Mental Model of AutoRent's Customer Satisfaction Course

Unit 2—Resolving Customer Problems
Part 2—Resolving Customer Problems
Facts, Concepts, Principles, Mental Model(s) and Procedure

Facts/Concepts

solution	reasonable solution	acceptable solution	problem	resolution
feedback	preferred solution	authorized person	negotiate	

Principles

- If the customer is asked to and provides a preferred solution to the problem, then the CSA more likely will have a better understanding of what the customer wants and also a basis or start for finding a satisfactory resolution.
- If the solution is reasonable, acceptable to AutoRent, and can be implemented, then the CSA will more likely be able to bring about a resolution of the problem that is satisfactory to both the customer and the company.
- If the CSA cannot implement the customer's preferred solution but transfers the transaction to someone who can, that is, an authorized person, then the solution more likely will be satisfactory to both the customer and the company.
- If at the conclusion of the problem resolution, the CSA asks the customer for comments on how the problem was resolved, thanks the customer, and invites the customer to use AutoRent again, then there is a good chance that the customer will have a more positive attitude toward doing business with the company again.

Procedure

1. Ask the customer how he/she would like the problem to be resolved. AutoRent calls this the customer's preferred solution.
2. Determine whether or not the customer's preferred solution is reasonable, acceptable to the company, and can be implemented. If the solution meets all three of the criteria, then execute the solution.
3. If the preferred solution doesn't meet any of the three criteria, find a person authorized to make higher-level decisions and transfer the transaction.
4. When the problem has been resolved, ask the customer (when diplomatically possible) for comments, thank the customer for using AutoRent, and invite the customer to use AutoRent again.

show you now is what we're going to cover in today's unit on resolving un-availability of rental car situations." [*Refer them to the appropriate page in their training manuals and also project the information in the training room. Tell them to read through the content and ask for questions.*]

Fact/concept definitions: vehicle upgrade, substitution, larger vehicle class, lower vehicle class, reduced rate, unavailability of rental car, customer satisfaction.

Principles

- If the vehicle that the customer has reserved is unavailable at time, offer the next larger vehicle class available at no additional cost.

- If the next larger vehicle class is not available, offer the next lower vehicle class at the reduced rate.

- If either of these transactions will take longer than the customer is willing to wait, then offer to either take the customer to a local destination or call and pay for a cab to do the same and drop off vehicle when it is available.

- If the customer cannot wait and doesn't have a local destination, find a like vehicle at another agency. If the other agency's rental rate differs from AutoRent's, ask the customer to mail or provide a copy of the receipt and advise the customer that he or she will be reimbursed and issue a $25 voucher on his or her next rental.

[*After the questioning period, again display each of the previous unit's contents. Explain how they will be using all of these elements when applying these principles in "unavailability of rental car" situations.*]

Lesson Element: Objectives

Description. The objectives should require the learner to use the principles in some way. Most common is to have the learner *predict* what will happen next when observing or manipulating an object or scenario or *explain* why something happened or why a particular decision is (or is not) justified. In response to a "why" question, the correct answer is often close to a statement of the relevant principle. Note that the event being observed or manipulated can be real or in a game or simulation, and it can be a normal or abnormal function.

AutoRent Example: [*Display the objective of the unit and call their attention to it in the training manual. The objective for this workshop is: "Given a series of 'unavailability of rental car' simulations and AutoRent's 'unavailability of rental car' principles, use the principles to resolve the situations, and when resolved explain why." This objective can be introduced at any time up to this point in any of the preceding sections.*]

Learner Task 4: Assimilate the New Knowledge into Existing Knowledge

Lesson Elements: Present New Knowledge and Examples

Description. Follow these guidelines for what to include and the sequence in which to include them:

Step 1. Show the principles in action, using prototypical examples in the form of stories (both about how it works when it works and how it works when it doesn't work). People usually remember the prototype (idealized or first) example, not the principle or mental model in verbal form. Make stories credible, vivid, and straightforward enough to highlight key principles. Tell the stories verbally with testimonials or with realistic video, photos, or illustrations.

Step 2. State the principles involved in the mental model and the mental model itself:

- Present the context for the principles and the mental model.

- Present the principles as if . . . then . . . statements or because . . . reasons.

- Display all principles in the mental model simultaneously to facilitate comparison and contrast and/or to show how the principles fit together in the mental model.

- Show how the principles integrate with existing mental models, concept structures, and fact structures to create the new mental model.

- Use some kind or diagram to show what the mental model looks like.

Be sure you are representing the system at the level of detail at which the learner will be operating. For example, don't show a full schematic diagram if a block diagram of the system shows what the learner will be manipulating. You should have determined the correct level of detail in your task/content analysis.

Step 3. Present as many additional examples as needed to assure that all applications of the mental principles and mental model in the desired context are exemplified.

Step 4. If the objectives include abnormal or emergency operation of the system, or if the learner will be troubleshooting the system, then present the failure modes of the system components. State:

- All the ways a component can fail.

- The probability of each type of failure (if necessary).

- The principle(s) of system operation with that failure mode.

Again, be sure you are representing the system at the level of detail that corresponds to what the learner will be manipulating about the system.

AutoRent Example: [*Show five short video scenarios to the group. Before playing the tape, tell the group that they have seen this first CSR-customer interaction and will see it again only before the appropriate principle is to be applied. Explain that you will stop the action and ask them to apply the proper principle. The CSR on tape goes through each principle, including the last one where she has to call another agency, secure a vehicle and transportation to the agency, and explain how to send the rental statement in for an adjustment and the $25 voucher. Verbally reinforce the context, mental model, and principles when and if necessary.*

[*The second video has the same format. In this one, however, active listening principles are displayed as they are modeled along with the "unavailability" principles. Verbally reinforce the integration of the active listening rules into the current context, mental model, and principles.*

[*The third video has the same format. In this one the "resolving transaction" principles are displayed as they are modeled along with the "unavailability" and "active listening" principles. Again, verbally reinforce the synthesis of these sets.*

[*The fourth video again has the same format with a slightly different scenario. As the CSR applies the three sets modeled in the previous videotapes, the customer resists the predictable solutions. At appropriate points in the transaction, the action stops and AutoRent's Customer Satisfaction Guidelines (Figure 7.3) are displayed. The CSR applies the appropriate guideline to that point of the transaction and the action resumes. The scenario continues until all of these major principles are shown in application. Process the scenario by reinforcing the idea of how these major principles fold into the previous elements.*

[*The fifth video again shows an "unavailability" situation. This time the CSR's voice is heard in a "think-aloud" narrative in which she models the thought process of recalling and applying the principles to decide what to do.*

[*To close this section, display the "unavailability" principles first; then add the other sets, explaining how they complement each other and combine to form a larger system of customer transaction guidelines.*]

Learner Task 5: Strengthen the New Knowledge in Memory

Lesson Element: Practice

Description. Practice with examples of system function. Use the principles to build the practice. Ask questions which require application of the principles to new situations. For example, you can ask the learner to:

- Predict how the system will respond to something the learner does or observes.

- Explain by stating the reason why the system behaved as it did.
- Generate or select another example of the system's behavior.

If you are teaching a mental model of a system that later will be used for abnormal or emergency operation of that system or to facilitate troubleshooting, *practice modeling the failure modes* of the system. Ask questions about system operation with the failure modes that ask the learner to predict, explain by stating the reason why, and generate or select another example of the system's behavior.

AutoRent Example: [*In the first practice and feedback exercise, direct the trainees to the section of their manuals that contains twenty statements of completed CSR-customer transactions concerning the "unavailability of rental car" situation. For each of them, tell the trainees to write which principle or group of principles was operating to bring about the final transaction. Once the CSRs have finished responding to the transactions in the manual about Mrs. Kingsbury, who had reserved a Toyota Camry, which was not available, process each one, being sure to emphasize all the principles operating in each case.*

[In the second practice and feedback exercise, have the CSRs create a situation similar to the ones they just worked on, partner up, and role play with one being the customer and the other the CSR, then switching. Select a number of them for presentation to the entire group. Give feedback and reinforcement.

[In the third and final practice, show them video scenarios where "unavailability" transactions are set up and the action stopped. Their task is to predict the outcome with a written response, given the specific situation. Once all have written their responses, play out each of the scenarios. Trainees can check their predictions against the example. This exercise will help you check on how effectively their mental models are operating.]

Lesson Element:
Feedback

Description. Let the learners know how well they've done in using the new knowledge, what problems they're having, and why.

AutoRent Example: [*Process their answers by reinforcing correct responses and asking them to vocalize their reasoning leading to those responses. For incorrect predictions, tell them where they reasoned incorrectly, what they left out, and/or why they arrived at their answers. Go over the exercises, elaborating on the processes for arriving at correct responses.*]

Lesson Element: Summary

Description. Present the structure of content, showing the complete new mental model, including context, principles, and structure, and incorporating existing mental model(s), concept structures, and facts (Figure 7.5).

AutoRent Example: [*Direct the trainees to the summary section of the unit in their manuals, which explains the situations or contexts where the principles will be used, lists all the principles as they appear in the structure of content section, and lists the principles already learned for active listening and resolving transactions and AutoRent's customer satisfaction principles. Reiterate the importance of incorporating these previously learned skill sets when using the newly learned "unavailability of rental car" principles.*]

Lesson Element: Test

Description. Have the learners use the new knowledge again to prove to themselves, the trainer, and the employer that they can perform the training objective.

AutoRent Example: [*Put trainees into groups of three. Two are trainees and the third is an experienced CSR. The trainees will role play customer and CSR. The "customer" uses a script to initiate the transaction. The CSR uses a performance checklist to grade the trainees on their ability to bring each transaction to a "satisfactory" close. The scripts used are structured to present a wide variety of situations requiring trainees to use previously learned principles with the ones underlying the current training session. After each role play, ask the CSR role player to explain why he/she handled the transaction the way he/she did.*]

Lesson Element: On-the-Job Application

Description. Have the learners use new knowledge in a structured way on the job to ensure they "use it, not lose it."

AutoRent Example: [*Inform the CSR managers how the new CSRs have been trained to respond to "unavailability of rental car" situations. Give the managers a number of scenarios they can use at slack times or meetings to reinforce the application of principles learned in the training session. Give them a copy of the performance checklist used in the training session for observational purposes. Tell the trainees what to expect when they go on the job.*]

A second principle and mental model lesson segment is shown in tabular form in Figure 7.6. It illustrates the design for teaching YourMart warehouse technicians how to predict what will happen when electrical components are connected in any way.

FIGURE 7.6. Job Aid for Teaching Principles and Mental Models

Lesson Element	Example
1. Select the Information to Attend To *Attention.* Explain that you are teaching the "how" and the "why" of the model or concept structure.	"You'll be able to explain how and why the robot uses its supply voltages and currents, and what the client must provide for source electrical power."
WIIFM. Explain how understanding the system will help later with procedural skills.	"When you know the basics of an electrical circuit, you'll be able to set up a YourMart robot at a client site, calibrate the supply voltages, and verify normal operation."
YCDI. Tell the learners that they will be able to absorb and apply the training content.	"We have thirty-five technicians out in the field who took this training. They all completed it successfully and that's out of thirty-five we've trained."
2. Link New Information with Existing Knowledge *Recall* concepts upon which the principles operate, if the learner already has learned them.	"Like water in a swimming pool, an electrical circuit needs pressure to make it work. There's resistance when the water flows through the filter. And you have to take out just as much water as you put in."
Relate new information by showing similarities and differences between it and old knowledge.	"An electrical circuit is something like the flow of water when you're circulating the water in a swimming pool."
3. Organize the Information *Structure of Content.* Show how the parts are related.	"In an electrical circuit, the pressure is called 'voltage' and the rate of flow is called 'current.' The resistance is called 'resistance' or 'load.' And all the parts have to be connected so the electricity can flow in a complete circuit. The current flows through wires, rather than pipes, of course!"
Objective. Usually has the learner predict or explain behavior of the system.	"Once you understand how an electrical circuit works, you should be able to predict what will happen when its components are connected in any way."
4. Assimilate the New Knowledge into Existing Knowledge *Present New Knowledge.* *Present Examples.* • Show all the concepts and components upon which the principles act • Use examples and analogies • If you are teaching operation or troubleshooting of a physical system, represent the system at the abstract (general) level, OR give an example of an actual (real) system, highlight the	"Here is a simple example of an electrical circuit, like the ones found in YourMart robots—or something as simple as a flashlight: Lamp Battery Current Flow Switch (shown open)"

FIGURE 7.6. (Continued)

Lesson Element	Example
attributes that are generally true of all such systems, and note where system-specific differences occur. • If the terminal objective calls for solving a class of abstract problems (for example, mathematical reasoning, communication), then develop an abstract diagram or other representation of how the components in the problem space interact OR show example(s) of typical problems, emphasize the attributes that are generally true of all problems in the class, and note where problem-specific differences occur. • If experts use a standard symbol system to represent the knowledge/system structure, then you should probably use it, too.	"The battery (voltage source) feeds current through the switch (when it is closed) to the lamp (resistance), with a return path to the battery. "You complete an electrical circuit like this one when you: • Turn on a light switch • Start a robot • Move the arm of the robot • Start your car • Turn on your TV" [*briefly show how the complete circuit works in each case*]
	Elaboration: [*For some skills (such as math), problem representation is a major part of the meta-procedure. If so, then your analysis should have included principles for both the problem structure and the process of representing the problem. You will need to include both kinds of principles, together or separately.*]
State principles as *if . . . then* causal statements *because* reasons	"*If* the switch is closed, *then* the current flows because that completes the circuit. *Because* the voltage supplies the 'electrical pressure,' it pushes the current through the load and around the circuit."
5. Strengthen the New Knowledge in Memory *Practice.* Have learners do something with the new knowledge. Ask questions that require application of the principles to new situations. For example, you can ask the learner to predict, explain by stating the reason why, or generate or select another example of the system's behavior	"What would happen to the current if the voltage were zero? Why can't the current flow if the switch is open? If you measured the voltage at each connection of the switch, and it is closed, what would it read? What would it read if the switch is open?"

(Continued)

FIGURE 7.6. Job Aid for Teaching Principles and Mental Models (*Continued*)

Lesson Element	Example
(*Optional*) *Present Additional New Knowledge*. State all the ways a component can fail, the probability of each type of failure (if needed), and the principle(s) of system operation with that failure mode.	"A circuit can be open or shorted. Either condition is equally likely. If the circuit is open, then there is no complete path for the current to flow, and no current will flow. If the circuit is shorted, then there is a path for the current to flow without going through the load."
(*Optional*) *Additional Practice*. Ask questions about system operation with the failure modes which ask the learner to predict, explain by stating the reason why, and generate or select another example of the system's behavior.	"If the circuit is shorted, and you measure the voltage between the connections of the load, what will it be? Why?"
Feedback. Let learners know how well they've done in using the new knowledge, what problems they're having, and why.	[*Tell the learners when their predictions, explanations, and examples of the system's behavior are on the mark. When their answers are not, explain where they made their error(s) and why.*]
Summary. Give them the structure of content presented earlier in the lesson with a brief summary of the main points.	[*Show how all the parts are related.*]
Test. Give learners the opportunity to use the new knowledge again to prove to themselves, to you, and to their employer that they can perform the training objectives.	[*Give them a variety of systems and principles and require them to predict failures, explain how and why failures occur, and generate examples of system's behavior.*]
On-the–Job Application. Have learners use new knowledge in a structured way on the job to ensure they "use it, not lose it."	[*Remind learners that in the next phase of this robotics course they will be applying the knowledge learned here. Give them additional problems that anticipate content in the next unit of instruction.*]

SUMMARY

In this chapter we explained what principles and mental models are all about, gave some specific training goals for designing principle and mental model lessons, and showed how to design a principle and mental model-level lesson segment by using the lesson elements.

We began by defining the term "principle" as a statement of a cause-and-effect relationship that explains why or how something works and then defined the term "mental model" as a network of facts, concepts, and principles synthesized into a purposeful knowledge network. This network reflects the behavior of some real-world aspect that serves as the basis for procedural knowledge.

Next, we explained three specific training goals for teaching principles and mental models:

- Ensuring that learners relate principles to one another and to existing knowledge in mental models.
- Helping learners to learn and/or create mental models related to context use.
- Helping learners to synthesize declarative knowledge to use it for problem-solving tasks as they move to learning procedural knowledge.

In the last part of the chapter, we integrated this knowledge into a principle/mental model-level sample lesson segment using the lesson elements. This sample teaches AutoRent's customer service representatives to perform a variety of tasks and functions formerly requiring supervisory permission.

We concluded the chapter with an example in job-aid format that illustrates the design for teaching YourMart technicians how to predict what will happen when electrical components are connected in any way.

FIGURE 8.1. Chapter 8 Structure of Content

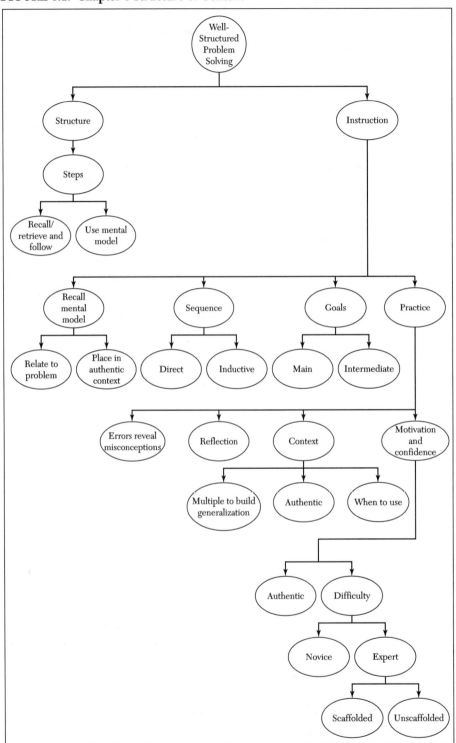

Chapter 8

Teaching Well-Structured Problem-Solving

Recall (from Chapter 1)

- Procedural knowledge is all about problem solving.

- Procedural knowledge is the ability to string together a series of mental and physical actions to solve a problem or, in other words, achieve a goal.

- Procedures vary in complexity along a continuum of how well the problem solving procedure is defined—at the precise end are well-structured problems; at the far end are ill-structured problems.

- Well-structured problems are solved by applying rote procedures or what we call procedures.

- Procedures can be applied without understanding why they work.

Relate to What You Already Know

- Examples of procedures you already know are programming your VCR to record a future program, making coffee using a standard coffee maker, buying gas at a self-serve station, or accessing your e-mail.

Structure of Content

- See Figure 8.1.

Objectives

- To describe what procedures are.

- To apply general strategies for teaching procedures.

- To design a lesson to teach procedures including all lesson elements.

ABOUT WELL-STRUCTURED PROBLEM-SOLVING

At AutoRent newly hired vehicle service specialists need to learn how to service incoming vehicles using the company's eight-step procedure.

At YourMart new hires need to learn basic word processing skills such as the procedure for creating mail merges.

You can think of well-structured problem solving as a completely defined step-by-step procedure. All of the problem-solving components (situation, operations, goal, and constraints) are well-defined. In other words, well-structured problem solving:

- Always has the same goal.
- Is always done the same way, with the same tools and information.
- Does not vary with context.

Examples include balancing a checkbook, many operations for using end-user software, many flight procedures, and some kinds of troubleshooting.

The instructional strategy in this chapter teaches the learners to perform the procedure. It does not teach them to generalize or modify it. Therefore, you should probably use this instructional strategy only if the well-structured problem-solving procedure you are teaching meets these three criteria:

- It is not likely to go out-of-date (doing it the same way in the future is desirable).
- It is not like many other procedures you are teaching (since teaching a large number of well-structured procedures that are very similar will be very repetitive and inefficient.
- It must be recalled from memory because it is too time-sensitive, complex, or critical to be simply looked up (and therefore automation or job aids will not work).

We agree that these caveats reduce the frequency of teaching well-structured problem-solving procedures, but we don't agree it will eliminate it. There are still many procedures that meet these criteria. For example, how to dial a phone number, many bookkeeping procedures, almost everything the crew at a McDonald's does, and so on. And note that all three of these examples often use job aids and the training is in how to do the procedure using the job aid!

GENERAL STRATEGIES FOR TEACHING WELL-STRUCTURED PROBLEM-SOLVING

Before we move into the specific events that go into a well-structured problem-solving lesson, it is appropriate to provide you with a "mental model" of the principles we use to guide our procedures for teaching problem solving.

What to Teach

1. For any "real-world" job or work skill, identify both the declarative and procedural knowledge components. Give each appropriate instructional emphasis.

2. Use contexts, problems, difficulty levels, and teaching styles appropriate to the learner and the task, and thus build interest, motivation, confidence, persistence, and knowledge about self and reduce anxiety.

3. A common error is to fail to teach and practice "when to use the procedure" (the conditions of performance for Step 1). Therefore, you should always include practice situations that allow the learner to choose the procedure from among other alternatives or to recognize that it's needed. The requirement for contextualized learning means that procedures always require a simulation or some kind of OJT or apprenticeship.

Present the Structure

4. First introduce a problem-solving context; then either alternate between teaching declarative and procedural knowledge, or integrate the two.

5. When teaching declarative knowledge, emphasize mental models appropriate to the problem solving to come by explaining knowledge structures and system behaviors and asking learners to predict what will happen or explain why something happened.

6. Use direct (deductive) teaching strategies for declarative knowledge and well-structured problem solving.

7. Within a problem exercise, help the learners understand (or define) the goal; then help them to break it down into intermediate goals.

8. The sequence of instruction described here is not the only one that has been shown to be effective. For example, "backward chaining" works too.

Build Procedural Knowledge

9. Teach problem-solving skills in the context in which they will be used. Use *authentic* problems in explanations, practice, and assessments, with scenario-based simulations, games, and projects. Do not teach problem solving as an independent, abstract skill that is free of context.

10. Give practice of similar problem-solving strategies across multiple contexts to encourage generalization.

11. Use the errors learners make in problem solving as evidence of misconceptions, not just carelessness or random guessing. If possible, determine the probable misconception and provide feedback to correct it.

12. Ask questions that encourage the learner to grasp the parts of the skill that can be generalized across many similar problems in different contexts.

13. Plan a series of lessons that grow in sophistication from novice-level to expert-level understanding of the knowledge structures used.

14. When teaching well-structured problem solving, allow learners to retrieve the procedure if appropriate (for example, from a reference card). If the procedure is frequently used, encourage memorization of the procedure and practice until it is automatic.

Practice

15. In algorithmic problem solving, if speed of performance or cognitive load is an issue (due to problem complexity, stress, fatigue, and so forth), add extensive practice to build automatic performance. Otherwise, don't bother, because it's expensive, obnoxious, and it's usually OK to cease training before "expert" level automaticity is achieved.

16. As with any kind of learning, the amount of practice depends entirely on the criterion. If required performance time is low, or if the procedure will later be folded into more complex ones, or if it must be performed under stress or fatigue, then practice should continue until performance is automatic. However, this takes a lot of repetitions—often hundreds. In many situations, it's OK to cease practice as soon as performance is fairly error-free, then let proficiency build on the job.

Discovery-Based Strategies

"Discovery-based" or "inductive" strategies may be acceptable. However, research indicates they are only effective if the learner:

- Already knows the principles and concepts (the mental model) of the problem space.
- Is motivated to solve the problem.
- Has good thinking skills.
- Is allowed to make errors on the first few trials.

If all these conditions are met, then training may need to consist of nothing more than providing a job aid, a demonstration, and perhaps a simulation that provides a view of the mental model being manipulated and feedback on how well the procedure has been executed under the right circumstances. This kind of "discovery" of the procedure can be motivating and much more efficient than a full procedure teaching strategy.

How much of the underlying concepts, principles, and mental models you teach is always a judgment call. It's possible to simply memorize (or follow) a well-structured procedure by rote, without ever understanding why it works or what the purpose of each step is. But the more the learner knows about the concepts, principles, and mental models, the easier the procedure will be to recall, to relate to other procedures, and to generalize to new situations.

USING THE LESSON ELEMENTS TO TEACH WELL-STRUCTURED PROBLEM-SOLVING

Example Scenario

A major part of an AutoRent's vehicle service specialist's (VSS) job consists of refueling, servicing, and cleaning or "prepping" returned cars for re-rental. New VSS hires are taught these procedures in a three-unit sequence. Here we assume they have completed training on the company's refueling procedure. In this unit, Unit 2, they learn the procedure for servicing the car. The unit after this one instructs them on cleaning the car. To avoid redundancy, Learner Task 1, Select the Information to Attend To, and its corresponding lesson elements, Attention, WIIFM, and YCDI, are not shown. For descriptions see Chapter 3. The lesson segment begins with Learner Task 2, Link the New Information with Existing Knowledge.

Learner Task 2: Link the New Information with Existing Knowledge

Lesson Element: Recall   *Description.* Recall concepts, principles, and mental model(s) needed to represent the procedure.

> AutoRent Example: "All of you have been tested out on all the parts of the cars you'll be servicing. You know what they look like, where they are, and what they do. For example, you know that the battery supplies the initial starting electrical power to the engine and the rest of the car. You also know that to operate properly the battery terminals have to be clear of crud and that the battery cables have to be clean and securely connected both to the terminals and to the engine. Finally, it has to have the right amount of fluid in its cells to keep up the required electrical charge. Also, we've given special attention to two parts of the servicing procedure that have given some people trouble in the past, the difference in location and appearance between the windshield reservoir and the radiator reservoir. Remember, they look very similar and in different vehicles their locations can be reversed." [*Remind them to refer to their job aid as the explanation proceeds. Go through each of the parts that make up the servicing procedure in like manner, again emphasizing the appearance and locations of the two reservoirs. The parts include the window washer reservoir, crankcase, transmission, brakes, power steering, battery, radiator reservoir, and tires.*]

Lesson Element: Relate

Description. Relate the concepts and/or principles and/or mental models to the purpose of the procedure.

> AutoRent Example: "Seven of these eight parts of the car need proper fluid levels to operate; the tires need proper air pressure to do the same. The purpose of this procedure we call 'servicing the car' is to check these levels and correct them when needed."

Learner Task 3: Organize the Information

Lesson Element: Structure of Content

Description. Name and number the steps in the procedure and highlight any branches.

> AutoRent Example: "This is AutoRent's servicing procedure. We'll go through each step in the order you see on the slide." [*Show slide. It displays the steps shown in Figure 8.2.*]

FIGURE 8.2. AutoRent Servicing Procedure

> Servicing Procedure
>
> *Check and, if necessary, correct these fluid levels in the following order:*
>
> 1. Window washer fluid reservoir (*white* cover).
> 2. Engine oil (wipe stick and reinsert for correct reading).
> 3. Transmission fluid (same as oil).
> 4. Power steering fluid (to marked line) if needed.
> 5. Battery (check indicator—if green, OK; if red, open, check, and fill).
> 6. Radiator reservoir *red* cover (to marked level).
> 7. Tires. Find correct air pressure. Tire inflation information is found on the manufacturer's label. The label may be located in any one of many places: on the driver's side door jam, inside the gas filler door, or inside the glove compartment door. Check pressure. Correct.

Lesson Element: Objectives

Description. Objectives should describe both the behaviors to be performed and the knowledge to be learned. Inform trainees of the objective at an appropriate time during the presentation.

> AutoRent Example: "At the end of this unit, you'll be able to perform the servicing procedure on a returned car. This includes all the steps listed in the servicing procedure handout and that pocket-sized job aid."

Learner Task 4: Assimilate the New Knowledge into Existing Knowledge

Lesson Elements: Present New Knowledge and Present Examples

Description. Follow these guidelines to present the new knowledge and examples:

1. Show a worked-out example, that is, a prototype example, as an application of the procedure;

2. include an explanation of each step in the procedure at the level of detail appropriate to what the learner already knows;

3. introduce, then show the individual steps, each with its own explanation;

4. point out the cue that signals the beginning of the step, the action, and the feedback that shows the step has been correctly completed;

5. relate the steps to facts and concepts as the steps use them; and

6. teach the concepts and facts as they occur if the learner does not know them.

AutoRent Example: [*Applying the above guidelines to the first step in the procedure, checking the window washer reservoir, the training sequence would go something like this.*] "At the beginning of the unit, you saw the complete procedure. It was presented a little faster than normal, but you all got the picture. Now we're going to go back through each step of the procedure individually and talk in detail about when you start the step, what you do in the step, and how do you know that you've done it correctly." [*During the explanation, use the appropriate video sequence to explain the details of the step. Start and stop the videotape at the appropriate times.*] "You check the washer fluid reservoir the first thing after completing the refueling procedure." [*The video shows an open hood with the reservoir highlighted.*] "In most of our fleet cars, it is in the left front of the engine compartment as you stand facing it. It's a plastic container. It has a white plastic snap-off cover with a rubber hose attached to it. The fluid should be right up to the lip of the container. Fill it up to the top if it isn't. Replace the cap tightly. As we've said before, in a number of our cars these reservoirs are located in different spots under the hood and have different shapes, but remember they all have white caps and covers. Let's look at these variations." [*Show slides of different engine compartments with variations. Either point out the reservoirs or ask the learners to do so.*] "After the reservoir has been checked, you're ready for the next step, checking the crankcase or oil level." [*Continue in this manner until all eight steps are covered.*]

Learner Task 5: Strengthen the New Knowledge in Memory

Lesson Element:
Practice

Description. Practice using additional examples. Use any or combinations of these kinds of practice: Present a new problem scenario and ask the learner to select or recall the procedure from among alternatives or broaden the practice to include content and irrelevant information so the learner is required to select only the relevant information.

AutoRent Example: [*Give learners a short quiz on the eight steps in the servicing procedure. This tests their recall of the knowledge component. Next, present them with a series of service eye view photos of a variety of engine compartments, closeups of fan belts and batteries, and possible locations of tire pressure specifications. Their tasks here are to interpret the photos and make appropriate discriminations and to find the right parts. Next, pair the learners up with an experienced VSS out in the shop. The purpose here is to give the learners practice under supervision. Have them practice with the VSSs for a two- or three-day interval until they are satisfied that the learners are following the eight steps competently. Company policy at this stage of the training does not require mastery or fluency of the procedures but the ability to perform at an intermediate level under supervision.]*

Lesson Element: Feedback

Description. Let the learners know how well they've done in using the new knowledge, what problems they're having, and why.

AutoRent Example: [*At the next training session, make sure that the experienced VSSs come into the training room after the practice interval and discuss any problems the trainees had in applying the procedure and explain possible reasons why they might have made some application mistakes.*] "Well, all of you did very well on all the steps, especially with checking and refilling the coolant and windshield washer reservoirs. Nobody made any mistakes there. That might have something to do with the color code system we began using with the two reservoir covers to prevent mix-ups. The white cover reminds us of snow and sleet and it covers the windshield reservoir. The red lid reminds us of heat and covers the radiator reservoir. Good job! Next, I'm sure you'll all be happy about this, we're going to see how well you do on your own—it's called a test."

Lesson Element: Summary

Description. Restate the structure of content, that is, the entire procedure.

AutoRent Example: [*Reassemble the group back in the training room. In this phase of the servicing procedure training, show visuals of the steps and have learners summarize them. Remind them again to keep their pocket-sized versions of the procedure with them and refer to them when needed.*]

Lesson Element: Test

Description. Have the learners use the new knowledge again, this time to prove to themselves, the trainer, and their employer that they have met the performance objectives.

AutoRent Example: [*By prior arrangement have experienced VSSs take the trainees out to the shop once more on a one-to-one basis and check their skills in applying the eight-step procedure using a performance checklist.*]

Lesson Element:
On-the-Job Application

Description. Have learners use new knowledge in a structured way on the job to ensure they "use it, not lose it."

> AutoRent Example: "You all have the results of your performance tests. You know where you need some refreshing on some of the steps and you know which ones you had no trouble remembering. You're going into the shop again tomorrow and will begin doing this vehicle maintenance procedure. Here's how it works—you'll partner up with a VSS in the shop. The two of you will do the maintenance procedure together for about ten cars. If your partner thinks you have the procedure down cold, you're on your own. If not, you'll continue to work with him or her until you can work on your own. Remember, you can use that pocket-sized list of the procedures as long as you want. After a while you probably won't need it. Good luck!"

The instructional components were presented in a typically deductive sequence. Depending on your lesson design, your implementation may vary. Remember also that it's common to embed fact, concept, and principle when teaching a procedure lesson—as long as the resulting lesson isn't too hard to follow.

A second procedure lesson segment is shown below in tabular form (Figure 8.3). It illustrates the design for teaching YourMart new hires to use the "mail merge" procedure.

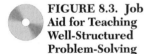 **FIGURE 8.3. Job Aid for Teaching Well-Structured Problem-Solving**

Lesson Element	Example
1. Select the Information to Attend To. Heighten and focus attention on the new knowledge. *Attention* component should explain you are teaching a procedure and when to use the procedure (hint: look at the name or goal of the procedure for information on when to use it).	"Now let's take a look at the procedure for setting up a mail merge. Use it whenever you need to create many versions of a document, each of which has a unique part."
WIIFM. Tell the learners the benefits of using the procedure.	"Using mail merge, all you have to do is type the main document once, and then type just the parts that are different. That's much easier than making many copies of the same document!"
YCDI. Reduce anxiety by telling learners that the procedure is not hard to learn.	"In Word, mail merge has been completely redesigned to make it more logical and easier to use."

(Continued)

FIGURE 8.3. Job Aid for Teaching Well-Structured Problem-Solving (*Continued*)

Lesson Element	Example
2. Link the New Information with Existing Knowledge. *Recall* concepts, principles, and mental model(s) needed to represent the procedure.	"You already know the principles of how it works." [*Repeat mail merge diagram used earlier in principles lesson.*] "You know how it matches variable names in the main document with those in the data table document and substitutes the data for the variable in each copy of the main document."
Relate the concepts to the purpose of the procedure.	"That means that setting up a mail merge involves creating the data document, then the main document file."
Optional Step If it's necessary to use principles and a mental model to understand the procedure, then relate the explanation to them here.	"Word makes it easy to make the variable names in the two files match."
3. Organize the Information. Organize the new knowledge so that it matches the organization of existing knowledge. *Structure of Content.* Name the number of steps in the procedure and highlight any branches.	"When you click on 'Tools . . . Mail Merge,' the mail merge helper dialog box first asks you what kind of merge you want to do. Then it shows you the three basic steps of the process: (1) create (or edit) the main document; (2) get (or create) the data source document; and (3) merge the data with the document."
Objectives. Specify both the desired behavior and the knowledge to be learned.	"If you follow the instructions as they appear on the screen, you'll be able to do the three-step procedure."
4. Assimilate the New Knowledge into the Existing Knowledge. *Present New Knowledge.* Present the procedure in a way that makes it easiest to understand. Show a worked-out example as an application of the procedure.	"First, let's look at how you create a data table. Although identifying the data source is Step 2 of the mail merge procedure, it has to be done before you can create a main document in Step 1. Here are the steps." [*Demonstrate the process as you explain the steps.*]
Present Examples. Demonstrate real-life application. Show one or more "prototype" examples of solutions that apply the procedure. Include an explanation of each step in the procedure, at the level of detail appropriate to what the learner already knows.	"First, click on the 'get data' button, and a submenu will appear. Then, click on 'create data source.' Your choice is confirmed by the black bar moving to that choice. A dialog box appears, which lets you add and remove field names from a list by selecting or typing until you have the ones you want.

FIGURE 8.3. (*Continued*)

Lesson Element	Example
	When you are finished, click on the OK button. A 'Save File' dialog box will appear, and you can type in a file name for the data file and save it by clicking on the 'SAVE' button. A dialog box will appear to give you the choice of adding data to the data file or returning to the main document. Click on the button for the choice you want." [*For each step, point out the cue that signals the beginning of the step, the action, and the feedback that shows the step has been correctly completed. Include references to the principles and mental model, if the learner knows the model. Or teach it now if you intend to. Relate procedure steps to facts and concepts as the steps use them. Teach them as they occur if the learner doesn't already know them.*]
Show additional "far out" examples of solutions using the procedure.	"Now, let's run through the procedure for creating a data file, but this time let's do mailing labels." [*Demonstrate the data source creation procedure without the above commentary, but with the "mailing label" choice selected in Step 1 of the main three-step dialog box for Mail Merge.*]
Elicit from the learner how the procedure was used to solve the problem in each case.	"How was the data source creation procedure different this time?" [*Answer: It was identical, except for the variable names you'd probably use.*]
5. Strengthen the New Knowledge in Memory. Involve learners by having them do something with the new knowledge. *Practice.* Use these kinds of practice: • Given a new problem scenario, ask the learner to select or recall the procedure from among alternatives. • Given the problem scenario and the problem-solving process, solve the problem. • Broaden the practice to include context and irrelevant information, so the learner is required to select only the relevant information.	"Now, create a data file for a mail merge letter which confirms a training class registration. It has name and address fields, and this sentence: 'You are confirmed for the training class [class name], meeting on [day] at [time] in the training center.'"

(Continued)

FIGURE 8.3. Job
Aid for Teaching
Well-Structured
Problem-Solving
(*Continued*)

Lesson Element	Example
Feedback. Let the learners know how well they've done in using the new knowledge, what problems they're having, and why.	[*Check the data files they've created. Reinforce correct applications and point out errors in application and the reasons why these errors occurred.*]
Summary. Summarize the new material by again presenting the structure of content, that is, the procedure.	"So now you know that when you are doing a mail merge, the first thing you need to do is create the data source file using this procedure." [*Include procedure steps here.*]
Test. Have the learners use the new knowledge again, this time to prove to themselves, the trainer, and to their employer that they can perform the training objective.	[*Have them create several data source files using the procedure just learned.*]
On-the-Job Application. Have learners use the new knowledge in a structured way on the job to ensure they "use it, not lose it."	[*Remind the learners that they have a job aid in the training packets that they can use when creating data source files back on the job. Tell them they can send a copy of their on-the-job applications to the instructor for evaluation.*]

SUMMARY

In this chapter we described well-structured problem solving, presented general principles for teaching well-structured problem solving, and illustrated how to apply the lesson elements to design a well-structured level lesson segment.

We began by defining well-structured problem solving as a step-by-step procedure in which the problem-solving components—situation, operations, goal, and constraints—are well-defined.

Next, we provided a "mental model" of a number of principles used to guide the methodology for teaching problem solving. The model specifies that one:

- Identify declarative and procedural knowledge.
- Teach in proper context and major knowledge sequences.
- Emphasize mental models in teaching declarative knowledge.
- Use authentic problems.
- Use deductive strategies for teaching declarative knowledge and well-structured problem solving.
- Help learners to define and break down larger goals.

- Provide practice of similar problem-solving strategies across multiple contexts.
- Ask questions aimed at encouraging the learner to understand and generalize the skills.
- Use appropriate teaching styles matched to learners and the task.
- Plan lessons of increasing sophistication.
- Allow job aids to recall the procedure if appropriate.
- Build automaticity when appropriate.
- Emphasize "when to use."
- Determine appropriate practice schedules.

In the last part of the chapter, we integrated these strategies into a well-structured problem-solving procedure-level training segment using the lesson elements. This segment demonstrates the application of the lesson elements to train AutoRent's vehicle service specialists how to apply an eight-step servicing procedure.

We concluded the chapter with an example in job-aid format that illustrates the design for teaching YourMart new hires to use the "mail merge" procedure.

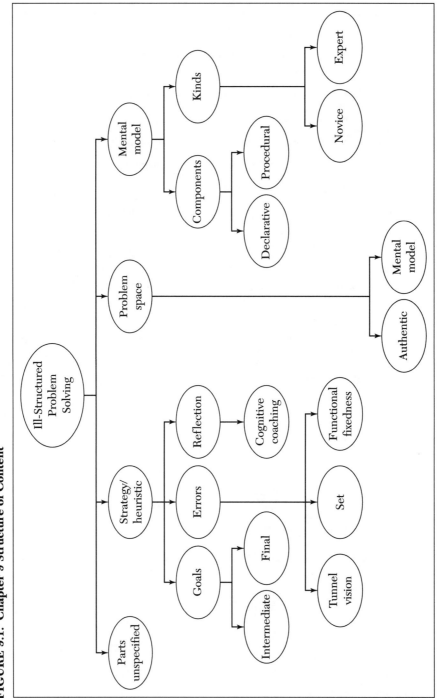

FIGURE 9.1. Chapter 9 Structure of Content

Chapter 9

Teaching Ill-Structured Problem-Solving

LINK AND ORGANIZE

Recall (from Chapters, 1 and 8)

- Procedural knowledge is all about problem solving.
- Procedural knowledge is the ability to string together a series of mental and physical actions to solve a problem or, in other words, achieve a goal.
- Procedures vary in complexity along a continuum of how well the problem solving is defined. At the precise end are well-structured problems; in the middle are moderately structured problems; and at the far end are ill-structured problems.
- In well-structured problem solving, defining the problem is relatively easy because all the components are given, the learner can recognize the problem as a certain problem type, and the learner can then recall the appropriate declarative and procedural knowledge to fill in the problem space.
- In ill-structured problem solving, defining the problem is not easy because to some degree three or four of the components are either not clear or not spelled out at all.
- The learner can't recognize the problem type or a clear goal.

Relate to What You Already Know

- Examples of ill-structured problem solving are:
  - Designing an automobile tire that will never wear out.
  - Planning a voyage to the planet Mercury.
  - Redesigning a work process.

Structure of Content

- See Figure 9.1.

Objectives

- To describe what ill-structured problem solving is.
- To apply general strategies for teaching ill-structured problem solving.
- To design a lesson to teach ill-structured problem solving using all lesson elements.

ABOUT ILL-STRUCTURED PROBLEM-SOLVING

An AutoRent task force must determine why the company's profits are going down and suggest solutions.

YourMart word processing new hires have to learn to apply the general strategy for mail merges to unusual jobs like the "quarterly fax."

You can think of an ill-structured problem as a completely undefined situation in which none of the problem-solving components is well-defined. In other words, an ill-structured problem has no clear or spelled out initial state, goal, set of operations, or constraints.

Examples include launching a new product, resolving political situations, developing a cure for a disease, analyzing a client's problem, and starting your own business.

You know you are dealing with ill-structured problem solving when the content domain and the training objective:

- Have many similarly structured procedures, which can be taught more efficiently as examples of a single strategy (for example, writing memos for various purposes, an example of *moderately structured* problem solving).
- Call for the ability to generate specific solution algorithms on the spot for new examples of a class of problems (for example, geometric proofs that are new enough that they can't be solved solely with use of a *rote procedure,* also *moderately structured*).
- Call for the ability to generalize and to solve a class of problems, even when details change due to changes in specifications, new or unknown equipment, new or unknown conditions, and so forth (for example, designing or upgrading computer networks, or an optimization dilemma such as expanding airport capacity while minimizing negative political consequences).
- Are new to the learner (remember that familiar problems will be treated as well-structured, since the learner can simply recall the solution algorithm).

In fact, the most meaningful and useful learning occurs at this level, and most learning for most adults has components of this type.

Definition of Problem Space

When learners are presented with a problem, the first thing they must do is represent it in their minds. They must create a mental representation of the initial state, goal state, constraints, and so on, of the problem. What they create is called a "problem space."

The most difficult part of the task, and one that contrasts greatly with well-structured problem solving, is defining the problem space. After recognizing there is a problem in the first place, the learner now tries to figure out "What kind of problem is this?"

Unlike with well-structured problem solving, the learner cannot just try to match the new problem with problems encountered in the past and use that match to define the problem space. The problem, by definition, is difficult, if not impossible, to classify. It is defined by the context or situation that presents it, and not by a specific set of declarative and procedural knowledge that one has learned. Therefore the problem space must contain information about many possible initial states, goal states, operations, and constraints of the problem. It also must contain a great deal of declarative and procedural knowledge that might be related to the problem.

Check the Results—Reflect

In ill-structured problem solving, since the "solution" is almost always one of many possible solutions, it is important for the learner to be able to justify why he or she reached the solution he or she did. This involves both checking the results of implementing the solution, to see if it solved the problem, and, more importantly, *reflecting* on the process of getting to the solution. This reflection activity is uniquely important to ill-structured problem solving. Reflection on the process becomes part of the mental model that is stored along with the problem and its solution. *And it is the reflection on the process that aids in both more effective problem solving next time, and in generalization of the process to new, related problems.*

PROBLEMS LEARNING ILL-STRUCTURED PROBLEM-SOLVING

What kinds of problems have you seen with people learning to solve problems on the job? Have you seen people apply solutions to other problems they've already solved—even if those problems are unrelated to the current one (for example, redesigning a sales process just like they did a manufacturing one)? Have you seen them define the problem as one kind of problem when it is really another kind (perhaps thinking "This is a problem of how to structure the organization most efficiently" rather than "This is a problem of how to design and organize work to get it done most efficiently")? Have you seen them define the problem as a well-structured one with a known solution when it is really an ill-structured one ("This is a downsizing/outsourcing problem" rather than "This is a reduce fixed costs in a down economic cycle while retaining quality, service, and intellectual capital problem")? Have you seen them define the problem in terms of the solution ("This is a training problem" rather than "This is a problem of how to improve performance")?

All of these are examples of errors common in ill-structured problem solving, and they often go right back to the way the learners learned to solve the problems originally. The problems people have in learning to problem solve include:

- Defining the problem space too narrowly or incorrectly.

- Assuming the problem is like another they've already solved when it is not.

- Not seeing that a problem is in fact like one they have already solved.

- Defining the problem in terms of the solution.

- Searching for an algorithm that will provide a simple solution to the problem, when only heuristics will work.

GENERAL STRATEGIES FOR TEACHING ILL-STRUCTURED PROBLEM-SOLVING

Before we move into the specifics of a lesson on solving ill-structured problems, it is appropriate to provide a "mental model" of the principles we use to teach problem-solving procedures.

Our training task is to aid the learner to (1) define the problem space, (2) generate the heuristics to solve the problem, and (3) reflect on the problem-solving process by:

- Providing an appropriate sequence of problems that fit the context in which the problem-solving skill will be applied.

- Providing instruction, examples, and practice in a sequence that allows learners to develop the problem-solving heuristics for themselves.

- Keeping cognitive load within the capabilities of the learners through problem type and format selection and the use of scaffolding.*

- Allowing for and encouraging reflection on the process.

To accomplish these goals, we recommend the guidelines below. Some are the same as those for well-structured problem solving, but some are new:

What to Teach

1. For any "real-world" job or work skill, identify both the declarative and procedural knowledge components. Give each appropriate instructional emphasis.

---

*Cognitive psychologists use the term *"scaffolding"* to refer to assistance given to learners in early stages of the problem-solving learning. It is defined in detail on page 217.

2. Teach problem-solving skills in the context in which they will be used. Use *authentic* problems in explanations, practice, and assessments, with scenario-based simulations, games, and projects. Do not teach problem solving as an independent, abstract, out-of-context skill.

3. Use contexts, problems, and teaching styles that will build interest, motivation, confidence, persistence, and knowledge about self and reduce anxiety.

4. Emphasize ill-structured problem solving when transfer is a goal of instruction.

Present the Problem

5. First introduce a problem-solving context; then either alternate between teaching declarative and procedural knowledge or integrate the two. Then present the structure.

Present the Structure

6. When teaching declarative knowledge, emphasize mental models appropriate to the problem solving to come by explaining knowledge structures and system behaviors and asking learners to predict what will happen or explain why something happened.

Generate the Heuristic

7. Use inductive teaching strategies to encourage synthesis of mental models and for ill-structured problem solving.

8. Within a problem exercise, help the learners understand (or define) the goal; then help them to break it down into intermediate goals.

9. Plan a series of lessons that grow in sophistication from novice-level to expert-level understanding of the knowledge structures used.

10. When teaching moderately structured problem solving, encourage the learners to use their declarative (context) knowledge to invent a strategy that suits the context and the problem. Allow many "right" strategies to reach the solution, and compare them for efficiency and effectiveness.

11. When teaching ill-structured problem solving, encourage the learners to use their declarative (context) knowledge to define the goal (properties of an acceptable solution), then invent a solution. Allow many "right" strategies and solutions, and compare them for efficiency and effectiveness.

Reflection

12. Use the errors learners make in problem solving as evidence of misconceptions, not just carelessness or random guessing. If possible, determine the probable misconception and provide feedback to correct it.

13. Ask questions and make suggestions about strategy to encourage learners to reflect on the problem-solving strategies they use. Do this either before or after the learner takes action. (This is sometimes called *cognitive coaching*).

14. Give practice in similar problem-solving strategies across multiple contexts to encourage generalization.

15. Ask questions that encourage the learner to grasp the generalizable part of the skill across many similar problems in different contexts.

In addition, the following general principles from teaching well-structured problem solving also apply:

16. "Minimalist" or discovery-based strategies may be acceptable. However, research indicates they are only effective if the learner:

    - Already knows the principles and concepts (that is, the mental model) of the problem space.

    - Is motivated to solve the problem.

    - Has good thinking skills.

    - Is allowed to make errors on the first few trials.

17. If all these conditions are met, then training may need to consist of nothing more than a job aid, a demonstration, and perhaps a simulation that provides a view of the mental model being manipulated and feedback on how well the procedure has been executed under the right circumstances. This kind of "discovery" of the procedure can be motivating and much more efficient than a full teaching strategy.

18. How much of the underlying concepts, principles, and mental models you teach is always a judgment call. But the more the learner knows about the concepts, principles, and mental models, the easier the procedure will be to recall, to relate to other procedures, and to generalize to new situations.

19. In designing simulations, games, and exploratory environments, *do not* present the solutions learners use in any of the phases of problem solving, from creating the problem space to testing the solution. Unlike in principle and procedure learning, the learners *must discover the approach to solving the problem themselves* if they are to transfer and retain the capability to solve problems over a long period of time; we must present the problem in such a way that we do *not* state the solution, but rather require

the learner to construct the solution with only the minimum of modeling and coaching. It's OK to begin by modeling the process of building a strategy (using the cognitive coaching techniques above), then change the problem and let the learner invent a strategy, then change the whole problem space and let the learner invent a similar strategy, and so on.

20. "Cognitive coaching" and learning environments in which the learners work in small groups on solving a problem and discuss their strategy may be particularly helpful. They can promote reflection on the key decisions and strategy and may help build confidence and persistence.

USING THE LESSON ELEMENTS TO TEACH ILL-STRUCTURED PROBLEM-SOLVING

Example Scenario

For the last two years, AutoRent's profits have been shrinking while competitors' are holding even or increasing. Concerned about these declines, the company CEO formed an executive task force. He charged it with first determining what the causes (problem) of the decline are and, secondly, recommending solutions. The task force consisted of top executives from the company's major units: marketing, sales, human resources, field operations, finance, research and development, and service operations.

In the initial meeting with the CEO, the task force members reached a number of conclusions. After much discussion, they agreed that, at that point, they had no idea what the problem was. Likewise, they determined that strategically their goal was to implement strategies to reverse this downward trend, but they had no idea what specific goals they were heading for. While all the executives were competent (at least in their own minds) in solving specific problems in their own units, they reluctantly agreed that, in this case, it was difficult to determine how to proceed operationally in "going after" the "declining profits" problem.

The human resources task force member suggested that they meet with the corporation's organization development specialist for consultation on a way to proceed. In this meeting the OD specialist convinced task force members that they were dealing with a special kind of problem-solving situation, that is, one where the problem was ill-defined. He suggested that there were methodologies they could apply to deal with this type of problem and that he would be willing to facilitate a number of "training" sessions that would give them the framework needed to tackle the project goals.

The group agreed to the proposal, and the training sessions were scheduled. What follows is the group's first training session in a typical deductive sequence. Depending on your lesson design, your implementation may vary.

To avoid redundancy, Learner Task 1, Select the Information to Attend To, and its corresponding lesson elements, Attention, WIIFM, and YCDI, are not shown. For descriptions of these, see Chapter 3. The lesson segment begins with Learner Task 2, Link the New Information with Existing Knowledge.

Learner Task 2: Link the New Information with Existing Knowledge

Lesson Element: Recall

Description. Recall related declarative knowledge that is part of the mental model and procedures that are analogous to the one you are teaching, in whole or in part.

> AutoRent Example: "The Rummler-Brache process improvement system uses processes and tools for determining organizational effectiveness and efficiency and solving organizational problems. These tools will require integration of AutoRent's organizational structures, process descriptions, and job and employee descriptions to enable task force members to learn and apply the general strategy. Let's display the data we currently have about AutoRent: Its organizational charts; each business unit's organizational chart; corporate and unit processes; employee position descriptions and functions; and performance evaluation methods." [*Post this data.*] "The problem-solving approach we are going to use is NOT like any you learned in business school. It does not involve reorganizing, downsizing, or moving people's offices. These are the strategies for improving profitability that you know, and you've agreed that you've tried them and they won't get us ahead of the competition."

Lesson Element: Relate

Description. Relate the current procedure to what the learner already knows about the mental model and the analogical procedure(s).

> AutoRent Example: "We're going to be closely examining all of the data we've posted around the room, using this data to figure out relationships within and between our units and create new diagrams and charts to reflect these relationships. It is like a complete physical of the organization. We do not just look at symptoms, but rather examine the complete organization in a systematic way, gathering data, making a hypothesis about the underlying cause of the illness, testing the hypothesis, revising it, and finally prescribing a remedy or series of remedies that get to the cause of the illness. The process is also like what strategic planners do, what marketing planners do, what financial planners do, and what systems analysts do. It is based on what we know about organizational psychology."

Learner Task 3: Organize the Information

Lesson Element: Structure of Content

Description. Structure of content should show the mental model or a heuristic for a class of abstract problems, develop an abstract diagram or other representation of how the components in the problem space interact, and/or present *worked examples* of typical problems, then articulate the strategy steps used to solve the problem(s). Worked examples can take many forms, including "think-alouds" and step-by-step solutions. Note features of the problem that are unique to that problem (as opposed to those that are typical of a class of problems). Not all of the typical features or exceptions need be covered in these initial worked examples, as long as they are covered elsewhere in the activity. Be sure that the cognitive processes (such as cues and decisions) are made clear in the example, as well as the performance.

> AutoRent Example: "Figures 9.2, 9.3, and 9.4 are models that can be used for diagnosing organizational performance problems, which is why the task force was formed." [*Introduce Rummler-Brache's models of organizational, process, and job/performer performance. Briefly explain each level and the matrix and how they determine an organization's effectiveness and efficiency.*]

FIGURE 9.2. The Organization Level of Performance

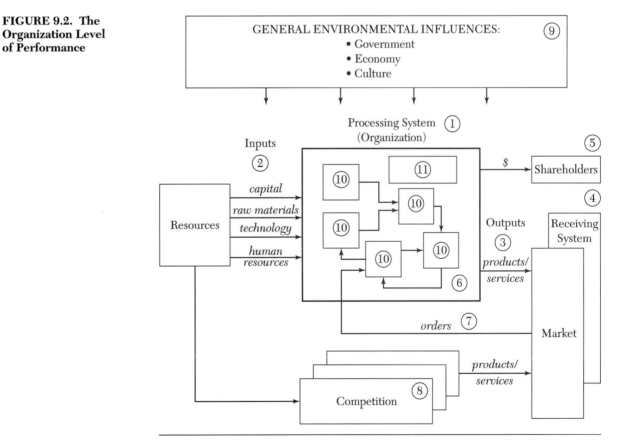

From G.A. Rummler & A.P. Brache, *Improving Performance: How to Manage the White Space in the Organization Chart* (2nd ed.). (San Francisco, CA: Jossey-Bass, 1995). Used with permission.

FIGURE 9.3. The Process Level of Performance

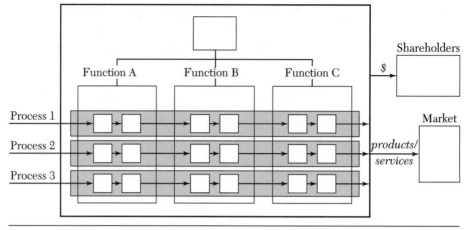

From G.A. Rummler & A.P. Brache, *Improving Performance: How to Manage the White Space in the Organization Chart* (2nd ed.). (San Francisco, CA: Jossey-Bass, 1995). Used with permission.

FIGURE 9.4. Job Level Chart

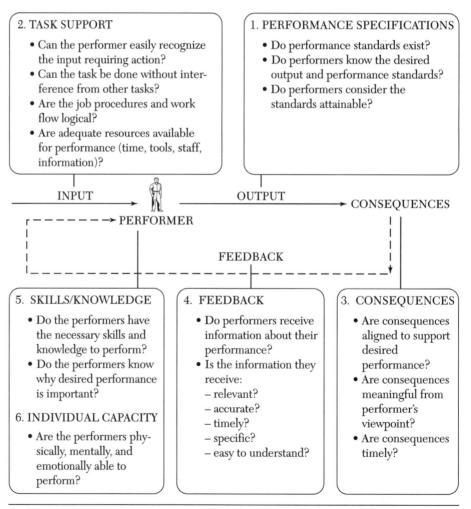

From G.A. Rummler & A.P. Brache, *Improving Performance: How to Manage the White Space in the Organization Chart* (2nd ed.). (San Francisco, CA: Jossey-Bass, 1995). Used with permission.

Lesson Element:
Objectives

Description. Tell the learners the purpose of this lesson is to understand a (particular) general procedure for solving a (particular) broad class of problems (which you name).

> AutoRent Example: "Let me just summarize what we're doing here. The purpose of these workshops is to help you understand and apply the Rummler-Brache strategies for solving organizational performance problems. Specifically, you will learn how to determine why AutoRent profits are declining and make recommendations for how to remedy this situation."

Learner Task 4: Assimilate the New Knowledge into Existing Knowledge

Lesson Elements:
Present New
Knowledge and
Present Examples

Description.

1. State the class of problems to which the heuristic applies;

2. show the heuristics;

3. show the steps or general approach of each heuristic;

4. explain that the heuristic is a guide the learners can use to generate a specific solution or procedure for a problem; and

5. teach the underlying principle(s) or stimulate recall on them.

Since problem representation is a major part of problem solving, the heuristic may have two major subparts (or two heuristics): one for representing the problem and one for solving the equation, once represented. Both heuristics need to be taught and practiced for each of the components below. Then show a specific example of application of the problem (a worked example), emphasizing the key decisions and information used in the step-by-step application of the procedure.

> AutoRent Example: [*State the class of problems to which the heuristic applies.*] "This heuristic approach works to solve organizational performance problems, whether at the organization, work process, or individual performer level." [*Show the heuristics in Figures 9.2, 9.3, and 9.4 and the steps or general approach of each heuristic. Explain each of the levels of performance, starting with organization, and introduce a set of diagnostic questions for analyzing goals, design, and management at this level. Illustrate with a company. Explain and demonstrate use of the relationship map at this level. Explain and exemplify the cross-functional processes that contribute to providing products and services to customers and introduce a set of diagnostic questions. Introduce, explain, and demonstrate the use of the process map for meeting needs at the process level. Continue to use the same company example introduced earlier. Introduce the use of the human performance system as*

a means of understanding and meeting performance needs and introduce a set of diagnostic questions. Emphasize the role of all company personnel in improving organizational and process performance.]

[*Explain that the heuristic is a guide the learner can use to generate a specific solution or procedure for a problem. Emphasize the point that all these elements can be thought of as tools for understanding performance at each level. Explain that the maps lead to an understanding of the specific problems at each level in the organization and specific solutions to address each problem identified.*]

[*Teach the underlying principle(s), or stimulate recall on them.*] "The principles underlying these heuristics are declining profits, which is a *symptom* of a problem, not the problem, and further analysis is required to determine the real problem. A systematic look is better than assuming an answer. You have to know how the organization works now before you can change it. For maximum problem-solving effect, the entire corporate system and all that the system entails would probably have to be looked at upside down and backwards with no limits. At the organization level, you should show the flow of work through the entire organization from inputs to outputs; at the process level, functional silos are a common cause of work-flow problems, and at the individual level, inadequate information, feedback, tools and resources, and incentives are the most common causes of performance problems."

[*Since problem representation is a major part of problem solving, the heuristic may have two major subparts (or two heuristics): one for representing the problem and one for solving the equation, once represented. Now that problems have been identified using the Rummler-Brache models, introduce the second set of heuristics—those for solving each of the types of problems identified. Introduce all the possible interventions in the following categories: financial systems, organizational design and development, job and work redesign, human resource development, organizational communication, performance support tools and information, and personal development.*]

[*Show a specific example of application of the problem (a worked example), emphasizing the key decisions and information used in the step-by-step application of the procedure.*]

Learner Task 5: Strengthen the New Knowledge in Memory

Lesson Element: Practice

Description. Practice using a range of similar problems. Use scenario-based simulations and games, on-the-job mentoring, and/or OJT. Use the following principles:

1. If necessary, provide part-task practice of relevant algorithmic methods (facts, concepts, principles, rote procedures). Part-task practice

can be wrapped into the scaffolding of the whole skill practice described below.

2. Provide scaffolded practice: Scaffolded problems can take several different forms. One form is to provide part of a solution and ask the learner to do the rest, such as by interrupting a think-aloud or completion problem (where we present a partial worked solution and ask the learners to complete it). Also possible are interactions where the sensitivity of feedback triggers is modulated so that feedback would be available at every step for early problems, but available later only on the final output.

3. Provide significant support to the learner on initial problems, slowly withdrawing that support until the learner is doing the whole task independently.

4. As you scaffold, do *not* distort the basic logical structure of the strategy. Each practice should be complete from beginning to end. Make the problem easier by providing direction, eliminating irrelevant detail, avoiding "branches" for special cases or extra steps, and avoiding or clarifying points of confusion.

5. Provide a range of problems, including prototypical problems, problems that require unusual uses of the heuristic, and problems where the heuristic is an inappropriate choice (non-examples).

6. Provide a range of contexts.

7. Do *not* increase problem difficulty while decreasing support. Modulate both difficulty and support, but only one at a time.

8. Be sure to include features that expose anticipated learner misconceptions.

AutoRent Example: [*Provide a simulation/case study involving a simple business. Provide a great deal of information about the organization and a partially filled out organization map. Build the simulation/case study so the problems are the most common and obvious ones and the most easy to discover (unclear strategy; no customer inputs; functional silos not communicating; excess "wait" time in processes; lack of information, feedback, and incentives for workers). Have learners work in groups of four and share their diagnoses and rationales; agree on a "class answer." After diagnosis is complete, have groups work on proposing interventions for each level of problems.*

[Now provide a simulation/case study involving a medium-size business in an industry completely unrelated to car rental. Provide some data about the organization and documents in which the rest of the needed information can be found. Build the simulation/case study so the problems are less common and obvious (lack of alignment among levels; internal policies and procedures not matching external requirements; more complex process and tools issues).

Have learners work in groups of four and share their diagnoses and rationales. After diagnosis is complete, have groups work on proposing interventions for all levels of problems, following the same pattern as above.

[Do a third practice in which you provide a simulation/case study involving a complex business (a Fortune 500 company). Provide only documents about the organization that contain some of the needed information, and people to role play corporate executives they can interview to get more information. Build the simulation/case study so the problems are the least common and obvious ones (globalization issues; internal political strife; industry restructuring; unionized workforce). Have learners work in pairs and present their completed diagnoses, proposed interventions, and rationales.]

Lesson Element: Feedback

Description. As you dialog with the learner about how he or she has defined each of the basic problem characteristics, ask the learner to explain why he or she made the decision, and what knowledge he or she used to make the decision. Listen to the explanations for gaps or misconceptions in the learner's mental model. When you find one, point it out. Look at the sequence of steps the learner is going through and check it against the heuristics identified in the cognitive task analysis. When the learner skips a step, does a step out of order, or does a wrong or unnecessary step, ask the learner to reflect: "Are you sure you want to do that now?" If that doesn't cause the learner to correct the error, then state the missing heuristic to the learner: "You don't have enough information to do that yet. Remember that [heuristic]." If that doesn't work, then model the solution and include a "think aloud" explanation of why the solution is as it is: "Here's how I think about problems like this. . . ."

> AutoRent Example: "What steps did you go through in each case? What wasted moves or mistakes did you do? How can you avoid them in future jobs? What should you always do when you solve problems like these? What should you do differently, depending on the specifics of each problem?"

Lesson Element: Summary

Description. The *structure of content* is the fully generated heuristic for problem solution. If possible, the learner should generate it.

> AutoRent Example: [*Repeat the three Rummler-Brache models and help everyone apply them to AutoRent.*]

Lesson Element: Test

Description. Problem solving has to be tested with a performance-based strategy: The only way to find out whether a learner can solve problems is to have the learner solve problems of realistic complexity and in realistic contexts, without extra scaffolding. You can do this with well-designed simulations, hands-on exercises, role plays, and projects. Paper-and-pencil testing formats usually favor open-ended (divergent or essay) questions that are scenario-based. In many content areas, however, paper-and-pencil formats are too limited to capture the context and complexity of the desired performance. In these cases, online simulations and various kinds of "live" group exercises, role plays, and projects are needed, depending on the content area.

> AutoRent Example: [*Provide the learners with a simulation/case study involving a complex business to analyze using the models. Provide only documents about the organization that contain some of the needed information and people to role play corporate executives they can interview to get more information. Build the simulation/case study so the problems are the least common and obvious ones and the most difficult to discover. Have learners work in pairs and present their completed diagnoses, proposed interventions, and rationales.*]

Lesson Element: On-the-Job Application

Description. In the first few weeks following training, make sure the learner encounters a wide range of tasks of typical difficulty and representative of the objective. It's helpful to have the learner do some tasks, and then review, critique, and troubleshoot similar tasks done by others.

> AutoRent Example: [*Have the class develop a work plan for doing an analysis of AutoRent. Have teams of learners begin the analysis, meeting frequently to share their findings and discuss both results and difficulties. Be available as a coach to provide expert feedback on progress and suggestions for improving performance.*]

Components of Practice Examples

In the example above, the instructional components used in this strategy were in a typical inductive sequence. Depending on your lesson design, your implementation may vary. Remember also that it's common to embed fact, concept, and principle teaching in a problem-solving lesson, as long as the resulting lesson isn't too hard to follow.

A second procedure lesson segment is shown below in tabular form (Figure 9.5). It illustrates the design for teaching YourMart word processing new hires the general strategy for applying mail merges to unusual jobs like the "quarterly fax." The numbers throughout the example refer to the numbered principle list on pages 132 through 135.

FIGURE 9.5. Job Aid for Teaching Ill-Structured Problem-Solving

Principle	Example
1. Select the Information to Attend To (#5) *Attention.* This component should explain you are teaching a general strategy for solving a class of problems, even if some of them are new.	"When you plan a complex mail merge, it's important to think about how best to do it."
WIIFM. Establish the context in which the problem is solved. This should be the framework for all explanations, examples, and practice throughout the lesson.	"At the end of every quarter, you must fax to all the regional sales managers. Different central office managers participate every time, and the details of the call's date, time, and topic change with every call. With the mail merge tool, you can set up the memo you need once and save a lot of time. But you need to plan your strategy carefully when you set up the data file."
YCDI. Encourage the learners by telling them it may be hard at first to learn this content but it is not really that hard.	[*Use a collaborative learning approach so learners see this is hard for everyone, so it's OK to be puzzled.*]
2. Link the New Information with Existing Knowledge *Recall* related declarative knowledge that is part of the mental model and procedures analogous to the one you are teaching.	"You already know how to set up a mail merge for a task such as a series of letters. You know how to set up a data file, with its variables, and how to embed the variable names in the text of the letter."
Relate the current procedure to what the learners already know about the mental model and the analogical procedure(s).	"The repetitive fax job uses the same principles, but how you set up the job depends on what's constant and what's variable about each quarter's run."
3. Organize the Information Organize the new knowledge so that it matches the organization of the existing knowledge. (#19) *Structure of Content.* Show the mental model for a heuristic for a class of abstract problems. (#6) • Develop an abstract diagram or other representation of how the components in the problem space interact, and/or • Present *worked examples* of typical problems, then articulate the strategy steps used to solve the problem(s). Worked examples can take many forms, including think-alouds and step-by-step solutions. Note features of the problem that are unique to that problem.	Salutation / Last name: Mr. / Smith; Ms. / Johnson; Dr. / Wilson; Mr. / Allison. Dear {Salutation} {Lastname}: Please plan on participating in the conference call for investors on Thursday, July 18, at 10 AM. At . . . Dear Ms. Johnson: Please plan on participating in the conference call for investors on Thursday, July 18, at 10 AM. At . . .

FIGURE 9.5. (*Continued*)

Principle	Example
(as opposed to those that are typical of a class of problems). Not all of the typical features or exceptions need be covered in these initial worked examples, as long as they are covered elsewhere in the activity. Be sure that the cognitive processes (such as cues and decisions) are made clear in the example, as well as the performance.	"The basic strategy is the same: 1. Set up your data file. 2. Use it to set up your main file. 3. Run the mail merge. But you need to do some thinking when you plan Steps 1 and 2. And you need to learn about some special Word functions, such as the *compare* function."
Objectives. Tell the learner the purpose of this lesson is to understand a (particular) general procedure for solving a (particular) broad class of problems (which you name).	"In this lesson, you'll see how to apply the general strategy for mail merges to unusual jobs like the quarterly fax."
4. Assimilate the New Knowledge into Existing Knowledge (#7–11) *Present New Knowledge.* Show the heuristics: • State the class of problems to which the heuristic applies. • Show the steps. • Explain that the heuristic is a guide the learner can use to generate a specific solution for a problem. • State the underlying principle(s) or stimulate recall on them. • Since problem representation is a major part of problem solving, the heuristic may have two major subparts (or two heuristics): one for representing the problem and one for solving the equation, once represented. Both heuristics need to be taught and practiced.	"To select only those employees who are participating in the call, you need a way to include in the merge only a certain subset of the possible managers on your list. You do this by using a logical function called *compare*. Compare works by checking the value of a variable against a value you specify, so if the value matches, then *compare* returns a 'true' statement. If you click on the 'Insert Word Field' button on the merge data button bar, you'll see all the variations of the *compare* function."
Present Examples. Show a specific example of application of the problem (a worked example), emphasizing the key decisions and information used step-by-step.	"For example, here's one I needed to do. I had a data field named 'call,' which I set up so you type 'x' if the person is not participating, and otherwise leave blank. I did this because it's often helpful to have a data field that includes the specific conditions for action. In this case, I want to fax only participating people. Then in the main document, I can" [*illustrate with*

(*Continued*)

FIGURE 9.5. Job Aid for Teaching Ill-Structured Problem-Solving (*Continued*)

Principle	Example
	screen prints or live demo] "(1) click on Insert Word Field; (2) click on the 'Skip Record If' choice (This form of the *compare* function compares a variable's contents to what you specify and skips the record if the *compare* function says it matches.); (3) for the Field Name, select 'call'; (4) for the comparison, select 'equal to'; and (5) for the 'compare to' type in 'x.' "Then when I run the procedure," [*click on the View Merged Data icon on the tool bar*] "it selects only the records of the participants and merges them with your meeting announcement document, like this" [*point out selected records*]. "You can select 'merge to fax' from the Mail Merge icon just as easily as you select 'merge to print,' like this" [*demonstrate*].
5. Strengthen the New Knowledge in Memory (#14) *Practice* using a range of similar problems. Use scenario-based simulations and games, on-the-job mentoring, and/or OJT. Use these principles: • If necessary, provide part-task practice of facts, concepts, principles, and rote procedures. • Provide scaffolded practice. One way is to ask the learner to provide part of a solution and ask the learner to do the rest, such as by interrupting a think-aloud or completion problem. Also possible are interactions where the sensitivity of feedback triggers is modulated (in early problems, feedback would be available at every step; in later problems, feedback would only be available for the final output). • Provide significant support to the learner on initial problems, slowly withdrawing that support until learner is doing the whole task independently.	"Now, you try planning and setting up a few mail merges in Word. Ask for help if you get stuck. [*Let the learners work on their own. If there is a problem, provide feedback using these strategies:* • *First, ask the learner what he/she intends to do and why.* • *If the principle is wrong, correct it. If it is missing, supply it.* • *Ask the learner to state the modified procedure to solve the problem by applying the principle.* • *Only if all else fails, model the action for the learner and state the principle as you describe the procedure step.*] "Set up a mail merge for a 'past due' billing notice that will skip the people who have already paid and print it." [*Note: the solution will be virtually identical to the example above.*] "Set up a mail merge that will fax a confirmation letter to all the invitees to a conference, so that it includes one paragraph if they have prepaid and another if they must pay at the registration desk." [*Note: the solution involves use of the "if . . . then" function and the "merge to fax" choice, but is otherwise similar to the example.*]

FIGURE 9.5. (*Continued*)

Principle	Example
• As you scaffold, do not distort the basic logical structure of the strategy. Each practice should be a complete beginning-to-end use of the strategy. Make the problem easier by providing direction, eliminating irrelevant detail, avoiding "branches" for special cases or extra steps, and avoiding or clarifying points of confusion. • Provide a range of problems, including prototypical problems, problems that require unusual uses of the heuristic, and problems where the heuristic is an inappropriate choice (non-examples). • Provide a range of contexts. • Do not increase problem difficulty while decreasing support. Modulate both difficulty and support, but only one at a time. • Be sure to include features that expose anticipated learner misconceptions.	"You're preparing to send a software upgrade to your customers. Set up a mail merge for your customer file that will automatically assign an order number to each customer that is the same as the customer's order among the customers who have ordered a free upgrade. Print it to mailing labels, with the order number showing, and also print out packing lists for each order from the same data file." [*Note: this is obviously more complex, but uses the same principles, except that in addition to the 'compare' function, this uses another function called 'merge sequence.' It also requires that the learner recall how to use the label templates.*]
Feedback (#12, 13, 15, 20) • As you dialog with the learner about how he or she has defined each of the basic problem characteristics, ask the learner to explain why he or she made the decision and what knowledge he or she used to make the decision. • Listen to the explanations for errors that reveal flaws (gaps, misconceptions) in the learner's mental model of the problem space. When you find one, point it out to the learner. • Look at the sequence of steps the learner is going through and check it against the heuristics identified in the cognitive task analysis. When the learner skips a step, does a step out of order, or does a wrong or unnecessary step, first ask the learner to reflect on the strategy in use ("Are you sure you want to do that now?"). If that doesn't cause the learner to correct the error, then state the missing heuristic to the learner ("You don't have enough information to do that yet.	"Now that you've worked three mail merge problems, it's time to think about how you designed each mail merge job. Answer these questions: What steps did you go through in each case? What wasted moves or mistakes did you do? How can you avoid them in future jobs? What should you always do when you solve problems like these? What should you do differently, depending on the specifics of each problem?"

(*Continued*)

FIGURE 9.5. Job Aid for Teaching Ill-Structured Problem-Solving (*Continued*)

Principle	Example
Remember that [heuristic].”). If that doesn't work, then model the solution and include a “think aloud” explanation of why the solution is as it is (“Here's how I think about problems like this . . .”).	
Summary. The *structure of content* is the fully generated heuristic for problem solution. If possible, the learner should generate it.	“Now you know how to use the basic merge procedure, to include variables for selection, substitution and numbering. What is your strategy?” [*Answer: set up your data file (with selection variables); use it to set up your main file (with compare or other functions); run the mail merge (to print, fax, or e-mail).*]
Test. Problem solving has to be tested with a performance-based strategy: The only way to find out whether a learner can solve problems is to have the learner solve problems of realistic complexity and in realistic contexts, without extra scaffolding. You can do this with well-designed simulations, hands-on exercises, role plays, and projects. Consequently, paper-and-pencil testing formats usually favor open-ended (divergent or essay) questions that are scenario-based. In many content areas, however, paper-and-pencil formats are too limited to capture the context and complexity of the desired performance. In these cases, online simulations and various kinds of “live” group exercises, role plays, and projects are needed, depending on the content area.	[*Construct another mail merge scenario of realistic complexity and difficulty. Give it to the learners with no special aids or suggestions, just instructions.*] “Now it's time to do the monthly newsletter, which goes to all clients. You want to customize the newsletter, so each client gets one which features articles about the products they purchased and other products clients like them purchase. Use the file generated by your client data base, and these source articles, and plan and address the personalized newsletters.”
On-the-Job Application. In the first few weeks following training, make sure the learner encounters a wide range of tasks that are of typical difficulty and are representative of the objective. It's helpful to have the learner do some tasks and to review, critique, and troubleshoot similar tasks done by others.	[*Develop a mentoring plan for mail merge jobs. Work with the supervisor to make sure the trainee is assigned at least three mail merge tasks representative of the full range of difficulty encountered in the task, beginning with the easiest one. Also, ask the supervisor to assign the trainee to help others in the office when they are having problems with mail merge tasks.*]

SUMMARY

In this chapter we described what ill-structured problem-solving procedures are, how to recognize them, how learners function when presented with problems, the problems in learning ill-structured problem solving, and general principles for combining declarative and procedural teaching.

We began by defining an ill-structured problem as a completely undefined situation—no initial state or goal or set of operations or constraints. We then elaborated on two major tasks learners must perform when presented with a problem—create a "problem space" and check the results.

Next, we listed and discussed five problems learners have in learning problem solving and listed and discussed general principles for teaching ill-structured problem-solving procedures, categorized by:

- Deciding what to teach.
- Presenting the problem first.
- Presenting the heuristics to solve the problem.
- Using reflection.

We explained the general principles for combining declarative and procedural teaching, reinforcing the discussion with sample lesson sequences. The final portion of the chapter illustrated the development of an ill-structured problem-level lesson segment using the lesson elements designed to teach AutoRent's executives how to solve the problem of why company profits are falling, how to remedy the problem, fix it, and determine that the problem is solved.

We concluded the chapter with an example in job-aid format that illustrates the design for teaching YourMart word processing new hires the general strategy for applying mail merges to unusual jobs like the "quantity fax."

FIGURE 10.1. Chapter 10 Structure of Content

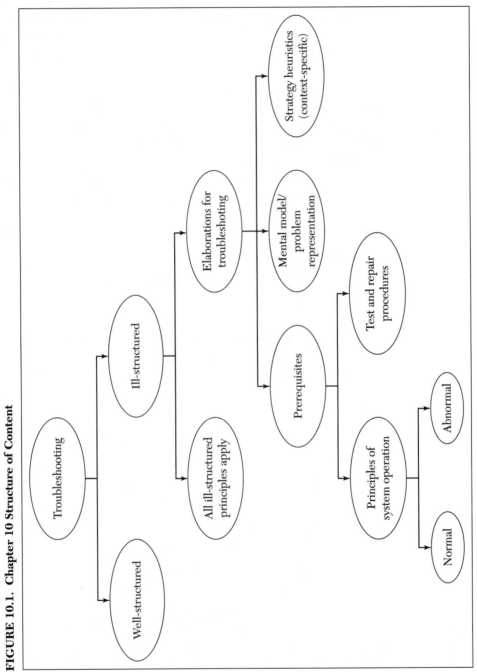

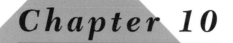

Chapter 10

Teaching Troubleshooting

Recall (from Chapter 1)

- Procedural knowledge is all about problem solving.
- Procedural knowledge is the ability to string together a series of mental and physical actions to solve a problem or, in other words, achieve a goal.
- Procedures vary in complexity along a continuum of how well the problem is defined—at the precise end are well-structured problems; in the middle are moderately structured problems; and at the far end are ill-structured problems.
- Troubleshooting is a special case of moderately structured problem solving.
- Most troubleshooting requires principle and mental model knowledge.

Relate to What You Already Know

- Examples of troubleshooting you already know are:
  - Fixing a desk lamp that won't light.
  - Repairing, or at least determining why the lawn mower won't start.
  - Figuring out why you are not receiving e-mail and fixing it so you are.

Structure of Content

- See Figure 10.10.

Objectives

- To describe what troubleshooting is.
- To apply general strategies for teaching troubleshooting.
- To design a lesson to teach troubleshooting, including all lesson elements.

ABOUT TROUBLESHOOTING

At AutoRent, the vehicle service specialists cannot properly diagnose and service rental cars that don't start.

At YourMart, new hires to the technical support staff cannot find and fix modem problems.

These types of training problems involve *troubleshooting*—finding out what's wrong with a product, system, or organization, deciding how to fix it, fixing it, and determining that it is fixed.

What kinds of troubleshooting problems might you see on the job? Have you seen some of the novice performers in your organization take too long to figure out what's wrong, never figure out what's wrong, always replace lots of parts, do too many tests, or always use the same fixes regardless of the problem? Does your company introduce new technology or release new models or versions so often that you can't retrain your service or support people fast enough?

You can solve those troubleshooting problems by turning your novice performers into experts, or at least helping them to acquire the expert-level knowledge needed to troubleshoot quickly and efficiently. By doing so, you will also equip them to master new equipment quickly, with little or no formal training.

In troubleshooting, the learner starts out with the following givens:

- It is clear how the product, system, or organization is supposed to work.
- The kinds of problems that can occur are limited.
- There are some definite signals (symptoms) that the problems are occurring.
- There are some strategies for figuring out what the problem is.
- There are some definite things to do to fix each problem in the product, system, or organization.

Troubleshooting is often taught as a cluster of well-structured procedures. However, extensive research on expert troubleshooters in a wide range of areas has shown that experts approach troubleshooting as moderately structured problem solving if they are dealing with a novel problem. Therefore, that is how we approach it in this chapter.

GENERAL STRATEGIES FOR TEACHING TROUBLESHOOTING

Our general instructional strategies include all those for ill-structured problem solving (see Chapter 9) plus some additional ones that duplicate the ways experts think when they troubleshoot:

- Teach the principles of normal and abnormal system operation as a prerequisite, including failure modes of components and their probabilities.
- Teach test and repair procedures as a prerequisite.
- Present troubleshooting heurisitics in such a way that the learners develop the desired mental model.
- Provide a wide variety of practice simulations they will encounter on the job.

USING THE LESSON ELEMENTS TO TEACH TROUBLESHOOTING

Example Scenario

Among the actions taken in a recent AutoRent company reorganization was the reduction of the number of mechanics at each of the locations. In order to maintain adequate servicing of the fleet and take some pressure off location mechanics, upper management decided to move some responsibilities for fleet maintenance to the vehicle service specialists (VSSs). These employees are not trained mechanics. They are responsible for preparing vehicles for re-rental by doing such tasks as washing and cleaning the cars, maintaining fluid levels (coolant, windshield wiper and so forth), and so on. One of these new responsibilities (formerly the mechanics') is to be able to determine why a vehicle won't start and either fix the vehicle within a range of possible problems or, if they cannot fix it, refer the problem to a mechanic. Because their backgrounds and experiences vary widely, the training department was asked to produce a training course in troubleshooting non-starting vehicles. In previous units the VSSs learned the parts (subsystems) of the starter system, their functions, how the system works normally (both principles and procedures) and abnormally, and repair procedures. To avoid redundancy, Learner Task 1, Select the Information to Attend To, and its corresponding lesson elements, Attention, WIIFM, and YCDI, are not shown. For descriptions see Chapter 3. The lesson segment begins with Learner Task 2, Link the New Information with Existing Knowledge.

Learner Task 2: Link the Information to Attend To

Lesson Element: Recall

Description. You should recall for the learners previous course and job-related content, facts, concepts, and their relationships, including components and subsystems and the failure modes of each, and procedural and heuristic knowledge, including how the system works normally, test and inspection procedures, and practice in predicting how the system will malfunction when each component or subsystem failure occurs.

Asking questions or presenting problems designed to recall this knowledge is generally more effective than just presenting it. The objective is to stimulate recall of the entire, working mental model.

AutoRent Example: "Now let's recall the information we went over in the first unit. This is important because you need to have a working knowledge of the starter system to practice the troubleshooting later in this lesson." [*Have them close their training manuals. Begin by asking them to define the basic parts (subsystems) of the starter system. These would include: fuel supply, ignition switch, safety switch, battery, battery posts, battery cables, solenoid switch, and starter motor. Then ask them to recall the principles that determine how a car engine starts (shown here in Figure 10.2).*]

FIGURE 10.2. Principles: How a Car Starts

> If:
> Fuel tank has at least one gallon of proper (summer/winter) octane in it
> And
> Automatic transmission is in "park" or manual transmission's clutch is disengaged
> And
> Ignition switch is functioning properly
> And
> Battery is at least three-quarters charged
> And
> Battery posts are clean
> And
> Battery cables are properly connected and not broken or corroded
> And
> Solenoid switch is functioning properly
> And
> Starter motor is functioning properly
> And
> Oil is proper viscosity
> Then, when ignition key is turned to "start," engine will start

[*Next get them to recall the procedures (the electric and mechanical steps) that occur during a normal car start (shown here in Figure 10.3)*].

[*After this first phase of recall, if you need to reinforce any of this material, have them open the manuals and examine the appropriate sections. Tell them to again close their manuals. In the second phase you're going to ask them to recall the modes of failure for each of the subsystems and predict how the system will malfunction (what the symptoms are) when each of the*

FIGURE 10.3. Steps: How a Car Starts

> How a Car Starts—Steps
> 1. When the ignition key is turned on, it sends an electrical charge to the safety switch.
> 2. The safety switch is opened if the vehicle's automatic transmission is in "Park" or manual transmission's clutch is disengaged.
> 3. The electrical charge drawn from the battery travels to the solenoid switch.
> 4. The solenoid switch activates the starter motor.
> 5. The starter motor turns the engine flywheel over as fuel enters the engine cylinders and spark plugs are activated.
> 6. Engine turns over, begins combustion process, and begins firing.
> 7. Vehicle starts.

subsystems fails. To do this give them a handout like the one shown in Figure 10.4, only blank.]

[Their task is to fill in on their own all the blanks for each of the subsystems. Process their answers. Once you are satisfied that the learners have recalled the entire working mental model, you are ready to relate it to the new knowledge.]

Lesson Element: Relate *Description.* Relate the new knowledge to the existing knowledge structures by:

- Identifying the similarities and differences between the new knowledge and the existing related knowledge—but at a high level of abstraction.

- Presenting analogies to the new knowledge that would be familiar to learners.

- Identifying previous job or real-world experience learners have related to the new knowledge, including:

    - Similar concepts and relationships and procedural or heuristic knowledge they already know and use.

    - The job situation in which learners use it.

    - How that job situation relates to the new knowledge they are learning.

AutoRent Example: "OK, everyone's up-to-speed on the starter system. You all just demonstrated that you're able to name and define the parts of the starter system, relate how the system works, explain how each of those parts can fail, what the symptoms of failure are, what the chances are of that part failing, how to confirm what's happening, and what to do once you know what's wrong. At this point some of you may be asking yourselves, 'So what else is there to know about this new responsibility? Let's get out of here and back on the line.' Good question. But before we let you go back on the line, there's one more crucial skill you need to have so that you don't unnecessarily

FIGURE 10.4. Starting System Troubleshooting Chart

Subsystem	Why It Fails	Symptom(s)	Failure Probability	Best Approach to Confirm
Fuel Supply	Empty Tank	Engine cranks, won't start	Moderate	Check fuel supply
	Wrong Octane	Same	Low	Check octane
Safety Switch	Shift lever not in "Park" or clutch not engaged	Dead silence	High	Check shift lever or clutch
Ignition Switch	Loose wire connections	Dead silence	Low	Mechanic
Battery	No charge	Dead silence	High	Inspect hydrometer (charge indicator) on top of battery
	Low charge	Same or slow crank	High	
	Cracked	Same or slow crank	Low	Inspect battery
	Corroded posts	Same or slow crank	Moderate	Inspect battery posts
Battery Cables	Broken	Dead silence	Low	Inspect cables
	Loose	Dead silence	Low	
	Corroded	Slow crank	Moderate	
Solenoid Switch	Defective	Cranks, won't start	Low	Mechanic
	Loose wire connections	Dead silence	Low	
Starter Motor	Defective	Cranks, won't start	Low	Mechanic
	Loose wire connections	Dead silence	Low	
Oil	Too thick for weather conditions	Slow crank, won't start	Moderate	Mechanic

refer a non-starting vehicle to a mechanic. The difference between what you know now about the system and what you need to know is what to do and how you do it when more than one fault could cause the symptom you see. What you're going to learn in this unit is how to use all of the material we just reviewed in as many situations as possible by thinking strategically, bouncing around the possible reasons why the car won't start, choosing the correct one, and either fixing it, if you can, or referring it to the mechanics if you can't—and doing this as quickly and efficiently as possible.

"Let me give you a similar situation to make the point about what we're going to do next. Most of you have some 'system.' I say that in quotes, such as knowledge of how a floor lamp works, right?" [*Ask for answers.*] "That's right, the light bulb is connected with a wire to an outlet that provides electricity. When you turn on the switch, electricity flows to the bulb and it lights. Good! Now, you're sitting reading the paper and the light goes out. Based on your knowledge of this system, what's the first thing you'd do? Right, check the bulb to see if it's burned out. But what if the bulb isn't burned out? What do you do next? OK, check to see if the lamp is plugged in. What if it is? What next? Here is my point—all of you are at this stage of troubleshooting with the starter system. You know a few symptoms of how parts fail but really don't know what to do when, like the lamp example, more than one fault could be causing the symptom you see.

"Just to summarize here—you've got the knowledge about the starter system, and now you're going to learn how to apply that knowledge in a variety of ways to keep the fleet rolling."

Learner Task 3: Organize the Information

Lesson Element:
Structure of Content

Description. Present material that shows the learner how the new knowledge is organized. The form you use should be structured or organized by the following:

- The learner's job tasks or what he or she already knows.
- Structures suggested by the knowledge itself.
- Suiting both the new knowledge and learner meta-cognitive strategies.

Keep in mind that the structure of content cannot be represented by an outline of the content or the sequence of the presentation. You're much more likely to use a representation such as a flowchart or decision table, in conjunction with a system structure diagram of some kind that captures the key elements of the mental model used for troubleshooting.

AutoRent Example: "Here's the training material we're going to use for this unit." [*Direct them to Figure 10.2 and Figure 10.5.*]
[*Quickly review the principles, the meaning of the chart, and the strategic plan.*]

Lesson Element:
Objectives

Description. Write the objectives so that they contain:

- The conditions accompanying the expected performance as close as possible to the real-world ones.

FIGURE 10.5. If . . . Then Table for Failure to Start*

If	Then Check	Failure Probability
Engine cranks or clicks but won't start	Battery	High
	Battery cables	Moderate
	Oil	Low
	Gas tank level	Moderate
	Gas octane	Low
Engine doesn't crank, no sound, dead silence	Battery	High
	Battery cables	Moderate
	Safety switch	High

Strategic Plan—When more then one fault could cause the symptom you see, first check the most probable and easiest to test.

- The performance itself, using an active verb that accurately states the knowledge, skills, or attitudes expected as a result of learning.
- The level of performance required by the job or expert judgment.

AutoRent Example: "The objectives for this lesson are 'Given a car that won't start for a reason you can fix, correct the problem and start it. And, given a car that won't start for a reason you can't fix, forward the car to a mechanic for service.'"

Learner Task 4: Assimilate the New Knowledge into Existing Knowledge

Lesson Element: Present New Knowledge

Description. Note: The complexity of this presentation strategy means that chunking considerations will usually keep you from doing all the presentation components below before doing any of the practice. We suggest that you insert practice after, or in parallel with, the "b" part of each presentation component. Depending on the complexity of the system and the prior knowledge of the learners, consider building the learners' mental models by sequencing the content "vertically" (that is, doing all forms of presentation and practice for one subsystem at a time), after only a general "horizontal" overview of the entire system structure and function. If your learners know enough about the system so this kind of sequence isn't confusing, your learners may find it

---

*N.B. The research is inconclusive on how effective it is to directly tell the learner the information, as in Figure 10.5. Some (constructivists) prefer that the learner construct the first two columns based on system knowledge and add the last column from experience (real world or with simulation).

easier to understand and more motivating, because they will quickly see how all the various learning tasks fit together into realistic troubleshooting tasks.

You also will want to use *worked examples* in Steps 4 and 5. These are examples of solutions, accompanied at each step by a full "think-aloud" explanation of the reasoning process that leads to that step.

1a. Present the system/process/object in which the troubleshooting will occur:

- Describe how the system/process/object works when it is working normally (including each normal operating mode or condition) in terms of its components (concept knowledge) and their interrelationships when operating normally (relationship knowledge).

1b. Present examples of and/or analogies for each of the concepts and their relationships (for example, "This content was reviewed in the 'recall' section").

2a. Present the categories of failure that can occur in the components of the system/process/object in which the troubleshooting will occur:

- Describe each category of failure that can occur in the components of the system/process/object when it is not working well.

- Describe (and get the learners to predict) how each category of failure affects the abnormal operation of the system/process/object in terms of its components (concept knowledge) and their interrelationships (relationship knowledge).

2b. Present examples of, and analogies for, the categories.

AutoRent Example: [*This content was also reviewed in the "recall" section, but you may want quickly to run through these categories of failure again, for example, one typical question would be, "If the battery has a low charge, what will happen when you try to start the car?" The learner's prediction should be, "Either there'll be dead silence/no cranking or slow cranking, but the car won't start." The extent of these exercises will depend on how well they know the categories of failure that can occur from the previous lesson and from the "recall" section.*]

3a. For each commonly occurring component failure, and a selection of rare failures, describe the probability of each failure mode and the cost (and risk) of each test or replacement procedure for each component.

3b. Present examples of, and analogies for, each failure.

AutoRent Example: [*Using the probability table in Figure 10.6, point out again the commonly occurring component failures—the battery and the battery cables (both high probability)—and a selection of rare failures—solenoid and starter motor (low probability). Emphasize the fact that the cost for testing or examining and, if necessary, replacing or charging the battery and/or replacing the cables is measured by the time it takes them to inspect and service these components.*

[Give them the replacement costs of the various batteries and battery cables. Remind them that the solenoid and starter motor failures are referred to the mechanics. Give them an idea of those replacement costs. Take them through a scenario where a VSS checks out a suspected dead battery. Tell them how much time it took him or her to check out the battery, determine that it needs to be replaced, take the battery from the shop, and replace it. Translate that time to a cost figure. Also (later on) you'll want to discuss the consequences of an incorrect diagnosis, such as replacing a battery that only was dead or had corroded connections.]

4a. For each subsystem, describe a strategy (general solution algorithm) for solving problems in that subsystem; it should be based on:

- The probability and modes of failure of components.

- The costs and risks of the tests.

- The costs and risks of the fix.

4b. Present examples of, and analogies for, the general solution algorithm.

AutoRent Example: [*Again using the "Starting System Troubleshooting Chart" (Figure 10.4), point out the general solutions (listed in the "Best Approach to Confirm" column) for specific problems in each of the subsystems. For example, in the fuel supply subsystem the general solution is to "check," for the safety switch it's to "check," for the battery and battery cable subsystems it's to "inspect," and so on. Demonstrate the various inspection and checking procedures. One highly effective technique to use in the demonstrations here is the "think-aloud" monologue, that is, giving a running commentary that emphasizes the cues and decision-making points, as well as the action taken. It's what the "color commentator" does at a baseball or football game: reconstruct why the shortstop or quarterback just made the decision he did and the action he took. One of your "think-aloud" monologues might go something like this:*] "So I get in the car, I'm in a big hurry to get it up to the front. It's just been serviced; I put the key in the ignition, turn it, and nothing happens—nothing, not even a crank. I look at the gas gauge; the tank is full. I look at the shift lever and realize that I'm in a car with a standard transmission. So what does this mean? In a standard transmission car, the starter safety switch needs to be turned off or disengaged by putting the clutch in, so I put the clutch in, turn the ignition key, the car starts, and I'm off!"

5a. Present heuristics learners can use to develop specific solution algorithms for specific problems within each failure category.

5b. Present examples of, and analogies for, each heuristic.

6a. Present a heuristic strategy for troubleshooting in general that emulates one used by experts for these types of problems, for example:

- Develop a mental model of the system/process/object being fixed.
- Add hypothetical component failures to it and predict resulting symptoms.
- Retain those possible failures that produced predicted symptoms that match the given symptoms.
  - Perform actual tests, using these heuristics, until a fault is found:
  - Work from highest to lowest probability fault.
  - Test from lowest cost and risk to the highest.
  - Use a strategy such as split-half or linear trace (output to input or input to output).

AutoRent Example: [*While displaying a diagram of a generic starting system, review the principles from Figure 10.2 governing why a car starts. Pair the learners up. Under your guidance have them generate a decision table they would use as a hypothetical job aid to determine from symptoms of a non-starting car what the causes are, along with chances of these failures happening (probability). In other words they have to generate symptoms, their causes, and probabilities. The finished chart should look something like Figure 10.6.*]

FIGURE 10.6. Symptom-Cause-Probability Table

Symptom	Cause	Probability
Engine clicks or cranks, won't start	Empty fuel tank	Moderate
	Wrong octane	Low
	Battery	High
	Battery cables	High
	Solenoid switch	Low
	Starter motor	Low
	Oil	Low
Dead silence	Safety switch	High
	Ignition switch	Low
	Battery	High
	Battery cables	High
	Solenoid switch	Low
	Starter motor	Low

[*Once they have generated these charts, move to the simulator. The simulator is programmed to re-create all the faults, with appropriate probabilities, in random order. After the simulator practice, go to the shop for practice on a few real cars to put the whole task together.*]

• Repair the fault, and test system operation to confirm normal operation.

AutoRent Example: [*After the fault has been determined, repair it and confirm normal operation. For example, this might consist of charging or replacing a weak battery or tightening a battery cable or cleaning the battery posts. Also demonstrate that, when the repair(s) doesn't result in normal operation, it becomes a "mechanic" referral. In this section also discuss the consequences of an incorrect referral (like referring for something you should have been able to fix or trying to fix something that should have been referred).*] "Think about what happens when you refer your vehicle to a mechanic just because you didn't check the connections at the lower end of the battery cable and that turns out to be the problem—a vehicle is taken out of service for who knows how long, a mechanic has to go over the initial checks you should have done, pulling him or her off a repair job, and some customer might be shorted a rental car somewhere down the line—time, money, and bad customer vibes."

6b. Present example of and analogies for the heuristic.

Learner Task 5: Strengthen the New Knowledge in Memory

Lesson Element: Practice

Description. During or immediately following each step in the presentation of troubleshooting content, procedure, and examples, have learners work in small groups, if possible. Have them:

• Underline the relevant text.
• Take selective notes on the elaboration and examples of each step in the procedure.
• Create their own outlines, maps, matrices, or other representations of the system structure and procedure.
• Give an example or analogy of the system or procedure and why it works in their own words.
• Give their own examples of the procedure.
• Demonstrate the procedure, using the real system or a simulator, with the appropriate fault.
• Demonstrate the procedure in a novel situation, again using a real system or simulator with the appropriate fault.

AutoRent Example: [*Have the learners demonstrate troubleshooting with the non-starting vehicles set up with the appropriate faults and also demonstrate these skills in novel situations.*]

Lesson Element: Feedback

Description. Let the learners know how well they've done in troubleshooting by using the symptoms as a basis for matching them to their causes, using the various tests, trying out the solutions, and testing for correctness. In addition to pointing out incorrect diagnoses and why, also point out failures to fix what should have been fixed, failures to refer what should have been referred, and fixing things that weren't a problem.

> AutoRent Example: [*Observe the learners as they troubleshoot the set-up vehicles. If possible, have them talk through what they're thinking as they go through the procedures. After the exercise is complete, reassemble in the training room and provide appropriate responses to their efforts.*]

Lesson Element: Summary

Description. Summarize the lesson by:

- Tying all the essential information together.
- Highlighting key points.
- Encouraging learners to make up their own memory joggers.
- Providing a job aid if one was not generated or used earlier.
- Requiring learners to apply new knowledge to similar but slightly different situations or problems.

> AutoRent Example: [*Present the same material as in the "structure of content" section. Also call their attention to the previous charts and the job aid they created earlier.*]

Lesson Element: Test

Description. Have the learners apply the troubleshooting knowledge to reinforce their learning and ensure their supervisors that they are able to handle this new responsibility.

> AutoRent Example: [*At the knowledge level, have them diagram their version of how a car starts and have them fill in a blank symptom/cause/probability/test matrix. At the application level, have them perform troubleshooting procedures on set-up cars as in practice session. Use a performance checklist to assess their competencies.*]

Lesson Element: On-the-Job Application

Description. Devise ways for learners to use troubleshooting knowledge in a structured way on the job to reinforce the learning and ensure they "use it, not lose it."

> AutoRent Example: [*For a period of time, when vehicles won't start have experienced VSSs require the newer trainees to troubleshoot the vehicles under their supervision.*]

A second procedure lesson segment is shown below in tabular form (Figure 10.7). It illustrates the design for teaching YourMart new tech staffers how to troubleshoot modems.

**FIGURE 10.7.
Job Aid for
Teaching
Troubleshooting**

Lesson Element	Example
1. Select the Information to Attend To *Attention.* Component should explain you are teaching a strategy, which the learner should be able to apply to a class of problems you define.	"You'll see the general strategies for all modems, and you'll be able to apply them whether you're using a Windows, Mac, or Unix computer."
WIIFM. Tell the learners the advantages of learning to troubleshoot the system they are learning.	"You'll be asked to deal with lots of different operating systems and lots of modems. But you can learn to troubleshoot them all with just a single general approach. It'll make you a real 'modem ace'!"
YCDI. Encourage the learners by telling them that they have previous knowledge about the content and learning troubleshooting won't be difficult.	"You already know a lot about how modems work, so learning how to troubleshoot them is easy, once you put on your thinking cap."
2. Link the New Information with Existing Knowledge Stimulate *recall* of concepts and principles needed for mental modeling and generating solutions.	"You've already learned what a modem is and how the device driver controls it."
Relate to the mental model (or present it if it's new). Show typical system components, typical component interactions, principles, concepts, and facts.	"Here's what happened to me last month: I got into a hotel in a new city, plugged in my modem, started the computer and the dialer, and clicked on 'connect'—but nothing happened! I know that right after I click on 'connect' I should hear a dial tone from the loudspeakers because the modem feeds its line audio to the speakers during the dialing sequence, but there was just silence. [*rest of story*] It was a loose wire."
3. Organize the Information *Structure of content* component should explain what the learner should expect to do in the activity.	"Now you're ready to learn how to correct failures to connect to your Internet service. First, we'll take a look at common causes of failures to connect and how to correct them. Then we'll put it all together in a troubleshooting strategy you can use, regardless of the type of computer you have."
Objective. Specify both the desired behavior and the knowledge to be learned.	"In this lesson, you can learn what you need to become an expert modem troubleshooter."
Transition	"First, I'll show you how to use all the strategies together, then we'll look at each one."

FIGURE 10.7. (*Continued*)

Lesson Element	Example
4. Assimilate the New Knowledge into Existing Knowledge *Present* the heuristic: • State the class of problems to which the heuristic applies. • Show the steps. • Explain that the heuristic is a guide the learner can use to generate a specific solution for procedure for a problem. • State the underlying principle(s) or stimulate recall on them.	"When I'm troubleshooting a modem problem, I know it's important to work from the phone line backward to the device driver, and I know I should look first at the things that are most commonly at fault, that are consistent with the symptoms I'm seeing." [*Stimulate recall on mental model of modem, faults of each part, and probability of each fault.*]
5. Strengthen the New Knowledge in Memory *Practice.* If necessary, provide part-task practice of relevant algorithmic methods (facts, concepts, principles, rote procedures). (See Chapters 6 and 7 for guidance in how to provide meaningful practice with concepts, principles, and mental models.)	[*Provide practice on any relevant concepts or principles here. This might include parts of the system (dialer, device driver, modem, speakers, phone line, telephone exchange, ISP dial-up port, Internet server), principles of operation*] "You tell the dialer what phone number to call and how to dial it and which modem to use." [*or failure probabilities and corrections.*] "The most common problem is with the phone line connection. Wiggle the plug at both ends to verify you have a good connection."

Practice. Provide significant support to the learner on initial problems, slowly withdrawing that support until learner is doing the whole task independently.
     As you scaffold, do not distort the basic logical structure of the strategy. Each practice should be a whole task, beginning-to-end use of the strategy. Make the problem easier by providing direction, eliminating irrelevant detail, avoiding "branches" for special cases or extra steps, and avoiding or clarifying points of confusion.
 • Provide a range of problems, including prototypical problems, problems that require unusual uses of the heuristic, and problems where the heuristic is an inappropriate choice (non-examples).
 • Provide a range of contexts.
 • Do *not* increase problem difficulty while decreasing support. Modulate both difficulty and support, but only one at a time.
 • Be sure to include features that expose anticipated learner misconceptions.
	"Here's a laptop computer that has been set up to dial, but there's no dial tone. What would you check first?" [*Discuss what to check and why that decision was made. Refer to a diagram of the mental model of the modem system.*] "What tests or corrections would you make to see if that's the problem?"
	
	 [*Go on to more difficult problems, such as: No dial tone due to phone service problem; wrong phone number; dial string problems; incorrect device driver; loudspeaker turned off; defective modem. In examples, vary the operating system used. Use simulations if needed, or do all practice on actual computers. Or, move from simulations to actual machines.*
	     Gradually reduce the scaffolding, until the learner is presented with nothing but a nonfunctional computer, with no supporting dialog or reference materials.]

(*Continued*)

FIGURE 10.7. Job Aid for Teaching Troubleshooting (*Continued*)

Lesson Element	Example
Elaboration: Scaffolded problems can take several different forms. One way is to provide part of a solution and ask the learner to do the rest, such as by interrupting a think-aloud) or completion problems (where we present a partial worked solution and ask the learners to complete it). Also possible are interactions where the sensitivity of feedback triggers is modulated (so in early problems, feedback would be available at every step; in later problems feedback would only be available for the final output). Another way to scaffold is to go from simple problems (with low cognitive load) to complex ones (with high cognitive load).	
Feedback. As the learner works on the practice, provide two levels of feedback: • Scenario-specific feedback, such as behavior of the system in a simulation. • Strategy-level feedback, such as a dialog on information gathered and decision-making strategy.	Example of scenario-specific feedback: After the learner fixes something in a simulation and clicks "connect," the simulation plays the audio heard through the speaker and shows the messages provided by the system under those circumstances. Example of strategy-level feedback: "Hmm . . . are you sure you know enough to try that fix now? Think about what you know about the problem and figure out what information you're missing."
Summary. The structure of content is the heuristic.	[*Show the complete heuristic one final time.*]
Test. Have the learners use the new knowledge again to offer evidence that they are capable of troubleshooting the system.	[*Repeat exercises similar to those used in the practice section to measure their troubleshooting skills.*]
On-the-Job Application. Have learners use new knowledge in a structured way on the job to ensure they "use it, not lose it."	[*Inform the group that by prior arrangement their supervisor has set up a number of laptops with problems and they will be asked to demonstrate their troubleshooting skills.*]

SUMMARY

In this chapter we described troubleshooting, showed how it can be used in training sequences, and gave an example of how to design a troubleshooting lesson segment using the lesson elements.

We began by categorizing troubleshooting as a special case of moderately structured problem solving. We defined troubleshooting as:

- Finding out what's wrong with a product or system or organization.
- Deciding how to fix it.
- Fixing it.
- Determining that it is fixed.

In your cognitive task analysis, you should have identified heuristics (moderately structured strategies) in three situations:

- Those in which the troubleshooting has many similarly structured procedures that can be taught more efficiently as examples of a heuristic (for example, writing memos for various purposes).
- Those in which the terminal objective is to be able to generalize—to generate specific troubleshooting algorithms on the spot, for new models of equipment (for example, troubleshooting without use of a rote procedure).
- Those in which the terminal objective is to be able to troubleshoot, even when details change due to changes in specifications, new or unknown equipment, new or unknown conditions, and so forth.

These are all examples of moderately structured problems: those for which a clear solution can be found, but the specific solution algorithm cannot be (or need not be) predetermined and recalled.

Next, we briefly explained some strategies that instructional designers should use to help learners become troubleshooters. These techniques are derived from research on what experts know and do. Instructional designers should make sure that, prior to the troubleshooting lesson, learners are familiar with normal and abnormal system operations and test and repair procedures. And then they should present the troubleshooting tasks so that learners develop the desired mental model, providing a wide variety of practice similar to those situations the learners will encounter on the job.

In the final part of the chapter, we put these strategies into a lesson segment on troubleshooting using the lesson elements for AutoRent's vehicle service specialists, who must know how to troubleshoot when cars won't start.

We concluded the chapter with an example in job-aid format that illustrates the design for teaching YourMart technicians how to troubleshoot modems.

FIGURE 11.1. Chapter 11 Structure of Content

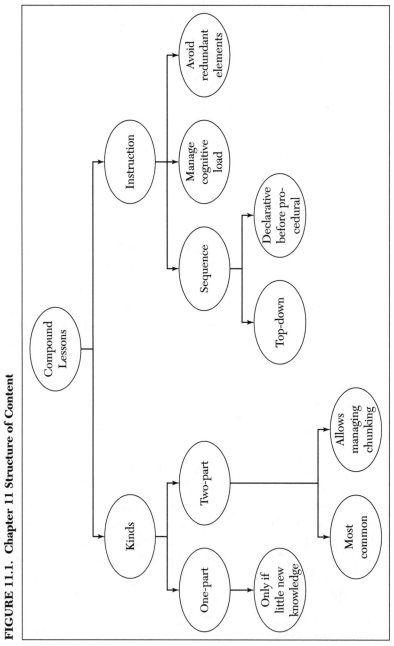

Chapter 11

Teaching Complete Lessons

LINK AND ORGANIZE

Recall (from Chapters 2 through 10)

- You have seen the model with seventeen lesson elements and how it is used to teach the six types of knowledge. The focus thus far has been on teaching each of those types of knowledge separately.

Relate to What You Already Know

- Just as when you started doing instructional design using the behavioral approach, you went through a series of steps and lesson elements for each type of knowledge. But after a while you figured out that there were more efficient ways to design lessons by combining objectives and eliminating some of the events—you became one of the "experts" who takes short cuts.

- Here, too, there are some efficiencies you can gain by developing lessons that combine several objectives. However, there are some differences in this approach about when and how to do that combining appropriately.

Structure of Content

- See Figure 11.1.

Objectives

- To create complete combined declarative/procedural knowledge lessons.
- To create complete procedural knowledge lessons with recall of declarative knowledge.

COMBINING DECLARATIVE AND PROCEDURAL TEACHING: TWO APPROACHES

As we said in Chapter 2, as an experienced instructional designer, you may want to try to teach many knowledge types as part of the same lesson. For example, you might want a lesson that ends up teaching well-structured problem solving, but teaches the appropriate principle, concept, and fact as part of the same lesson.

In the cognitive approach, there are really two possible scenarios for lessons that combine knowledge types:

- A lesson that combines all the procedural and declarative knowledge into one continuous lesson.
- A lesson that has two parts: the first part teaches the declarative knowledge through the mental model; the second part teaches the procedural knowledge after first recalling the declarative knowledge.

One Combined Lesson

It is difficult in most cases to develop a lesson that combines all six types of knowledge. Although it makes theoretical sense, combining declarative and procedural teaching is often difficult for designers. Sometimes it's feasible, and other times it is too confusing to the learner. We recommend that you use the following heuristics for how to combine lessons involving both procedural and declarative knowledge.

There are a few cases when you can combine all the objectives into one lesson. You can do this if it will make sense to the learners based on what they already know, their motivation, and the amount of new knowledge that does not exceed the learners' cognitive load capacity.

You begin with the ill-structured procedure to establish context, then digress to well-structured procedures and declarative knowledge.

For example, if you are teaching learners how to write a report, then you could use this sequence (but see the qualifier below):

1. Start by teaching the ill-structured task components in report writing, such as determining the purpose and the audience.
2. Next teach argumentation (how to state a conclusion and justify it with supporting evidence).
3. Next help the learner outline a simple and short report within a well-scaffolded* exercise.
4. Next help the learner write the first paragraph. Provide a template to scaffold it.
5. Continue to the next paragraph, and so forth, until the whole report is written.

A sequence such as this keeps the learner oriented to the "big picture" (whole task), but if there are too many substeps that are new to the learner, it's

---

*Scaffolding is discussed in more detail in Chapter 14.

likely that the learner will get lost among the trees and lose track of the forest. If this is the case, see the next recommendation.

There is considerable controversy over the best way of combining them. Some authors favor combining all knowledge types, often using an inductive sequence. We disagree, because experimental evidence favors deductive sequences (tell–show–do) over inductive ones (do–tell or do–tell–show) as more efficient and effective, especially when the learning outcome is specified and far transfer is not a major goal.

Separate Declarative and Procedural Knowledge Lessons

Therefore, we recommend that, in most cases, you teach the declarative knowledge and/or well-structured procedures first in a separate lesson before teaching the ill-structured procedures in a later lesson. Note, however, that in the early lessons, you'll probably want to inform the learner about the terminal objective of the sequence of lessons.

Example: Writing a Report

1. Teach how to identify the parts of a report. (*Note:* In the statement of the objective, include both the terminal objective of writing a report and the lesson objective of identifying parts of a report.)
2. Teach how to map the structure of a well-formed argument that supports a main point.
3. Teach how to structure a simple report that makes a simple argument, using a simple scenario.
4. Teach how to assemble a paragraph from component sentences.
5. Teach how to assemble paragraphs into an argument.
6. Teach how to use an argument to construct a simple report.
7. Expand to more complex reports.

TWO KEY ID ISSUES

Manage Cognitive Load

Regardless of which approach you use, manage cognitive load carefully, so the learner is never dealing with more than seven ± two new chunks at a time. Do this by teaching prerequisites first or by using novice/scaffolded versions of problems and their solution procedures and views first. If a procedure has many branches, teach each branch in the context of a full run-through of the procedure. Don't teach the branches in isolation. (See the example above.)

Use your cognitive task analysis to explicitly reference and provide practice on declarative knowledge use, mental model manipulations, and so forth.

Avoid Redundancy in Compound Lessons

Any time you combine separate lessons into a single, multi-part one, it's usually not necessary to include every lesson element separately for each sub-lesson.

This is especially true when you teach more than one knowledge type in the same lesson. In these cases, it would be redundant to repeat all the select, link, and organize lesson elements with every new sub-objective or knowledge type. Instead, you'll probably be able to build these lesson elements—just once— into the main lesson introduction, then use them as themes that carry throughout the lesson. For example, it's often good practice to build a structure of content graphic (such as a hierarchy or geometric shape or analogy to a physical object) that includes all the declarative knowledge to be taught—and perhaps some of what the learner already knows to which the new knowledge must relate. In this case, it's good practice to introduce the whole graphic in the lesson introduction as the organize element. Then, as you move through the lesson, return to the graphic and, for organize and summary lesson elements, simply highlight the relevant portions of the graphic. Similarly, often you can establish themes for WIIFM, YCDI, recall, and relate and carry them through the lesson. This avoids redundancy and gives overall unity to the lesson.

Most of the time, you will be creating lessons that have two parts: the first part teaches the declarative knowledge through the mental model; the second part teaches the procedural knowledge after first recalling the declarative knowledge learned in the first part.

TEMPLATE

A sample lesson plan that summarizes what we have said above is used in the example that follows. A blank plan is on the CD for you to print out and use. We suggest you use this template as you develop all your lessons.

We show one possible sequence for a two-part combined lesson structure to teach all declarative knowledge types together, followed by all procedural knowledge together. Our example is about conducting meetings. We recommend that when the amount of declarative knowledge new to the learner is relatively large (more than seven ± two teaching points), then it's probably best to teach the declarative knowledge as prerequisite using a structure similar to this one.

A similar precaution applies to embedding well-structured procedures within ill-structured ones. If the well-structured procedure has more than seven ± two steps or if it is particularly unfamiliar and difficult for the learners, then teach the well-structured procedures as prerequisites. The template presented in text can be adapted to teaching either declarative or well-structured procedural knowledge as a prerequisite to ill-structured procedure.

We intend these templates only as "initial skill modeling," not a definitive statement of the one best way to combine teaching of declarative and procedural knowledge in lessons.

Because of the length of the example, we will omit the narrative example from AutoRent that you have seen in previous chapters and present only the tabular example from YourMart that ends every chapter in this part.

AN EXAMPLE OF THE RECOMMENDED APPROACH TO COMBINED LESSONS

The YourMart Scenario

As part of the drive to meet and beat competition, YourMart senior management requires each of its stores to hold one storewide meeting a week along with weekly departmental meetings. Part of management's rationale is that these meetings give store personnel and local management more of a chance to communicate problems, ideas, competitive suggestions, and marketing strategies that have local or regional significance. Having as much input as possible at the local level could give the company an edge on their closest competitor, a highly centralized organization.

The local store managers and their department heads are free to structure and run the meetings as they see fit. There are no central corporate guidelines they have to follow. They are required to send minutes of the meetings to corporate headquarters.

Corporate officials are not happy with the quality of the departmental meeting minutes they are reading. Nothing of any strategic value—or of *any* value—seems to be generated from these meetings. The departmental meeting minutes that are attached to the storewide minutes appear even less valuable. Store managers are resisting these meetings.

In a series of meetings between YourMart management and the training department, a decision was reached to train management employees to plan and conduct effective and successful company meetings. Their task was to design and develop the first half of this "meeting conducting" course, that is, the plan successful meetings phase. The first part of the lesson, the declarative knowledge, is shown in Figure 11.2, which shows the training objectives:

- Fact: To be able to state the definitions of meeting types, meeting purposes, and meeting participants.

- Concept: Given examples and nonexamples of meeting types, purposes, and participants, label those that are examples and explain why.

- Principle: Given effective meeting planning principles and a number of scenarios predict what will happen in each of the scenarios and explain why.

The second part of the lesson, the procedural knowledge, is shown in Figure 11.3, which presents the training objectives:

- Well-Structured: Given a number of case studies that require planning a meeting apply the nine-step procedure for planning meetings that result in fully planned meetings for each of the case studies.

- Ill-Structured: Plan an emergency meeting to solve a crisis involving fifteen global offices.

**FIGURE 11.2.
Two-Part Lesson:
Part 1: Declarative
Knowledge**

Lesson Element	Example
Lesson Overview and Mental Model Presentation	
1. Select the Information to Attend to *Attention.* Attention component should explain you are teaching concepts and principles you need to solve the problem just presented in the scenario.	[*After title screen, begin the lesson with a video clip of people in a confusing store meeting; then show them emerging from the meeting and complaining about it.*] "Has this ever happened to you?" [*If yes—go on.* *If no—state*] "You've been lucky so far. It will. "Good meetings begin with a plan. That's what we'll concentrate on in this lesson.
WIIFM. Establish the context in which the problem is solved. This should be the framework for all explanations, examples, and practice throughout the lesson.	"Actually, [*characters in meeting video*] don't have to suffer through meetings like this. By understanding the elements of good meetings, you'll be able to assure this bad experience doesn't happen to your groups. Your store meetings can be a valuable way to make things work better—and to beat the competition.
YCDI. Build their confidence that this is a skill they can learn by showing them how they have already done similar things.	"Planning meetings well isn't much harder than planning them badly—it's just a matter of knowing what to do. It's a skill any successful professional develops, and you can, too."
2. Link the New Information with Existing Knowledge *Recall.* Recall related declarative knowledge that is part of the mental model and concepts the learner already knows which are analogous to the one you are teaching, in whole or in part.	"You probably already know many of the concepts involved in planning from other contexts: [*Show visual (hierarchy or actual graphic), which is first approximation of the structure of content. Have learner click on each element for a label.*] Agenda Decision making Record keeping" [*and other components the learners already know*]
Relate. Relate the mental model to what the learner already knows, often by use of an analogy.	"Planning a meeting is like planning a party, a card game, or a home improvement project. Click on the drawings below [*of planning a party, etc.*] to see what they have in common. "In each of these examples, you see that planning involves: Why you're doing it What you'd like the goal to be Who's going to be involved Time, place, and expense The steps to follow from beginning to end."
3. Organize the Information *Structure of Content* should show the mental model, including	[*Show complete visual diagram of the parts of a successful meeting, with arrows that show how they interact. Pop on each meeting plan part and*

FIGURE 11.2. (*Continued*)

Lesson Element	Example
concepts, principles, and skills. Develop an abstract diagram or other representation of how the components in the problem space interact, AND/OR present *examples* of typical concepts and principles.	*arrow as you name it, until the whole model is built.*] "Here's an example of a plan for a successful meeting. Roll your cursor over each part and you'll see its name. Roll your cursor over the arrows and you'll see what to call the ways the parts interact." [*Show example store meeting plan parts with arrows that show how they interact. When learner rolls mouse pointer over each part or arrow, its name pops up. When all names have been displayed, activate the "go on" icon.*]
Principle Lesson 1	
1. Select the Information to Attend to *Attention:* Transition to first principle (*WIIFM/YCDI* redundant and are omitted).	"Take a look at the first arrow in the diagram. It stands for the first rule for successful meetings [*the rule of meeting purpose*]. Click on it to see how it works."
2. Link the New Information with Existing Knowledge *Recall/relate:* (this is a great time for an analogy).	[*Show video of basketball team in huddle.*] "When you're playing basketball, the first thing you have to know is how points are awarded. Having a clear meeting purpose is like knowing how you'll score points."
3. Organize the Information *Structure of Content:* Show how the principle fits in the mental model.	*Structure of Content:* [*Show mental model, with first arrow (purpose) highlighted, and pop on the plan parts it connects to.*] "When you have a clear purpose, it's possible to develop all these parts of the plan: Agenda; participants; logistics . . ."
Concept Lesson 1 (remember, it's always best to teach concept structures, rather than isolated concepts).	
1. Select the Information to Attend to *Attention:* Transition to first concept structure (*WIIFM/YCDI* redundant).	"Let's see what the different purposes of meetings are and what they mean."
2. Link the New Information with Existing Knowledge *Recall/relate:* (another great place for an analogy).	[*Show posterized still photo of basketball video.*]

(*Continued*)

FIGURE 11.2. Two-Part Lesson: Part 1: Declarative Knowledge (*Continued*)

Lesson Element	Example
	"Meetings are like discussions you have with your teammates in a basketball game. Sometimes you're just talking about how the game is going. Sometimes you need to decide what play to use . . . and so on. Just as different conversations have different purposes, so do meetings"
3. Organize the Information *Structure of Content:* Show the concept structure.	*Structure of Content:* [*Bring up diagram next to basketball photo.*] [*Diagram of meeting purposes should include these, indicating arrangement from simple to complex, and with information flow coming in, going around within, and coming out of each pop on components individually*]: Information sharing Discussion Project-Review Operations-Review Decision-Making Problem-Solving *Objective:* At the end of this lesson, you'll know the differences between meetings with these six different purposes—you'll be able to define them and pick out examples of each.
Fact and Concept Lesson 1 (Remember that only presenting definitions is needed when teaching facts. Examples are needed for teaching concepts.)	
4. Assimilate the New Knowledge into Existing Knowledge (For facts:) Present explanations. *Step 1.* Show the facts. Use the structure you presented above. *Step 2.* Explain the structure. Include an explanation of the structure you presented.	*Present Definitions: Learner chooses sequence* [*Delete basketball visual. Add one meeting icon for each meeting purpose.*] "Click on each meeting purpose icon to see its definition" *Information Sharing*—objective/content is to disperse news, intelligence, policy, etc., to appropriate participants. *Discussion*—Objective is to share various points of view about an issue. *Project-Review*—examines or reexamines proposed current projects as to soundness, management, progress, and success. *Operations-Review*—systematically examines the soundness, management, progress, success of business procedures and processes. *Decision-Making*—Choose among several options to proceed with an action. *Problem-Solving*—main goal is to consider a question or statement or situation proposed for solution and achieve a resolution to it.

FIGURE 11.2. (*Continued*)

Lesson Element	Example
4. Assimilate the New Knowledge into Existing Knowledge (For facts:) Present explanations. *Present Examples* (remember there are no examples for facts, only the facts themselves. Examples are included here because this is a combined fact and concept lesson) (Note that in this medium, sequence of definitions (Fact lesson above) and examples (concept lesson here) can be learner controlled unless you deem a particular sequence to be critical to understanding).	[*Meeting type icons still on screen*] "Click on each meeting purpose icon to seen an example." [*Each example is a short video clip*]
5. Strengthen the New Knowledge in Memory *Practice* (For Fact, learners define. For concept, they select or classify.)	[*First, define each of these meeting types:* *Information Sharing* *Discussion* *Project-review* *Operations-review* *Decision-Making* *Problem-solving* *Practice (concepts)*] "Here are some more meetings. See if you can correctly identify the purpose of each one." [*Show eight video clips of meetings, each followed by a question asking "What meeting purpose did the example show?"*]
Feedback: For each incorrect answer, provide an explanation which corrects the probable misconception which caused the learner to select that choice; For each correct choice, tell the learner the choice is correct. Then move on to the next example and question.	(Example of incorrect answer feedback) "This is not an example of decision-making, because the participants are sharing information, but they are not trying to reach consensus."
Summary: Place concept structure back into the mental model.	[*Show the full mental model, with the concepts just taught highlighted.*] "So, now you can see all the types of meeting purposes and how they relate to the rest of the meeting plan."

(Continued)

FIGURE 11.2. Two-Part Lesson: Part 1: Declarative Knowledge (*Continued*)

Lesson Element	Example
Test: (great time for progressively more far-out positive examples and close-in negatives).	[*Fact test*] "Define the six types of meetings." [*Concept test*] "Here are some more meetings. See if you can correctly identify the purpose of each one." [*Show video clips of meetings, followed by question asking "What meeting purpose did the example show?"*] [*Score test*]
Transition back to the principle.	*Transition:* "Now let's see how the meeting purposes drive the rest of the parts of the meeting plan."
Principle Lesson 1	
4. Assimilate the New Knowledge into Existing Knowledge *Present principle,* using the concepts just taught; *present ± examples* of operation.	[*Continue with full mental model graphic, but change highlighting to include principle arrow.*] "If a clear-cut meeting purpose is specified, then you can clearly specify the meeting plan's participants, logistics, and agenda." "Here's Ginny. [*Show video still.*] Let's see how she decides on the participants, logistics and agenda for her meeting." [*In audio, play narrative in which Ginny introduces herself and explains her meeting's need, how she decided on a purpose, and how she used the purpose to decide on participants, logistics, and agenda. Pop on handwritten notes listing participants and agenda items as she talks.*]
5. Strengthen the New Knowledge in Memory *Practice:* Predict or explain; (great time for simulation).	"Here's George planning another meeting in the same company. [*Show example.*] "How do you think he decided on his agenda, logistics and participants? Did he do it right? If not, why not?" How do you think the meeting will go?"
Feedback: Diagnostic feedback as in concept lessons.	[*Be sure the system provides diagnostic feedback for wrong answers! Repeat with as many examples as the learner needs to correctly explain and predict.*]
Summary: Place principle and related concepts back into the mental model.	[*Show mental model diagram, with concepts and related principle highlighted.*] "So, now you can see how a clear meeting purpose really drives the rest of the meeting plan."

FIGURE 11.2. (*Continued*)

Lesson Element	Example
Test: Same as Practice.	[*Scenario-based examples for which the learner needs to correctly explain and judge the purpose (in the agenda) and predict the outcome.*]
Transition to the second principle.	"Now let's take a look at the second principle of meeting planning: Ensuring you have the right participants."
Principle Lesson 2	
1. Select the Information to Attend to *Attention:* Transition to first principle (*WIIFM/YCDI* redundant)	"Take a look at the second arrow in the diagram. It stands for the second rule for successful meetings [*the rule of correct attendees*]. Click on it to see how it works."
2. Link the New Information with Existing Knowledge *Recall/relate:* (this is a great time for an analogy).	[*Show video of football team in huddle.*] "When you're playing football, the second thing you have to know is what types of players you need to put on the field at any given time. Knowing which participants need to be at a meeting to accomplish a purpose is like having a clear idea of the football team composition."
3. Organize the Information *Structure of Content:* Show how the principle fits in the mental model.	[*Show mental model, with second arrow (purpose) highlighted, and pop on the plan parts it connects to.*] "When you have the right participants, it is possible to accomplish the purpose of the meeting . . .
Concept Lesson 2	
1. Select the Information to Attend to *Attention:* Transition to first concept structure (*WIIFM/YCDI* redundant).	"Let's see what the different types of meeting participants are and what they can do."
2. Link the New Information with Existing Knowledge *Recall/relate:* (another great place for an analogy).	[*Show posterized still photo of football team on field.*] "Participants are just like players at offense positions in a football game. Some play offense, some defense, one is the main play caller, some perform special functions. Just like teams have different types of players, so do meetings."
3. Organize the Information Objective and *Structure of Content:* Show the concept structure.	[*Bring up diagram next to football photo.*]

(Continued)

FIGURE 11.2. Two-Part Lesson: Part 1: Declarative Knowledge (*Continued*)

Lesson Element	Example
	[Diagram of meeting participants should include these, indicating arrangement from least to most influential, and with information flow coming in, going around within, and coming out of each.]
	[Pop on participants individually:
	Subject matter experts
	Stakeholders
	Decision makers
	Decision influencers
	Appropriate participants
	Facilitator
	Chairperson]
	"At the end of this lesson, you'll know the differences between these types of meeting participants—you'll be able to define them and pick out examples of each."
Fact Lesson 2 (Only Present Definitions is Needed)	
4. Assimilate the New Knowledge into Existing Knowledge Present definitions. *Step 1.* Show the facts. Use the structure you presented above. *Step 2.* Explain the structure. Include an explanation of the structure you presented.	*[Delete football visual. Add one participant icon for each meeting participant.]* "Click on each meeting participant icon to see its definition. *Subject matter experts*—individuals with highly specialized skills and/or knowledge in specific fields or subjects. *Stakeholders*—individuals who have a vested interest in meeting decisions, outcomes, and/or actions. *Decision makers*—those empowered with making judgments, reaching conclusions, and having the intuitional authority to make decisions that stand as a final. *Decision influencers*—those who directly or indirectly may shape decisions by reason of their expertise, vested interest, or other factors. *Appropriate participants*—subject-matter experts, stakeholders, decision makers, and influencers, that is, all those needed to achieve a meeting's objective(s). *Facilitator*—individual who specializes in running groups gathered for specific purposes. In most cases this individual participates only indirectly in a meeting's business by moving things along. *Chairperson*—individual who runs the meeting and participates in discussion and decisions."

FIGURE 11.2. (Continued)

Lesson Element	Example
4. Assimilate the New Knowledge into Existing Knowledge Present definitions. Present examples. (Note that in this medium, sequence of definitions [*Fact lesson above*] and examples [*concept lesson here*] can be learner controlled unless you deem a particular sequence to be critical to understanding.)	[*Meeting participant icons still on screen.*] "Click on each meeting participant icon to see an example of that person in a meeting [*each example is a video clip.*" *Subject matter experts* *Stakeholders* *Decision makers* *Decision influencers* *Appropriate participants* *Facilitator* *Chairperson*]
5. Strengthen the New Knowledge in Memory *Practice* For fact, learners define.	(Facts) "First, define each of these meeting types: Subject matter experts Stakeholders Decision makers Decision influencers Appropriate participants Facilitator Chairperson"
For concept, they select or classify.	(Concepts) "Here are some more participants in a meeting. See if you can correctly identify who each one is." [*Show eight video clips of a meeting, each followed by question asking: "What type of participant is (participant name)?"*]
Feedback: For each incorrect answer, provide an explanation that corrects the probable misconception that caused the learner to select that choice; For each correct choice, tell the learner the choice is correct. Then move on to the next example and question.	[*Example of incorrect answer feedback*] "Perhaps you thought Joe is the chairperson because he spoke the most. But a chairperson doesn't necessarily have the most to say; it's what the chairperson says that defines this role. Try again."
Summary: Place concept structure back into the mental model.	[*Show the full mental model, with the concepts just taught highlighted.*] "So, now you can see all the types of meeting participants and how they relate to the rest of the meeting plan."
Test: (great time for progressively more far-out positive examples and close-in negatives).	"Define the seven types of participants" (*fact test*).

(*Continued*)

FIGURE 11.2. Two-Part Lesson: Part 1: Declarative Knowledge (*Continued*)

Lesson Element	Example
	"Here are some more meetings. See if you can correctly identify the roles of the people in the meeting." (*concept test*). [*Show video clips of meetings, followed by question asking "What type of meeting participant did the example show?"*] [*Score test*]
Transition back to the principle.	"Now let's see how the meeting participants influence the rest of the parts of the meeting plan."
Principle Lesson 2	
4. Assimilate the New Knowledge into Existing Knowledge *Present principle*, using the concepts just taught; *present ± examples* of operation.	[*Continue with full mental model, but change highlighting to include principle arrow.*] "You must have meeting participants from all categories in a meeting for it to be successful; if any are missing, the meeting is likely to fail." "Here's Ginny. [*Show video still.*] Let's see how she decides on the participants to invite to her meeting." [*In audio, play narrative in which Ginny introduces herself and explains her meeting's purpose and how she decided on which participants in the organization to invite and why Pop on handwritten notes listing participants as she talks.*]
5. Strengthen the New Knowledge in Memory *Practice:* Predict or explain; (great time for simulation).	Here's George planning another meeting in the same store." [*Show example.*] [*Ask these questions:*] "How do you think he decided on his participants? Did he do it right? If not, why not? How do you think the meeting will go?"
Feedback: Diagnostic feedback as in concept lessons.	[*Be sure the system provides diagnostic feedback for wrong answers! Example feedback message: "George only invited four people to his meeting, so you may think that he couldn't possibly have people in each role. But remember that one person can fill more than one role. Try again." Repeat with as many examples as the learner needs to correctly explain and predict.*]

FIGURE 11.2. (*Continued*)

Lesson Element	Example
Summary: Place principle and related concepts back into the mental model.	[*Show mental model diagram, with concepts and related principle highlighted.*] "So, now you can see how having the right meetings participants is necessary for meeting success."
Test: Same as *Practice.*	"Here's George planning next month's meeting for his store." [*Show example.*] [*Ask these questions:*] "How do you think he decided on his participants? Did he do it right? If not, why not?" How do you think the meeting will go?
Transition to the second principle.	"Now let's take a look at the third principle of meeting planning: Ensuring you have the agenda items." (*NOTE:* This and the rest of the principle lessons, and their subordinate concept and fact lessons, will NOT be illustrated here since the pattern repeats).
Mental Model Testing and Lesson Summary	
5. Strengthen the New Knowledge in Memory *Practice/test* the concepts and principles taught so far and provide feedback. Activities should include classification or generation of examples, and prediction and explanation of system behavior (a good way is to ask questions such as "why do you have to do this?" or "what would you have to do if . . .?").	"Here's Dani planning another meeting for her store." [*Show example of Dani planning a meeting employing all the principles and concepts [purpose, participants, agenda, etc.]*] [*Ask these questions:*] How do you think she decided all the meeting elements? Did she do each element right? Did the whole set of elements fit together correctly? If not, why not? How do you think the meeting will go? Why?"
Summary: Refer back to the mental model.	[*Show complete visual diagram of the parts of a successful meeting, with arrows that show how they interact. Pop on each meeting plan part and arrow as you name it, until the whole model is built.*]

**FIGURE 11.3.
Two-Part Lesson:
Part 2: Procedural
Knowledge**

Lesson Element	Example
Well-structured procedure for planning a routine meeting	
1. Select the Information to Attend To *Attention*. Attention component should explain you are teaching a specific procedure for solving a type of problem.	"Now let's put it all together and start planning some meetings! There are lots of variations, but here's a simple way you can use to plan a meeting."
WIIFM. Review the context in which the problem is solved.	"There's a temptation to pooh-pooh this procedure or to shortcut some of the steps. Even the pros follow this procedure to ensure meeting success!"
YCDI. Build their confidence.	"It's a simple procedure—a lot like the ones you probably use already for planning other kinds of events, from group outings and carpools to vacations to household projects."
2. Link the New Information with Existing Knowledge *Recall/Relate*. Recall related declarative knowledge that is part of the mental model used in the procedure and the analogical procedure(s).	"Planning a meeting is just like the way you would plan a dinner party." [*Show stills of steps of planning a party.*] "First you have to decide why you want to have it, then you decide whom to invite, then you decide when to have it, then what food to serve, and so forth. In planning a meeting you have to do essentially the same steps." [*Party steps dissolve to meeting steps automatically or as mouse goes over steps.*] "You have already learned what to call these steps and the principles involved in doing them." [*Show mental model of meeting from declarative knowledge lesson.*]
3. Organize the Information *Structure of Content*. Show the structure of the procedure and state the objective.	[*Show procedure diagram.*] "Now let's see how you do the steps, in order to figure out how to plan your meeting: 1. Clarify the meeting's purpose(s). 2. Choose appropriate participants. 3. Establish date, time, and length of meeting. 4. Arrange for room setup and equipment. 5. Create the agenda, which must include all the information from Steps 1 through 4 and any additional meeting activities. 6. Send agenda to all concerned. 7. Appoint person responsible for taking minutes and person responsible for providing a permanent official record of the meeting. "You'll be able to plan meetings just like Ginny."

FIGURE 11.3. (*Continued*)

Lesson Element	Example
4. Assimilate the New Knowledge into Existing Knowledge *Present New Knowledge and Present Examples.* Show a worked-out example. Include an explanation of each step. Introduce, then show the individual steps, each with its own explanation. Point out the cue that signals the beginning of the step, the action, and the feedback that shows the step has been correctly completed. Relate the steps to facts and concepts as the steps use them.	"Let's rejoin Ginny as she plans her meeting, and we'll see how she uses these seven steps. Click on each step to see what she does." [*Clicking on each of the steps plays a video clip with Ginny explaining her thought process as she performs the step. Handwritten notes appear to show the output of each step.*] "Now let's look at each step in detail. Click on each step to learn how to do it." [*Show each step. Explain how to do it and show another positive example. Each of the steps is accompanied by a second positive example that shows how Dani applies the technique of that step to plan her meeting. Begin this sequence by introducing Dani's scenario.*] "Now let's look at another example of how people use this strategy to plan their meeting. Dani needs to decide how to plan a meeting for [*describe scenario*]. She will have to follow the same steps: Step 1. Clarify the meeting's purpose(s). Recall the types of meeting purposes and principle of aligning everything with purpose." [*Show video clip of Dani doing the first step of the procedure and verbalizing aloud the purpose of her meeting. Show list of substeps for doing this step as she verbalizes them:* *a. Think about the need that prompted the meeting.* *b. Match the need with the meeting purposes using a job aid.* *c. Decide which purpose will match the need best.* *d. Select the purpose.*] "Step 2. Choose appropriate participants. Recall the types of meeting purposes and principle of aligning everything with purpose." [*Show video clip of Dani doing the second step of the strategy and verbalizing aloud why she's doing it that way, as well as what she's doing. Show list of sub steps Dani is using for doing this step as she verbalizes her thought process:* *a. Think about the purpose of the meeting.* *b. Match the need with the seven meeting participants using a job aid.*

(Continued)

FIGURE 11.3. Two-Part Lesson: Part 2: Procedural Knowledge (*Continued*)

Lesson Element	Example
	c. Decide who in the organization fulfills each of the meeting participant categories for this meeting purpose. d. Decide who in the organization could be a backup for each participant category in case the primary person is not available. e. If there is no person to fill the category, go to the project leader to have an additional person added to the project. *Repeat for all strategy steps in this manner.*]
5. Strengthen the New Knowledge in Memory *Practice/test* the procedure steps taught so far and provide feedback. Summarize by referring back to the mental model and transition to the ill-structured problem-solving lesson.	"Now you try it. Here's the setup:" [*Show scenario, which opens with a narrative over the visual of a small group of people discussing hiring matters. Read aloud from the visual.*] "You are part of a human resource team at Knox Company. The team has decided to do some work process redesign and asked you to set up the work process redesign team and the first meeting. Decide what you should do first as leader of the *team*. Type in your answer after the question and click on 'What's the answer?' "What steps do you think would be best for planning this meeting?" [*Answer: a list of steps that are like the standard procedure.*] "What should you do for the first step?" [*Continue using this format until all steps of the planning a meeting procedure are covered. Then transition to an ill-structured procedure for meeting planning.*] "Now that you've practiced planning a meeting in a simple situation, let's see what happens when you have to plan a meeting in a situation that is not so cut-and-dried—one in which you have to do things on the fly and create your own procedure."

Here the lesson generalizes to an ill-structured procedure for planning non-routine meetings.

1. Select the Information to Attend To *Attention.* Explain that you are teaching a general strategy for solving a class of problems, even if some of them are new.	[*Show video clip: Joe is home in bed asleep; phone rings in middle of night. His boss says: "Governments in three of the fifteen countries in which we have global offices have found a serious defect in one of our products and are going to shut us down; it's only a matter of time until the other twelve countries do the same. You and Joyce must call an emergency meeting at 8 a.m. Eastern time of all the people we need to fix this and come up with a plan by noon to address the crisis."*]

FIGURE 11.3. *(Continued)*

Lesson Element	Example
WIIFM. Establish the context in which the problem is to be solved. This should be the framework for all explanations, examples, and practice throughout the lesson.	"This could be you facing this new kind of problem. What would you do in this kind of situation?"
YCDI. Build confidence.	"You can solve this problem because you already have the skills to figure out what elements need to be brought together and how to bring them together. You need to develop your own procedure for planning this unusual meeting, applying the principles of meeting planning you already know."
2. Link the New Information with Existing Knowledge *Recall* related declarative knowledge that is part of the mental model and procedures that are analogous to the one you are teaching, in whole or in part. *Relate* the current procedure to analogical procedure(s) the learner already knows.	"You already know the strategy for planning a meeting and the related principles and concepts." [*Show mental model of meeting elements from declarative knowledge and procedure lessons.*] "But this situation is different. There isn't time to use the routine process for planning this meeting, and you have to act before you know all the details. The problem you are facing is one of a class of problems you will face throughout your career—one where it's easy to solve them if you have the time and resources, but in reality you do not have all the elements you need to solve the problem and you have to create a way when you are missing some of the key elements. This is like cooking when the main ingredients did not arrive, the store is closed, the refrigerator power is off, and the gas stove is on the fritz. It's like playing football when five of your top players are injured, the weather is abysmal, none of your plays is working against the opposition, and you are forced to play one man short in a must-win game. Conventional recipes and plays will not work."
3. Organize the Information *Structure of content* should show the mental model for a heuristic for a class of abstract problems: (a) develop an abstract diagram or other representation of how the components in the problem space interact, and/or *Objective*. State ill-structured objective.	"In an emergency business situation, you have to juggle these elements that are crucial to resolving the crisis."

(Continued)

FIGURE 11.3. Two-Part Lesson: Part 2: Procedural Knowledge (*Continued*)

Lesson Element	Example
	"There are guidelines for manipulating these elements by how crucial they are and by how they should be sequenced, among others. The purpose of this lesson is to understand a general procedure for creating a meeting for a type of problem—getting people together to solve an emergency."
4. Assimilate the New Knowledge into Existing Knowledge *Present New Knowledge.* State the class of problems to which the heuristic applies. Show the heuristics. Show the steps or general approach of each heuristic— for representing, then solving the problem. Explain that the heuristic is a guide. Recall the underlying principle(s). *Present Examples.* Show specific sample applications of the problem.	"You already know from prior lessons that you need these elements to makes good business decisions, and where each of these elements can reside in an organization." [*Show the following example and definitions.*] "So what do you do in a crisis when you cannot have all of them? Some guidelines are: Based on the type of crisis, decide which are most important; for example, in this crisis, authority to make decisions and expertise about what to do are the most important elements. Based on the type of crisis, decide whether you can access the elements in sequence instead of simultaneously; for example; in this crisis, you need expertise and documents first, and might need authority after some recommendations have been developed. Watch Joe and Joyce as they think through how to resolve this crisis and plan a series of meetings." [*Show video of Joe and Joyce brainstorming; show "think aloud" balloons of principles as the video shows each; show both negative uses of heuristics, with Joe and Joyce correcting themselves and explaining why to each other. Show final plan on screen with mental model. Play audio of Joe and Joyce presenting this plan to the CEO, including their reasoning.*]

FIGURE 11.3. (*Continued*)

Lesson Element	Example
5. Strengthen the New Knowledge in Memory *Practice/Test*. Provide scaffolded practice, supporting the learner on initial problems, slowly withdrawing that support; provide a range of problems, including prototypical problems, and a range of contexts; modulate both difficulty and support, but only one at a time.	"Using what you know about meeting plans, and your experience in planning routine meetings, how should you go about planning this emergency meeting? Click on the planning steps you need to take, and place them in order. If you need to skip a step, drag it to the trash can." [*Learners select planning steps and place them in order. For each step that is dropped in the trash can, ask:*] "Why do you think you should no⁺ do that step this time?" [*For each step which is dragged into the plan, ask:*] "Why do you think you should take the time to do that step?" [*If the plan will generate all the components of the mental model, then show or read this scenario:*] "It's 8 a.m., and the meeting participants assemble. They're looking harried, and no one has slept well. The boss looks at the learner and says, 'OK, looks like a good plan for this meeting. Let's go!'" [*If the strategy will not lead to a sound meeting plan, then run this scenario:*] "It's 8 a.m., and the meeting participants assemble. They're looking harried, and no one has slept well. The boss looks at the learner and says, 'We've got an emergency here, and your plan will just waste our time. I'll take over from here.'"
Summary. Repeat mental model. *On-the-job application*. In the first few weeks following training, make sure the learner encounters a wide range of tasks that are of typical difficulty and that are representative of the objective.	[*Repeat mental model diagram.*] "You can see that, no matter how flexible you need to be to accommodate the situation, any planning strategy that gets you all the components of a good meeting plan will work. Now you're ready to try it on your job." [*Give the learners a checklist (rubric) for recording the next meeting they plan and rating how well the meeting went. The next week, bring the learners back together to recount their meeting planning processes, why they did it that way, and to judge the effectiveness of the meetings which resulted. Discuss how to do it differently next time.*]

SUMMARY

First, this chapter has provided you with two key sets of guidelines for your design efforts: guidelines for how to create lessons that combine different kinds of knowledge into multipart lessons and guidelines for what you could combine and what you probably should not. Second, we gave you detailed templates with examples to follow as you design lessons on your own.

Part III

Using the Cognitive Approach: The Research Issues

While Part II was written for all instructional designers and explained how to develop lessons, this part has a different focus and audience.

This part is the "theory" or "why" portion of the book, with three chapters that go into some detail on the theory and research issues underlying the cognitive approach presented in the "how to" chapters. It explores in depth the issues summarized in Part II, citing and explaining the research that led to the instructional design guidelines in Part II. In this part we explore other research issues not addressed earlier because of their complexity.

Given our focus, the main audience for this part may be instructional technology masters' and doctoral degree students who have completed at least an introductory ID course using a textbook such as Dick and Carey (2001), Seels and Glasgow (1998), or Smith and Regan (1999). Certainly ID practitioners who are curious about research can read and learn a great deal from this part as well.

The careful reader will notice that this part takes a more scholarly tone and that reference citations are given to point the reader to the works of other authors from whose work ideas are derived.

This part may be read before Part II, providing a theoretical underpinning for the how-to guidelines provided there, or may be read after Part II, using the guidelines therein as a mental model to elaborate on the theory presented here.

The three chapters in this part of the book are organized in this manner:

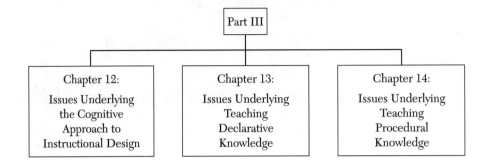

FIGURE 12.1. Chapter 12 Structure of Content

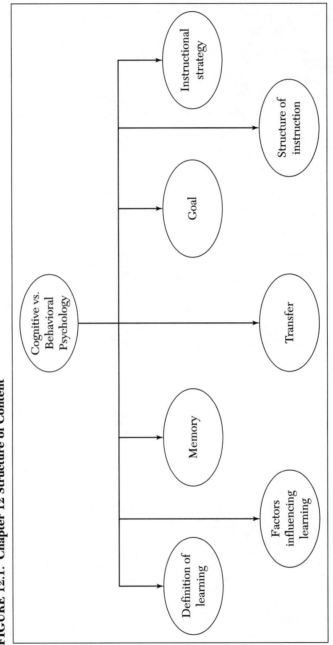

Chapter 12

Issues Underlying the Cognitive Approach to Instructional Design

---

LINK AND ORGANIZE

Recall (from Chapter 1)

- In Part I we presented a description of the cognitive approach to instructional design, including explanations of how people learn according to cognitive psychologists. Some of it may have been familiar to you, but most of it was probably new.

Relate to What You Already Know

- In this chapter, we'll go into more depth about a new way of thinking about the cognitive approach to training. This chapter will provide you with a more detailed, research-based description of the cognitive approach that relates this new approach to one you already know—the behavioral approach. By showing how the new approach is similar to, and different from, the one you already know, we hope to make the transition to the new approach a little easier.

Structure of Content

- See Figure 12.1.

Objectives

- To explain the differences between the cognitive and behavioral approaches to learning on the key elements of how people learn and how we design instruction to facilitate their learning.

PURPOSE AND APPROACH

In this chapter we revisit the subject of Chapter 1, "The Cognitive Approach to Training Development," at a more theoretical level. We intend the chapter for those interested in understanding the approach in more depth. Our discussion is based on the large available theory and research base.

We follow two principles from Chapters 5 and 6 ("Teaching Facts" and "Teaching Concepts") in providing this information. First, we move from the already known to the new knowledge by presenting a detailed comparison between the behavioral approach you are familiar with and the newer cognitive approach to instructional design. Second, we present the information in the form of a table (Figure 12.2) that clearly delineates the similarities and differences between the approaches.

For those familiar with the behavioral approach, this chapter will review what you already know and show how the cognitive approach differs. For those who have never had a formal study of the assumptions underlying the behavioral approach, this chapter will provide you with a theoretical understanding of the approaches you have been using to date. For those interested in pursing the subject matter further, references to sources from which the table is drawn are provided at the end of the book.

HOW THE BEHAVIORAL AND COGNITIVE APPROACHES DIFFER

To understand the cognitive approach to ID, it helps to contrast it with the current approach, based mostly in behavioral psychology. Words of caution: Defenders of the behavioral and the cognitive approaches can justifiably criticize what follows as an oversimplification. Also, yet another theoretical position of current note, constructivism, is beyond the scope of this book.

Of course, few instructional designers follow a purely behavioral or cognitive approach when designing instruction. Furthermore, in many cases the behavioral approach and the cognitive approach lead to similar design solutions. Therefore you may find, as we do, that you are already using some elements of the cognitive approach in designing your instruction.

Generally speaking, *behaviorism* is a set of principles concerning both human and non-human behavior. One major behaviorist goal is to explain and predict observable behavior. Behaviorists define learning as the acquisition of new behavior, as evidenced by changes in overt behavior. Behaviorists draw conclusions about behavior from research on external events: stimuli, effects, responses, learning history, and reinforcement. These behaviors are studied and observed in the environment and are explained with little or no reference to internal mental processing.

In dramatic contrast, a major tenet of *cognitive psychology* is that since internal thought processes cause behaviors, they can therefore best explain human behavior. Cognitive psychologists consider learning to be based on mental operations, including internally attending to (perceiving), encoding and structuring, and storing incoming information. Cognitive psychologists interpret external stimuli in terms of the way they are processed. They make use of observable behavior to make inferences about the mind.

The difference in focus between the behavioral and cognitive theories has important implications for instructional designers who seek design principles based on theory. The biggest differences are in the following theoretical areas:

- What learning is.
- Factors influencing learning.
- The role of memory and prior knowledge.
- How transfer occurs.
- The goal of instruction.
- The structure of instruction.
- Specific instructional strategies.

Different types of learning are best explained by each approach, and each approach provides basic principles that guide instructional design under different circumstances.

The implications for each area and how they differ in approach are shown in Figure 12.2 (based on Anderson, 1995a, 1995b; Ertmer & Newby, 1993; Fleming & Bednar, 1993; Foshay, 1991; Hannafin & Hooper, 1993; Silber, 1998; West, Farmer, & Wolff, 1991). It is important to note that some of the differences are merely semantic (for example, "fluency" and "automaticity" both describe degrees of learning proficiency), while some are more substantive

 FIGURE 12.2. Differences Between Behavioral and Cognitive Approaches

Instructional Design Area	Behavioral Approach	Cognitive Approach
What Learning Is	"Changes in form or frequency of observable performance" What learners *do*	Internal coding and structuring of new information by the learner Discrete changes in knowledge structures What learners *know* and *how* they come to know it
Factors That Influence Learning	"Arrangement of stimuli and consequences in the environment" Reinforcement history Fluency in responding	How learners attend to, organize, code, store, and retrieve information as influenced by the context in which information is presented when it is learned and when it is used Thoughts, beliefs, attitudes, and values Automatic responding

(Continued)

FIGURE 12.2.
Differences Between
Behavioral and Cognitive
Approaches (*Continued*)

Instructional Design Area	Behavioral Approach	Cognitive Approach
The Role of Memory and Prior Knowledge	Not addressed in detail Function of the person's reinforcement history Forgetting results from lack of use	Learning occurs when information is stored in memory in a meaningful manner so it can be retrieved when needed Forgetting is the inability to retrieve information from memory because of interference, memory loss, or inadequate cues to access the information given the way it is organized in memory Therefore, meaningfulness of learning directly affects forgetting
How Transfer Occurs	Focus on design of the environment Stimulus and response generalization to new situations	Stress on efficient processing strategies to optimize cognitive load Function of how information is indexed and stored in memory based on expected use of the knowledge Applying knowledge in different contexts by reasoning analogically from previous experiences Construction/manipulation of mental models made up of networks of concepts and principles Learners believe knowledge is or will be useful in new situation
Types of Learning Best Explained by the Approach	Discriminations (recalling facts) Generalizations (defining and illustrating concepts) Associations (applying explanations) Chaining (automatically performing a specified procedure)	Complex forms of learning (reasoning, problem solving, especially in ill-structured situations) Generalization of complex forms of learning to new situations
Basic Principles of the Approach Relevant to ID	Produce observable, measurable outcomes such as task analysis, behavioral objectives, criterion-referenced testing Existing response repertoire and appropriate reinforcers such as learner analysis Mastery of early steps before progressing to complex performance such as simple to complex sequencing; practice and mastery learning Reinforcement or practice followed by immediate feedback and rewards Use of cues and shaping by prompting, fading, sequencing	All of the behavioral principles Student's existing mental structures or learner analysis Guide and support for accurate mental connections or feedback Learner involvement in the learning process or learner control; meta-cognitive training; collaborative learning Identify relationships among concepts/principles to be learned and between them and learners' existing mental models or learner analysis; cognitive task analysis Emphasis on structuring, organizing, and sequencing information for optimal processing or advance organizers, outlining, summaries Connections with existing knowledge structures through reflective processing through analogies, relevant examples, metaphors

FIGURE 12.2. (*Continued*)

Instructional Design Area	Behavioral Approach	Cognitive Approach
Goal of Instruction	Elicit desired response from learner presented with target stimulus	Make knowledge meaningful and help learners organize and relate new information to existing knowledge in memory
Structure of Instruction	Determine which cues can elicit the desired responses Arrange practice situations in which prompts are paired with target stimuli that will elicit responses on the job Arrange environmental conditions so students can make correct responses in the presence of target stimuli and receive reinforcement	Determine how learners' existing knowledge is organized Determine how to structure new information to mesh with learners' current knowledge structure(s) Connect new information with existing in meaningful way through analogies, framing, outlines, mnemonics, advance organizers Arrange practice with structurally meaningful feedback so new information is added to learners' existing knowledge
Specific Instructional Strategies	Teach fact lesson first, then concepts, then principles, then problem solving Focus on algorithmic procedures for problem solving, including troubleshooting Teach each concept, procedural chain, troubleshooting approach separately; when mastered go on to next Focus on deductive learning Present principles and attributes Build generalization with extended realistic practice, often after initial acquisition	Teach problem solving in authentic (job) context; teach principles, concepts, and facts in context as appropriate within the problem-solving lesson Focus on heuristic problem solving and generalization, even in troubleshooting Teach overall mental model, then use coordinate concept, principle, procedure/problem-solving teaching to teach all related knowledge at or near the same time Focus on inductive learning Present examples Build generalization through practice in additional problems and contexts that require similar but not identical problem-solving procedures

From The Cognitive Approach to Training Development: A Practitioner's Assessment. *Educational Technology Research and Development, 46*(4), 58–72. Reprinted by permission of ETRD.

(for example, "emphasis on knowledge structures" reflects the cognitive theory's recognition of the need to think about the parts of knowledge in any given subject and how they fit together).

SUMMARY

In this chapter we have shown, in tabular form, the differences between the cognitive and behavioral approach to ID in the areas of what learning is, factors that influence learning, the role of memory and prior knowledge, how transfer occurs, the goal of instruction, the structure of instruction, and specific instructional strategies.

FIGURE 13.1. Chapter 13 Structure of Content

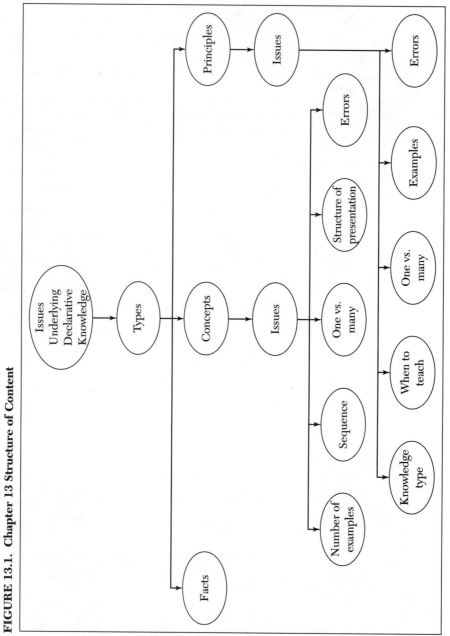

Chapter 13

Issues Underlying Teaching Declarative Knowledge

Recall (from Chapters 1, 5, 6, 7, and 11)

- In Parts I and II, we explained what declarative knowledge is and presented an approach to teaching it. Some of the concepts we discussed are probably familiar to you (particularly the part about facts), and some of it is probably new (the part about structure of content and perhaps the teaching of concepts and principles in mental models).

Relate to What You Already Know

- For most training, it's true that problem solving is the payoff—the part of training that directly results in improved performance. But declarative knowledge is the foundation, especially when you need to build real expertise or when you have to train to solve problems you can't anticipate—or even when there are too many problems to train to solve each one. So it's important to know *when* you need to teach declarative knowledge, as well as *how* to teach it.

Structure of Content

- See Figure 13.1.

Objectives

- To define facts, concepts, principles, and mental models in more detail.

- To explain some key issues about designing lessons for declarative knowledge.

- To describe some principles underlying the design of instruction for facts, concepts, principles, and mental models.

HOW DECLARATIVE AND PROCEDURAL KNOWLEDGE DIFFER

Declarative knowledge has been called *passive*, because you use it to describe, to state, or perhaps to understand something. *Procedural* knowledge is *active*, because you use it to do things such as solve problems.

There is good evidence that declarative knowledge is different from procedural knowledge. You can learn everything there is to know about a subject but still not be able to use that knowledge to do anything. For example, learning the rules of Italian grammar (declarative knowledge) does not mean you can speak the language. That requires procedural knowledge.

This distinction is not widely understood. Trainers and educators often describe rather than show, and they often ask learners to state or describe rather than do. Often, both teaching and testing are declarative, when the intended learning outcomes of the course are procedural.

But while declarative knowledge often receives too much attention in training, you should not ignore it. A certain amount of declarative knowledge is necessary. In fact, you might think of declarative knowledge as the "framework" upon which procedural knowledge is built. For example, to drive a car, you have to know what the steering wheel is, what it does (how it works, at least at a superficial level), and what it is called. Simply knowing about steering wheels does not mean that you can use one to drive a car, but it would be harder to learn to drive if you didn't already know what a steering wheel was.

You already know that there are three kinds of declarative knowledge: facts, concepts, and principles and mental models. Let's look at each of them in more detail.

FACTS

The literature does not have much to add to what we discussed in Chapter 5 about teaching facts. Basically, research has shown the following:

- Depending on how the facts are used, it is often more efficient to give learners a job aid so they can look up facts as needed, rather than requiring them to memorize large amounts of information. Your learners' performance may be slow at first while they look things up, but they will soon have memorized the facts they frequently use. If slow initial performance is acceptable and the work situation allows the use of job aids, keep fact teaching to a minimum and use "open book" tests, allowing learners to use the job aids during the test.

- Facts don't exist in isolation. Look for a logical structure that ties together a group of facts in a way that is related to how the facts are used. The structure you find will determine what fact-teaching strategy you use.

CONCEPTS

You already know that you can think of a concept as a way of grouping similar examples and giving them a common name. The key test for deciding whether a given piece of knowledge is a fact or a concept is this: If the learner has to recall literally from memory, it's a fact. If the learner has to identify, classify, or construct new examples, then it's a concept. This can be tricky, because we often use the same name to apply to facts and concepts (and principles, for that matter). For example, if I ask you, "What's your computer password?" then the answer is a fact. If I ask you, "What's an acceptable password for your computer?" then the answer is a concept definition.

Problems in Learning Concepts

Three types of problems crop up when people have to learn concepts: overgeneralization, under-generalization, and misconception.

Overgeneralization occurs because someone thinks (generalizes) that something is part of a group when it is not. This happens because the person is not looking for all the critical and variable attributes. For example, people might think a certain type of automobile is a "compact car" when in fact it really is not.

Under-generalization occurs because someone does not generalize far enough and thinks that something is not part of a group when it really is. This happens because someone has added additional critical attributes: he or she has either confused an irrelevant attribute for a critical or variable one or ignored acceptable variable attribute values. For example, people might not classify a certain type of automobile as an SUV because they think it is too small, when in fact size is not a critical attribute.

A *misconception* occurs when people seem to miss the point and put some ins out and some outs in. Misconceptions happen because the learner confuses critical and variable attributes, and then the learner decides whether something is in or out based on a variable that is not critical. For example, classifying all red automobiles as mid-life crisis cars, when color is a variable attribute not a critical one (Clark, 1999; Fleming & Bednar, 1993; Merrill, Tennyson, & Posey, 1992; Tiemann & Markle, 1983).

Instructional Design Issues

There are many ID issues in the teaching of concepts using the cognitive approach. Some are age-old issues, and some have been newly raised by the cognitive psychology research.

1. How Many Examples Should You Use? One of the most difficult judgment calls in instructional design is to determine how much help with definitions and examples learners will need to understand a concept structure. Experience seems to show that if you know more about the concepts than the learners do, you will probably underestimate the amount of help needed, and if you know less, you'll probably overestimate what's needed.

The best practice is one that has been around since programmed instruction: Write the first draft of the instruction "lean," then try out the instruction on some typical learners, adding definition and examples only where the learners make errors that show misconceptions.

2. What Teaching Sequence Is Best? Is an inductive teaching sequence (example followed by attributes) better than a deductive teaching sequence (attributes followed by example)?

Cognitive psychology puts a new spin on this old question, asking: "What do learners actually store in memory, the prototypical example (according to image theory) or the attributes (according to schema theory)?" No one really knows for sure (Anderson, 1995; Fleming & Bednar, 1993), but it probably depends on the "type" of content. Since this is not very prescriptive for an instructional designer, we will make the following brief recommendation, based on the specific guidelines in Chapter 6, "Teaching Concepts." Our recommendation is consistent with both theories, and with the "lean" approach recommended above:

1. Present the prototypical example.

2. If it appears that learners will have a little to some difficulty in learning the concepts, present the attributes.

3. Present additional examples/non-examples, depending on how much difficulty learners will have in learning the concept.

3. Should We Teach One Concept at a Time, or All Related Concepts Together? Fortunately, this is an issue for which the evidence all points in the same direction. Teach all the related concepts in a knowledge structure together. Even though it may seem like more to learn at once, it's actually easier for the learner. When the overall knowledge structure and the relationships among its concepts are presented along with the prototypical examples (and attributes if appropriate), learners can more easily understand how the concepts relate to each other and to the job on which they will apply the concepts. However, be sure to chunk the presentation and practice properly.

4. If We Present the Attributes of Concepts, How Should We Do It? Again, the evidence is clear. Writing a dictionary definition of a concept is definitely a non-example of how to analyze and present a concept. What does work is one of the following:

- Present a bulleted list of attributes of a single concept, as we did at the beginning of the chapter.
- Present an attribute matrix for all the related concepts.

PRINCIPLES AND MENTAL MODELS

You already know that a *principle* is the reason why something works: it states a causal relationship between two or more concepts. Often you can think of a principle as an "if . . . then" statement. A mental model is the synthesis of principles (and supporting facts and concepts) for a given purpose.

Differences Among Concepts, Principles, Mental Models, and Procedures

Just as we find it difficult to distinguish between facts and concepts, we also often confuse concepts with principles and mental models. As we said above, it's particularly confusing because people often use the same words to refer to a fact, a concept, and a principle. For example, "hot air rises" *could* be a fact, a concept, or a principle. The critical test is to ask yourself what you want the learner to *do*. To expand your understanding, we'll discuss the contrasts among them in more detail.

Principle and Concept. A simple test is to try to express the idea as an if . . . then statement or mathematical equation. If you can, it's a *principle*. For example, you know that *if* you turn the steering wheel clockwise, *then* your car will turn to the right. That statement is a principle. The concepts involved are steering wheel, clockwise, car, turn, and right.

Principles often are stated as assertions (rules) rather than if . . . then statements, so you may need to rewrite them in an unfamiliar form. For example, a principle is: "You can add numbers together in any order." Although it would be awkward, it is possible to rewrite the statement as an if . . . then statement: "If the numbers are added together in any order, then the total does not change."

Principle and Mental Model. If a *principle* is presented in isolation, then it is only a principle. Even if a series of principles is presented, unless there is a context or relationship among them, they are still only principles. But when a series of principles is presented in a context, with a purpose and an expressed relationship among them (and the subordinate facts and concepts), it is a *mental* *model.* For example, as we discussed in Chapter 7, you could separately learn all the various principles associated with the functioning of a car's steering mechanism:

- If the steering wheel turns clockwise, then the car turns right.
- If the wheel turns farther clockwise, then the car turns more to the right.
- If the steering wheel turns counterclockwise, then the car turns left.
- If the wheel turns farther counterclockwise, then the car turns more to the left.

. . . and so on. Or you could learn a mental model, which might be something like the one shown in Figure 13.2.

FIGURE 13.2. Mental Model of Steering Function

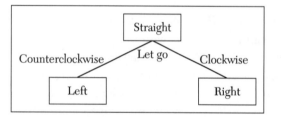

Principle and Procedure. A *principle* explains how something works, but there is no action involved. A *procedure,* on the other, involves action based on the principle. For example, if you're driving from home to the grocery store, your mental model of steering won't tell you when to turn the wheel clockwise and counterclockwise or how many times to do it. But if you know the route from your home to the store (a fact network), and if you have a mental model of steering (a principle network), then you can combine them to derive your own procedure for when to turn the wheel each way in order to get there.

Principle or Mental Model. The classical learning exercise for a mental model is to explain why a given phenomenon happened in the real world or to predict what will happen next. While these are some of the same things you also do when troubleshooting, the difference is that when teaching principles you are only asking the learner to explain or predict the behavior of a system, not to take any actions to fix it. For example, the mental model of steering makes it clear that it's impossible to go directly from right to left without going through straight. If learners have learned only the isolated principles instead of the whole mental model, have never observed a car being driven closely, or have not tried it themselves, then they might think it was possible to do so. To tell whether the learner has acquired the whole mental model, you could ask a question such as: "To avoid an accident, John needs to switch his car from a right turn to a left turn without going straight for even a few centimeters. Will he be able to do it? Why or why not?" Even better would be to build a simulation that involves this behavior and then ask the learners if the simulation is realistic.

When to Teach Principles and Mental Models

You can teach principles any time after the learners know the concepts on which the principles operate. This means you can teach principles:

- In stand-alone lessons, after stimulating recall of the concept structure the learners already know.
- Embedded in a concept-teaching sequence, as a way of showing how and why the whole concept structure interacts, behaves, or operates. This is often the case when teaching how or why a system operates.
- Embedded in well-structured or ill-structured a procedure teaching sequence.

Cognitive scientists differ on how much weight they give to the direct teaching of principles and the synthesis of mental models. Some (Schank, 1988, for example) tend to leave it implicit in the solving of problems. Others (Anderson, 1995a) advocate direct teaching of declarative knowledge and with it include principles and a "starting" mental model.

Our position is that direct teaching of principles and mental models is important, especially for learners who do not yet have an initial understanding of the knowledge structure for a given context. Embedding the principle and mental model teaching in the procedure teaching will work, but it's very likely that it will be difficult to do it without violating the principle of chunking. If you violate the chunking principle, then teaching concepts and principles will be so much of a digression from teaching procedures that the learner will be overwhelmed. Unless there are very few new concepts, principles, and mental models involved, we recommend teaching them before you teach the corresponding procedure.

One Principle at a Time vs. Mental Model

As with facts and concepts, you could probably learn the principles individually and then learn or create the mental model that relates them to one another. But it's much more efficient to learn all the related principles together in a mental model. Even though it may seem like it's more for the learner to learn at once, it's actually easier for the learner. If the mental model and the relationships among the principles in it are presented together, it is easier for learners to understand and incorporate the knowledge. For the same reason, you may want to combine the teaching of all the related declarative knowledge into a single, seamless learning experience.

Examples vs. Principles/Mental Models

In the behaviorist days of instructional design, we used to believe that the most important part of learning principles was learning the "if . . . then" rules as algorithms. Many cognitivists, however, assign a greater value and role to the examples. Under at least some circumstances, they believe that what many learners really remember is the prototype (idealized or first) example of a principle they encounter, not the (verbal) rules of the principles or the mental model. Learners store in memory an idealized version of the first example(s) they see as a prototypical example. Examples, then, are critical in learning, storing, and retrieving mental models.

Thus, it is important for instructional designers to select a first example based not necessarily on its possession of certain attributes, but on the context in which the principle/mental model will be used. Then the prototypical example will relate directly to the knowledge structure the learner already has, and the learner will be able to retrieve it from memory in the appropriate context on the job.

The difference between *concept examples* and *principle examples* is that examples for principles/mental models take the form of "war stories"— situations that went well and situations that went poorly. These stories are memorable precisely because they illustrate the system operating according to the principles. They are particularly memorable when they illustrate a principle or mental model feature not previously understood.

One example is not enough, however. People often learn principles by watching real systems behave and building a mental model of the system that "behaves" as the real one does. Just as with concepts, if all the learners have ever seen is one real-world example of a system, there's a good chance that the mental model they build will match the one example they've seen in ways that make it difficult to generalize to other examples of the model. Since we usually want learners to transfer what they learn to a range of situations, we want their mental models to be abstractions, rather than literal representations of real-world systems. Therefore, we would prefer that people watch or play with more than one real-world example of a system described by the mental model we want the learner to build.

COMMON ERRORS IN TEACHING DECLARATIVE KNOWLEDGE

The use of the guidelines discussed above and the specific recommendations for the lesson elements in Part II will help instructional designers avoid the following errors that inhibit the ability of learners to complete their learning tasks effectively:

- Teaching all declarative knowledge as if it were facts.
- Teaching concepts with a single positive example.
- Teaching declarative knowledge components in isolation, rather than in knowledge structures (the relationships among the parts that are important for how they will be used).
- Failure specifically to anticipate and deal with common misconceptions (applies to presentation, practice, and testing).
- Deliberate or unintentional teaching of misconceptions to novices in an effort to "keep it simple," thus creating a need to "unlearn" something later in training.
- Teaching out of context (principle of contextualized learning).
- Failure to provide whole task practice.
- Terminating presentation and practice too early, with artificially simplified contexts, problems, tools, and so forth (principle of authentic learning).
- Misalignments of presentation, practice, and test events that are supposed to use the same knowledge (for example, examples that don't "examp," low-level questions on high-level knowledge and skills).
- Failure to build sufficient fluency to manage cognitive load.

SUMMARY

You should now have a deeper understanding of the types of declarative knowledge and some of the issues and controversies related to teaching it. It's critical to clearly understand the distinctions and relationships among facts, concepts, principles, and mental models. We have identified a number of issues and controversies surrounding teaching of declarative knowledge and mental model formation, and we have offered our opinions on how to address these issues (of course, you are at liberty to come to different conclusions based on your own reading of the research we've referenced). Finally, based on our experience, we have listed a number of common errors we see instructional designers make when they teach declarative knowledge. We hope you will avoid them!

FIGURE 14.1. Chapter 14 Structure of Content

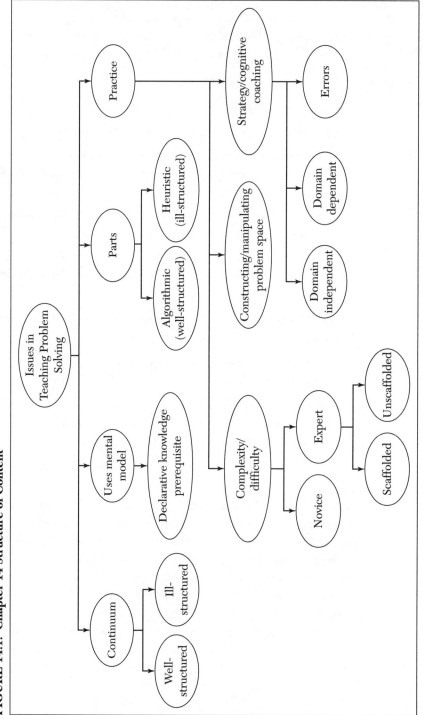

Chapter 14

Issues Underlying Teaching Procedural Knowledge

LINK AND ORGANIZE

Recall (from Chapters 1, 8, 9, 10, 11)

- In Parts I and II, we presented an approach to teaching problem solving. Some of it was probably familiar to you (particularly the part about well-structured problem solving), and some of it may have been new (the part about mental models and ill-structured problem solving). For most training, problem solving is the payoff—the part of training that directly results in improved performance. Taken together, the strategies we describe will give you ways of teaching problem solving that are much more powerful.

Relate to What You Already Know

- In this chapter, we'll go into more depth about a new way of thinking about problem solving that underlies our approach to training. This chapter is like an exploratory voyage or research venture. You will read what some of the issues are and what some of the leading thinkers in the field have to say about them; but you will probably not leave this chapter with answers—just with a deeper understanding and, we hope, a desire to pursue this subject further.

Structure of Content

- See Figure 14.1.

Objectives

- To state what psychologists agree on about problem solving.

- To explain the relationship between problem solving and declarative knowledge and mental model manipulation.
- To define six key terms related to problem solving.
- To describe how learners solve problems.
- To identify weak and strong strategies for solving problems.
- To explain ID issues in teaching problem solving procedures.

ABOUT PROCEDURAL KNOWLEDGE

AutoRent's newly promoted managers need to figure out how to develop their unit's budget for next year. The company's executives have to decide whether or not to add a different vehicle make to the fleet. They're also trying to figure out why the fleet task force committee isn't making recommendations. Meanwhile, AutoRent's secretaries are trying to figure out how to use the new word processing system.

A YourMart department head needs to implement the new corporate mission and vision within her department. Store cashiers need to calculate and include the new local sales tax in sales transactions until the cash register computer can automatically calculate it. The company's national headquarters executive task force is trying to determine why sales are down.

These examples involve solving problems and using procedural knowledge to solve them. Why do we use procedural knowledge, not declarative knowledge?

As we pointed out in Chapter 1, while declarative knowledge is knowing *that,* knowing *what,* and knowing *why,* procedural knowledge is knowing *how.* Knowing how means knowing how to perform rote procedures, solve problems of all types, and troubleshoot problems in machines and systems.

Most cognitive psychologists tend to equate procedural knowledge with problem solving, and most of the literature on learning and using procedural knowledge is contained in articles on learning to solve problems. Although some instructional psychologists consider that problem solving uses more than procedural knowledge, (Jonassen, 1997) and some consider that procedural knowledge is the know-how that underlies a broader class of problem-solving skills, there is no uniform distinction between the two.

We therefore have used the phrases *procedural knowledge* and *problem solving* interchangeably.

The Continuum of Problems

As we said in Chapter 1, with procedural knowledge, there's a continuum from *well-structured* problems to *ill-structured* problems (Newell & Simon, 1972). It's sometimes useful also to consider an in-between class of moderately structured problems. In Chapter 1, we discussed some differences between well-structured and ill-structured problems. Jonassen (1997) adds further detail on the characteristics of the well-structured and ill-structured problems; these are shown in Figure 14.2.

FIGURE 14.2. Two Classes of Problem Characteristics

Well-Structured	Ill-Structured
Present all elements of the problem	One or more of the problem elements is unknown
Presented as well-defined problems—parameters of problem specific in problem statement	Have vaguely defined or unclear goals and unstated constraints
Presented as a problem with a probable solution	Possess multiple solutions, solution paths, or no solutions
Engage the application of a limited number of rules or principles	Present uncertainty about which concepts, rules, principles are necessary for solution, or how they are organized
Principles are organized in a predictable and prescriptive arrangement, with well-defined parameters	Possess less manipulatable parameters; have no prototypic cases because elements are different in different contexts
Involve concepts and rules that appear regular and well-structured in domain of knowledge that also appears well-structured	Possess relationships among concepts, rules, and principles that are inconsistent between cases
Possess correct, convergent answers	Offer no general rules or principles for describing or predicting most of the cases
Possess knowable, comprehensible solutions	Have no solutions defined
Have a preferred, prescribed solution process	Have no explicit means for determining appropriate actions; require solvers to make judgments about the problem and defend them; possess multiple criteria for evaluating solutions

From D. Jonassen, Instructional Design Models for Well-Structured and Ill-Structured Problem Solving Learning Outcomes. *Educational Technology Research and Development*, 1997, *48*(4), 63–85.

Widely Agreed-On Premises About Problem Solving

Most writers in the field agree on the following premises about teaching procedural knowledge/problem solving:

- We know much less about how procedural knowledge works and how to teach it (especially in the form of ill-structured problem solving) than we know about declarative knowledge and teaching it; we know a fair amount about teaching well-structured problem solving, but less about teaching ill-structured problem solving.

- Mastering the component parts and subskills in a learning hierarchy is not enough to learn to do ill-structured problem solving. There is a separate and different skill involved in ill-structured problem solving, although it also includes declarative knowledge and well-structured procedural subskills.

- There are great differences between novice and expert problem solvers as they think about and solve problems.

- While the cognitive and behavioral approaches to teaching declarative knowledge are fairly similar, there are great differences among the approaches used to teach well-structured and ill-structured problem solving procedures.

- Teaching ill-structured problem solving that generalizes to new situations is not easy.

- Within well-structured and ill-structured problem-solving categories, there are subcategories of problems, but authors disagree about what the subcategories are.

- The research does allow us to generate some guidelines for designing instruction to teaching ill-structured problem solving, but authors disagree about what those guidelines are.

And that's about the extent of what writers agree about. There are great debates in the literature about whether deductive, inductive, or constructivist strategies are best for teaching problem solving, about what kinds of problems to use in teaching problem solving, about what kinds of practice to use, about how much/many "heuristics" and "scaffolding" (see below) to give learners, and so on.

The disagreement is enough to frustrate one at best. At worst, it might cause one to give up and return to the behavioral approach, despite its apparent limitations. In this book, we have attempted to include the simplest, most powerful, and most agreed-on guidelines for teaching problem solving. We also add what we consider to be some powerful, but overlooked, guidelines for relating declarative and procedural knowledge.

Declarative Knowledge, Mental Models, and Problem Solving

Procedural knowledge uses declarative knowledge. That is, the full continuum of procedural knowledge/problem solving uses facts, concepts, and principles—synthesized into a mental model—as the basis on which the procedures are recalled, generated, and applied to solve problems. The mental model is the synthesis of declarative knowledge into a structure, which is optimized for solving a certain class of problems (Anderson, 1995a/b). Solving problems typically requires problem solvers to restructure and "run" their mental models of the system dynamically in order to predict the effect of a proposed action on the system or to explain an observed system behavior. Thus, developing a mental model with the right kind of structure for solving a particular class of problems is a key to successful problem solving. Manipulating the mental model is a key step in problem solving, because it helps the learner predict the effects of various possible actions and then select the one that will move him or her closer to the solution.

We believe the importance of mental models, their development, and their manipulation has been under-emphasized in the literature. Since development of problem-solving skills depends on prior development of an effective mental model, we believe instructional designers should treat development and manipulation of an appropriate mental model as the main prerequisite for learning to solve problems—especially ill-structured problems. We believe that development and manipulation of mental models usually doesn't happen incidentally; there is only weak evidence to support the assumption often made by constructivists that learners are able to develop their own mental models with relatively little support and no direct instruction on the initial mental model that maps a problem space.

Instruction on the mental model can occur before the actual procedural knowledge instruction begins or can occur as a part of the procedural knowledge instruction. But it must occur.

TERMINOLOGY

Six key terms are important to discussion of problem-solving instruction. Each is explained below.

Algorithms (Well-Structured Problems)

Another term for a well-structured procedure is *algorithm* (also called "sets of production rules"). Algorithms are "first you, then you, then you" step-by-step procedures. There is always a clear "right" outcome of an algorithm. Algorithms are embedded in most everyday tasks. Examples include doing multiplication, balancing your checkbook, or commuting to work (without compensating for construction or bad weather). Algorithms are nice because, even though they may be long and complicated to learn, they always work to produce the solution we want. Because they never vary (although they may have branches), if you do them enough they become so *automatic* you can literally do them without thinking about it. (Have you ever driven to work and realized you don't know how you did it?)

Heuristics and Ill-Structured Problems

Ill-structured problems are problems you can't anticipate, because they never happen the same way twice, there is no single correct solution, there is a single correct solution but the way to reach the solution is undefined, or perhaps just because the problem is new to you and you don't know an algorithm for solving it. Examples of ill-structured problems include most kinds of design tasks (from writing a novel to designing a building or a computer program), because the best solution is not clear. The hardest part of design is to define the characteristics of a good solution, and there is always more than one good solution possible.

Since you can't use algorithms to solve ill-structured problems, you use a set of guidelines or "rules of thumb" called *heuristics* (related to "expert production rules" and "cognitive strategies"). Heuristics are abstractions from a set of more specific production rules derived from past experience solving similar problems. You apply heuristics to invent a particular algorithm to solve the problem at hand (remember that because the problem is ill-structured, by definition, you have never seen it before and cannot recall an algorithm to solve it). Some everyday examples of heuristics include statements such as, "Keep your boss informed of anything that could come back and catch her by surprise," "Troubleshoot from output back to input," and "Tell 'em what you're going to tell 'em, then tell 'em, then tell 'em what you told 'em."

In contrast to algorithms, heuristics are less well-structured, more general guidelines for how to go about solving a problem. Their attributes are:

- They are guidelines, not "must do's."
- They are based on declarative knowledge principles (as are algorithms).
- They may include steps, but the steps are of a different kind from those in algorithms:
  - The steps can be done in the recommended order, or in any number of modified orders, based on the needs of the problem and the ability of the user.
  - Steps can be skipped, and new steps can be added.
- If the heuristic is big enough, it can contain components that are algorithms.
- When teaching heuristics, we have to teach (or recall) both the underlying principles and the steps.

Note that the steps in the design model presented in Chapter 2 of this book are heuristics. There are a certain number of elements (steps) to teaching a lesson, but they are guidelines. You can change the sequence of the elements, combine several elements into one instructional event, and add elements. Some of the elements contain algorithms (such as the one for writing objectives); all elements are based on instructional strategy principles (an example is: "For concept teaching, if you present a prototype example before attributes, the learning is likely to be more effective"). Because the model is heuristic, this text teaches you the steps and how to use them (in Chapters 3 through 11), but there is lots of explanation of the underlying principles (in those chapters and here), and the examples of the application of the heuristics are intended to be only examples of one way you *could* design a lesson, not *the only* way to design a lesson, and still be consistent with the model.

Heuristics don't make sense by themselves; to understand them, you have to already know the declarative knowledge and algorithms on which they are built. The solution to any design problem is a context-specific application of heuristics. Furthermore, heuristics often tend to be applicable only in certain types of situations, which makes them even more context-specific. Heuristics often, but not always, lead to the solution you want. They can be applied to a wider range of problems than an algorithm, however, so they are more powerful.

Scaffolding

Using the analogy of the wooden scaffolding that builders use to help hold up a building (as well as those building it), cognitive psychologists use the term "*scaffolding*" to refer to assistance given to learners in early stages of the problem-solving learning. For those old enough to remember programmed instruction, the analogy to thematic prompts is somewhat applicable.

Scaffolding can include one or some combination of learning prompts, such as partially solved problems, hints on which heuristic to apply, analogous problems the learner has already solved, frequent feedback as each step is taken—almost anything short of actually either solving the problem for the learner or telling the learner how to solve the problem.

You apply scaffolding early in the learning sequence and gradually remove it (in a process that used to be called *fading*) until the learner can do the fully complex task with no extra scaffolding.

Problem Space

If we (not the learner) as experts look objectively out in the environment at a problem waiting to be solved and define all of its elements, we are said to be looking at a "complete representation of the problem," or its *task environment*. The learner, however, as a non-expert, has to create an "internal representation" of the problem by selecting certain portions of it to attend to and organizing them into a new knowledge structure. We call this the *problem space*. The problem space is the structure where the elements of a problem we discussed earlier are stored.

Creation of the optimum problem space is key to solving the problem, and there is much discussion about how it is created, about the differences between expert and novice problem spaces, and about teaching the creation of problem spaces.

Cognitive Load

Cognitive load is the amount of cognitive processing, or "brain power," a particular task requires of the learner. The more familiar the information or problem presented, the more familiar the task required, and the smaller the size of the information and the task, the lower the cognitive load. In learning situations, however, the reverse is usually true: The amount and newness of the information and task required typically means that cognitive loads are high for the learner.

Other things can happen that reduce the cognitive processing capacity of the learner, thereby effectively increasing cognitive load. These include stress, fatigue, lack of confidence, distraction, and even "lack of focus" on the problem at hand. That's why it's important to create a learning environment free of distraction, which helps the learner to be refreshed, relaxed, confident, and focused.

If the load is too much for the learners, they reach a state of cognitive overload and their concentration shuts down. Managing cognitive load is a key issue for us and is related to the use of scaffolding, one technique for reducing the cognitive load. Carefully controlling rate of presentation of content new to the learner and allowing time for the learner to reflect on new content (in the "relate" step) also reduce cognitive load. Another technique is to teach some subskills or knowledge as prerequisites, so they only need to be recalled when teaching the whole problem-solving skill. This is especially effective if the prerequisites are practiced to a high state of automaticity (fluency) so the learner can literally "do them without thinking about it."

Cognitive Coaching

Cognitive coaching is an approach to teaching problem solving in which, as part of the lesson, a "coach" talks to the learner throughout the problem-solving process (either automatically or on demand, depending on the medium) providing the learner with hints, suggestions, comments, feedback, ideas, and reflection about strategy—something like what a good "color commentary" does at a football game, discussing the decisions the coach and the quarterback are making and why.

HOW LEARNERS SOLVE PROBLEMS

To do problem solving, the learner has to go through a number of steps. Although different researchers define the steps differently, most would probably agree with this seven-step process:

1. *Form an initial representation* of the problem, called a "problem space," including all the elements of a problem (as described above).

2. *Recall declarative knowledge* (in the form of a mental model) and procedural knowledge (in the form of problems solved) appropriate to the problem space just created.

3. If the learner has previously solved a similar problem, he or she will probably just recall the procedure used last time and follow it in a rote manner.

4. If the learner doesn't see a match to something previously encountered, then he or she has to generate a new solution using one or more strategies, both *general* problem-solving strategies (called *domain independent*) and strategies *specific* to the content of the problem (called *domain specific*), to plan to solve the problem. The learner integrates the mental model, prior procedural knowledge, and these strategies to generate an algorithm or a heuristic for solving the problem.

5. The learner then implements the algorithm just created.

6. The learner then checks the results of the problem-solving efforts against the goal state to see if they match. If so, the problem is solved.

7. If the problem is solved, the learner is happy and quits; if not, the learner goes back to either Step 1, to reformulate the problem, or Step 2, to recall other declarative and procedural knowledge, or Step 3, to plan to solve the problem using a different strategy.

There is a variation on this basic process that some researchers advocate: early hypothesis formation. At the beginning of the problem-solving process, you generate seven ± two hypotheses about the solution and pick them off one at a time, going from most likely/cheapest to solve the problem to least. This has been especially proposed as a mechanism for troubleshooting and diagnosis, but might be a general strategy as well. It is controversial in either application, but worth considering.

Also, remember that many problems cannot be solved in one algorithm. They have to be broken down into component sub-problems, which usually have clearer goals and more structure than the "main" problem.

Note also that determining a goal in an ill-structured problem effectively transforms it into a moderately structured one. Determining a strategy in a moderately structured problem effectively transforms it into a well-structured one. Therefore, all problem-solving *performance* is actually at the well-structured level, and all ill-structured problem solving is essentially a problem-transformation task.

Initial Representation of the Problem: Creation of the Problem Space

The definition of the problem space is so important to problem solving that there are several issues. For *well-structured problems,* problem solving is basically a pattern-recognition task: You recognize the initial and desired end state of the problem as one for which you already have learned an algorithm and simply recall it (Step 5 above). Accessing a search engine on the Internet is an example. You recognize the initial state as your browser being at some other location. You recognize the end state as your browser being at the desired search engine location. Your algorithm consists of the series of mouse clicks and key strokes to get to the search engine.

For *any* problem type, but especially for ill-structured problems, problem representation is *the* key step. If the learner does not formulate the problem successfully, then the learner will have no idea when a solution has been found—or which of several possible solutions is the best. So learners spend a lot of time on identifying that there is a problem in the first place and formulating (and reformulating and re-reformulating) what that problem is (including defining the qualifying characteristics of a sound solution). For example, suppose your drip coffeemaker has the correct amounts of water and coffee in it. You turn it on and the red "on" light turns on, but nothing happens. What's the problem? It's broken, right? Your first reaction might be that there's a loose wire or "something." Unless you know that the problem most likely is that the hot water doesn't drip from the drip tube, you won't be able to apply a series of possible solutions, such as cleaning the scale from the coffeemaker.

The learner can err in the other direction, also, by incorrectly recognizing an ill-structured problem as an already-learned (and therefore well-structured) one. In this case, the learner will recall and use an inappropriate algorithm (literally solving the wrong problem), and be unpleasantly surprised when the solution achieved isn't satisfactory. Continuing with the above example, you recall that when the water doesn't drip from the drip tube, it probably is clogged with minerals from the water you've been using. The solution you apply is to pour a combination of vinegar and water into the water reservoir, let it set for a while, and turn on the coffeemaker to try to dissolve the minerals in the tubes. This doesn't work so, depending on how expensive the appliance was, you might throw it out or put it in the garage. Because of your limited knowledge of the coffeemaker's innards and what can go wrong and with what probability, you formulated a wrong problem. The actual cause could be anything from a defective thermostat to a faulty heating assembly.

Recall Declarative Knowledge (Mental Model)

There are several issues involved in representing ill-structured problems. The elements in the problem space are in the form of declarative and procedural knowledge. The declarative knowledge includes:

- Opening conditions.
- Desired states.
- Underlying principles.
- Relevant facts and concepts.

Recall Procedural Knowledge

The procedural knowledge includes well-structured procedures, which may become components of the solution strategies. They may be in any state of automaticity, but the more automatic they are, the more likely it is that the learner will have the cognitive resources to use them. Procedural knowledge also includes strategies gained from experience with similar problems. And remember that there are the "weak" strategies: general strategies for solving many problem types.

Let's take a look at a familiar problem space and name its components. You're having a gala party in your back yard. You want to decorate the bushes with a 100-bulb string of miniature lights. You retrieve the lights from the basement, plug them in, and they don't light:

- *Opening conditions:* Light string plugged into live electrical outlet; lights don't turn on.
- *Desired state:* One hundred light bulbs lit.
- *Underlying principles:* If bulbs, sockets, wires, and plug are intact, bulbs are properly fitted into the sockets, and the wire is supplied with correct amount of electricity (voltage and current), than all bulbs should light. If not, then all or some of the lights will not light.
- *Facts and concepts:* Bulbs, sockets, wire, plug, wire connections, wired in series, wired in parallel, electricity, filament, electrical contact, loose socket, proper fit of bulb in socket, electrical short, electrical open circuit, resistor in parallel with each bulb's filament.
- *Procedural knowledge:* How to test a light, how to test a socket, how to measure voltage, how to operate test instruments and tools, and troubleshooting strategies such as "space splitting" (using a strategy that rules out as many possible causes as possible with a single test or decision).

The steps of problem solving really involve a search of that problem space for the declarative and procedural knowledge that will change the initial state of the problem into the goal state of the problem within the constraints of the problem. With well-structured problems, you do this by recalling the right procedure. With ill-structured problems, you have to invent a procedure specific to the problem at hand.

Therefore, the contents of the problem space, how the problem space is organized, and the types of search strategies chosen to facilitate the search through the large number of options are the keys to problem-solving expertise.

Expert's vs. Novice's Problem Spaces

Not all problem spaces are created equal. Those of experts are quite different from those of novices:

> "Problem solving is a context-bound skill, in which experts synthesize their rich declarative knowledge to generate a dynamically changing, personal, working mental model of the system (problem space) suitable for solving a particular class of problems; they draw on an extensive reservoir of past experience solving analogous problems in the same domain, and they can set intermediate goals and switch between their corresponding sub-problems according to strategies appropriate for problems of a given type. Novices don't know as much, and therefore have mental models that are less complete, poorly structured, and even misleading. Therefore, novices can't simply imitate what experts do, because it doesn't make sense to them. The instructional challenge is to help novices develop initial mental models which are not misleading, and then to help them enrich their mental models to an expert's level. Simply recalling (or retrieving) well-structured solution algorithms is not enough [if transfer/generalization/problem solving in novel problem spaces is the goal]. (Foshay & Gibbons, 2001)

It should come as no surprise that there are big differences between how experts and novices categorize ill-structured problems and represent them in problem spaces. What may be a surprise, however, is what the difference between an expert's and a novice's problem space really is. The issue is NOT, as we might expect, just that experts have bigger problem spaces with more knowledge in them. So what are the differences? Six are discussed below.

1. In general, experts do have more declarative knowledge, but of a specific kind. They have more principles in their problem spaces, at a higher level of automaticity. This allows them to synthesize the declarative knowledge they have and bring it to bear more systematically on problems.

2. Experts have better links between the declarative knowledge structures (mental models) and their procedural knowledge structures (if . . . then statements) in their problem spaces. These links allow them to bring principles and procedures together to solve problems more efficiently. The structures resulting from these links are sometimes called mental models of the problem space.

3. Experts are really great at organizing their problem spaces. Recall that solving a problem (except when blindly following a rote procedure) involves constructing and manipulating the mental model of the system within the problem space. Experts do it so there are more associations among the declarative and procedural knowledge structures in the problem space. These allow them to more efficiently and quickly get around in those problem spaces to bring the needed knowledge to bear on the problem. It provides them with what others see as "mental shortcuts." Note that these "mental shortcuts" often involve insights about the problem space that novices could not possibly understand because they don't have the supporting knowledge structure.

4. Experts categorize and group problems differently from novices. While novices look at surface, perceptual issues in putting problems in the same category, experts extract the abstract problem features (underlying meaning) from the problems and categorize them based on their deep structure—making it easier to apply the right existing declarative and procedural knowledge structures to bear on solving them.

5. Experts generate heuristics for solving problems by "working forward" from the initial state, generating hypotheses, and then carrying them through to see if they lead to the goal. Learners, on the other hand, try to generate them "working backwards" from the goal state, generating operations that include the goal and a path to get there (Jonassen, 1997; Newell & Simon, 1972).

6. Complicating the issue of novice versus expert are the issues of situational and individual differences. They are believed to affect processing capacity, thus making cognitive load and automaticity a huge issue. We already mentioned factors that affect cognitive processing capacity, including stress, fatigue, confidence, motivation/persistence, and so forth. Thus, for example, an expert is more likely to persist if the first strategy doesn't work, but a novice may give up.

We can illustrate these six differences between expert and novice problem spaces by examining the problem space of a refrigeration expert and his or her approach to solving the problem of a refrigerator that's not cold enough. We'll also take a look at a novice's problem space and approach to the problem.

The Expert. Our expert has a whole lot of declarative knowledge about the parts of a refrigerator, for example, the structure and function of condenser coils, water inlet valves at the icemaker thermostat, the drain and its pan, icemaker motors, doors, door seals, gaskets and switches, temperature controls, on and off switches, types of icemakers and their parts, the compressor and mountings, condenser fan, breaker strips, evaporator fans, and defrost heater and timer.

Our expert knows how all these parts work together: Refrigerators work using a sealed cooling system. A compressor pumps refrigerant under high pressure into evaporator coils . . . and so on.

Our expert knows principles and procedures of refrigeration: If liquid refrigerant is pumped under pressure into evaporator coils, then it will boil. If it boils, it will expand into a gas. If it expands into a gas, it will absorb heat from inside the refrigerator box. If it absorbs heat from the refrigerator box, it will cool it . . . and so on.

All of these elements (plus a whole lot more) comprise the refrigeration expert's mental model of refrigeration and refrigerators. He or she knows how the system works, how refrigerators (in general) work, and how this particular refrigerator works.

Remember the problem? The refrigerator temperature isn't cold enough. Our expert has been informed of the problem. To solve it he or she constructs and manipulates his or her mental model of refrigeration and refrigerators within the "problem space," that is, the box should cool to between 32 and 40 degrees (goal state). The unit is cooling to 45 degrees and won't go lower (initial state). Our expert looks at underlying meanings and subsystems and begins to abstract problem features and categorize them based on deep structured knowledge so that he or she can apply the right declarative and procedural knowledge structures to solve the malfunction. For example, our expert would recognize that, since the refrigerator is cooling some, a number of subsystems must be working (the first space splitting). The expert would also recognize that only certain problems would be capable of causing poor cooling, while allowing some cooling to take place. Furthermore, the expert would know what the likelihood is of each of these problems occurring and how difficult or costly it is to verify each possible cause of the problem. The troubleshooting sequence might include the following steps—check temperature control, check the condenser coils, check door seals, test door switch, test evaporator fan, test defrost heater, test defrost timer, check all aspects of compressor. Based on this knowledge, the expert would sequence the appropriate measures for maximum efficiency and least cost to achieve the goal state.

The Novice. How would our novice solve (or try to solve) the problem? Here our novice would probably be an average householder. The novice's response, like the expert's, would also depend on his or her mental model of refrigeration and refrigerators. This model would probably consist of some or all of the following facts, concepts, principles, and procedures—knowledge of the temperature control and its function; of the electrical plug and its function; of the condenser coils and their function (maybe). The novice might also know that if the door seal is faulty, cold air will leak out of the box. If cold air leaks out of the box, the temperature will be warmer. Based on this profile, our novice might try to solve the problem by using these troubleshooting attempts: check the temperature control by turning it up or down and checking the box temperature; maybe clean the condenser coils; maybe check the door seals. The novice would also probably perform unnecessary operations, such as making sure the plug is properly positioned in the outlet. If our novice is lucky, correcting one of these may solve the problem. But if the cause is something else (such as loss of coolant due to a leak), the novice will be unable to diagnose the problem.

Both expert and novice know the initial and goal states. The critical difference here is that the expert's mental model of the subject matter makes it much easier for him or her to apply the right existing declarative and procedural knowledge structures in a comprehensive way to solve problems. This is the truth behind the old joke about a mechanic who charges $100 to fix a car for a few seconds' work tightening a nut. "That's $5 to fix the nut," he tells the distraught car owner, "and $95 for knowing which one was loose."

Based on these issues, our challenge in training, then, is to assist (but not tell) learners to categorize problems the way experts do.

Blocks Created by Problem Spaces

How a problem is represented in the problem space determines how the learner looks at all elements of the problem. When learners represent a problem in a certain way, they look at the initial state, goal state, operations, resources, and constraints in ways consistent with that representation and how they've solved problems like that before. This can make problem solving more efficient, or it can create blocks for learners trying to solve problems. The blocks come from "thinking only inside the box." That is, learners look at all problems the same way, whether it is appropriate or not. The blocks come in three forms:

- First, they tend to look at "objects" in the way they always have before, and they miss looking at other, novel ways of using tools given in the problem. This is called *functional fixedness.*

- Second, they tend to recall and use certain ways of solving the problem that are like the ways they have solved problems in the past—whether or not that way is the most effective way of solving the new problem; this is called *set*.

- Third, they can look at the problem as having certain constraints it really does not have, due to certain perceptions, assumptions, or boundaries they create for themselves (as in the classic model where people stay within the "perceived square" while connecting nine dots with four lines); this is called *unnecessary constraints* or *tunnel vision*. Discounting disconfirming evidence is another symptom of tunnel vision (Elstein, 1978).

All three of these blocks are causes of over- and under-generalization by the learner. The key issue for us as trainers is to assist learners in avoiding these blocks to effective representation of the problem. Here again, however, remember that simply telling the learner isn't enough—and may actually inhibit formation of the needed insights.

PROBLEM-SOLVING STRATEGIES

As we said above, in describing the fourth step of what learners do when they solve problems, they use one or more strategies, both *general* problem-solving strategies (called *domain-independent*), and strategies *specific* to the content of the problem (called *domain-specific*), to plan to solve the problem—to get from the initial state to the goal state. Let's look at those two types of strategies now, because the one most popular in problem-solving courses is neither the one that is most effective, nor the one we have included in our recommendations.

Domain-Independent. These strategies are general problem-solving heuristics that apply across all types of problems and therefore are called *domain-independent*. These are the strategies taught in "general problem solving" books and courses. Many people believe they are important and effective. However, the research indicates they are *not* as useful or powerful as people believe. They are *weak strategies* that are some use in helping solve problems, but the less structure the problem has, the less efficient they are. They are useful to problem solvers because of their wide applicability, but they are *not* as powerful as the domain-specific heuristics in solving specific problems.

This means they are necessary to solve problems, but not sufficient to solve problems. And unlike domain-specific strategies, there is no difference between expert and novice problem solvers in their ability to use them. See Figure 14.3 for some examples of domain-independent strategies.

Domain-Specific. These strategies apply only to problems in a specific content area or domain and are therefore called *domain-specific*. They do not transfer from one content area to another. They are, however, the most important strategies because research indicates that solving problems in a

FIGURE 14.3. Domain-Independent Strategies

Domain-Independent Strategy	Examples
Break into subgoals: In going from the initial state to the goal state, there are frequently intermediate states. If the learner can identify one or more of these, it reduces both the complexity of the problem (going from A to C to E to G rather than A straight to G) and the number of operations to try (any that start off heading from A to G, but veer off-track can now be eliminated when they miss C, instead of waiting to find out if they make it all the way to G).	Initial state: Nursing home applies for federal reimbursements. Goal state: Determine eligibility. Procedure divides into six stages. Learner taught to identify and implement stages and how they relate to eligibility.
Difference reduction: Identify the difference between the initial state and goal state and perform an operation that reduces that difference by just one step; then identify the difference again and operate again.	Initial state: 100 Italian light bulbs won't light (sound familiar?). Goal state: 100 Italian lights lit. After each of these checks, plug the string into an outlet to see if current is flowing and the string works (which indicates that you reduced the difference to zero and achieved your goal). (1) check plug, (2) check for wire breaks, and (3) work from the plug end to the other of the string and check the bulb, the socket, and the connection for each. It is important to emphasize that of the three possible tests described, the difference reduction strategy would cause you to choose the one that might get some of the lights on.
Working backward: Begin with the goal state rather than initial state and work backward, frequently through a series of subgoals (mazes and mathematical proofs).	A dispatcher needs to figure out the quickest and most economical cross-country routes for the company's truck drivers. Initial state: No planned cross-country routes. Goal state: All drivers have specific directions for getting to and from their assigned destinations. These routes will take the least time and money to deliver the goods. The dispatcher, armed with atlases and maps, plans each route by starting at the destination city and working backward to the trucker's beginning point.
Analogical reasoning: Use the approach that works to solve one problem to solve another problem that is seen to similar in nature/structure. The only catch here is that learners are pretty bad at seeing the analogies between problems on their own, and therefore must be led to discover (not told) the analogous relationship between the problems.	Initial state: An aneurysm (bulging blood vessel) is in danger of bursting. Goal state: Repaired aneurysm. The surgeon, early in training, likens an aneurysm to a weakened section of a water hose that bulges and uses the analogy to run through possible courses of action, for example, complete removal of that section or sewing up the weak tissue or "sleeving" the affected section.

domain relies on cognitive operations that are specific to that domain (Jonassen, 1997). *Therefore, what differentiates experts and novices is not general problem-solving skills, but domain-specific declarative and procedural knowledge, mental model manipulation skill, and domain-specific strategies—as well as motivational factors such as confidence.* It is their use of these strategies (as well as their better-organized problem spaces, discussed above) that makes the difference in experts' problem-solving ability. (See Figure 14.4 for some examples of domain-specific strategies.) Therefore, we can conclude that teaching general problem-solving strategies is not enough—and may not even be very important.

FIGURE 14.4. Domain-Specific Strategies

Domain-Specific Strategy	Electronic Troubleshooting: Strategies needed to find problem and repair a VCR
Activate existing structures.	Divide and check power inputs, power outputs, switching circuitry, circuit boards, mechanical systems, wiring systems, recording and playback processes, video and audio components. These are the names of the subsystems, which would be activating existing structures.
Break into sub-problems.	Breaking into sub-problems would be asking "Are the symptoms mechanical (tape does not move, gets tangled) or electrical (tape moves but does not play or record)?" For troubleshooting, the main strategy for breaking into sub-problems is space splitting like this. For example, suppose you are troubleshooting a string of one hundred mini holiday lights. By taking advantage of the fact that a 100-light string usually is actually three thirty-three light strings in parallel (the bulbs are usually 2.5–4 volts each), and each bulb usually has a resistor in parallel with the filament so if the filament goes the bulb will pass current and allow the rest of the bulbs to run (albeit a bit dimmer).
Model the problem space.	Use a series of if . . . then statements based on symptom(s) to determine problem. More specifically, add faults to your mental model of the system and then predict the system's behavior with the fault. Then check to see if the predicted and observed behavior match. For example, "If the belt for the tape drive is broken, then the tape can't pass over the playback head. Check to see whether the tape is passing over the playback head. Once established, use problem space to solve problem.
Probability of failure.	First check that all bulbs are good. Second, check all of the sockets. Third, check all the wire connections to the sockets. Fourth, check the wire for breaks. Fifth, check the plug for defects.

Let's elaborate a bit on these points. The domain-specific strategies are built around activating as many related existing declarative and procedural knowledge structures as possible (remember that experts can do this better than novices, so you need to help novices more). Once enough related knowledge structures are activated, the learner is able to go beyond the information given to fill in the blanks in the given information.

A second domain-specific strategy is based on how people solve defined problems. They try to break them down into a series of smaller, more solvable sub-problems. The more knowledge structures they have in a content area, the more they are able to do this.

A third domain-specific strategy is building a mental model of how the system in question (a computer program, a car or airplane, a building, a work process, or even a human body) operates when it is operating correctly or incorrectly. This is particularly useful for troubleshooting: The expert can mentally add faults to his or her model of the system and predict how the system with those faults would operate. Once the model is built, he or she can compare the current state with this constructed goal state and identify operations that will close the gap.

The key issue for us as trainers is two-fold: Of course you need to assist all learners in developing and using domain-free strategies. But most important, you need to help learners develop domain-specific problem-solving strategies for whatever content domain they work in.

TEACHING PROCEDURAL KNOWLEDGE TO SOLVE PROBLEMS

Now that we've discussed what to learn about problem solving, we can turn our attention to what to teach and how to teach it. Learning to use procedural knowledge to solve ill-structured problem solving differs from learning to solve well-structured problems. There are differences in how learners learn and remember the operations they use to solve them.

With well-structured problem-solving learning, retention and transfer to very similar problems are most effective when the training includes statements of the procedures. Furthermore, the way in which the well-structured procedure is taught has a direct influence on how well the learner generalizes and on how easy it is to learn generalizable strategies later (Scandura, 1977).

Ill-structured problem solving, which has as its goal far transfer to new problems, requires that the learners generate the appropriate specific or general strategy themselves and assemble previously learned well-structured procedures in a new way. If we tell the learners the strategy during training, we short-circuit the opportunity for procedure construction, and the learners end up no better than untrained novices for solving future problems. If, on the other hand, learners generate the strategy themselves during training, they are much better than untrained novices in solving new problems that are different in some ways from what they encountered in training. For example, if we teach you only how to type a letter in your word processor, you won't be able to figure out how to type a report. If, however, we teach you strategies for formatting text in your word processor, you'll be able to type any format of document.

So the strategies for teaching moderately and ill-structured problems are very different from those for well-structured problems. For ill-structured problem solving, then, we should *not* simply present the solution steps, but at the same time *not* just leave the learner alone floundering. We must recall, relate, and present enough declarative and procedural knowledge to *guide the learner in constructing the solution to the problem.*

ISSUES IN TEACHING ILL-STRUCTURED PROBLEM SOLVING

As we said earlier, there are a great many issues, and little agreement, related to designing instruction for ill-structured problem solving. Foshay and Gibbons (2001) and Jonassen (1997 & 2000) address some of the key issues.

1. Types of Problems

We've said that there are well-, moderately, and ill-structured problems, with troubleshooting as a special case of moderately structured problems. Other authors (Jonassen, 2000) suggest that there are eleven types of problems, each of which differs on six criteria (see Figure 14.5). While this classification is new, if it is empirically demonstrated and generally accepted, it could have major implications for the design of problem-solving training.

2. Problem Formats

Regardless of where the problems fall on the continuum, it is possible to use various combinations of the elements of a problem that may be useful to guide instructional design. Van Merrienboer (1997) suggests that there are two major types of problem examples, each with several subtypes.

The first major type is *product-oriented* worked out examples. These include the initial state, goal state, constraints, and problem solution, but they do not include the operations/heuristics used to solve the problem.

The second major type is *process-oriented* worked out examples (also called *modeling* examples), which do pay attention to, and illustrate, the process for applying the heuristics to solve the problem.

Van Merrienboer (1997, p. 187) then lists subtypes under each type in the order in which they place increasing "cognitive load" on the learner.

Product-Oriented Problem Formats

- Worked out examples.
- Reverse problems.

FIGURE 14.5. Problem Types

	Logical Problems	Algorithmic Problems	Story Problems	Rule-Using Problems	Decision-Making Problems	Trouble-shooting Problems	Diagnosis-Solution Problems	Strategic Performance Problems	Case Analysis Problems	Design Problems	Dilemmas
Learning Activity											
Inputs											
Success Criteria											
Context											
Structuredness											
Abstractness											

From D. Jonassen, Instructional Design Models for Well-Structured and Ill-Structured Problem Solving Learning Outcomes. *Educational Technology Research and Development,* 1997, 48(4), 63–85.

- Imitation problems.
- Goal-free problems.
- Conventional problems.

Process-Oriented Problem Formats

- Modeling examples.
- Problems with performance constraints.
- Problems combined with process worksheets or cognitive tools.
- Conventional problems.

The author says that the importance of both of these problem example types is that they "scaffold the learner by lowering the cognitive load associated with performing the learning task and by stimulating inductive processing and . . . [mental model] acquisition" (p. 187).

It is clear from this list that the conventional problems that instructional designers are used to presenting are the most difficult for learners to learn from, and that there are alternatives. Again, should this distinction be empirically proven and generally accepted, it will have implications for the design of problem-solving training.

3. Sequence of Teaching Problems

To those who think of learning categories in terms of hierarchies such as Gagne's, it would make sense that, in learning problem solving, one would begin with well-structured problems, then move to troubleshooting, and then to ill-structured problems.

It turns out, however, that is not the best practice. Instead, it seems that well-structured problem solving and ill-structured problem solving involve the use of different skill sets, and that being well-structured is not a prerequisite to successful ill-structured problem solving (Jonassen, 1977, 2000; van Merrienboer, 1997).

In addition, simple-to-complex sequencing of problems does not work either, because it gets in the way of building appropriate mental models and reflections of the complex problem-solving process one is trying to end up with (van Merrienboer, 1997).

The general strategy for sequencing (based on cognitive load, the problem formats described above, and not unlike the old behaviorist notion of "fading prompts") has two steps:

- To avoid cognitive overload, begin with problem formats that have lower cognitive loads. You can scaffold real-world (authentic) problems to reduce cognitive load, rather than using unrealistically simplified problems.

- Then, gradually diminish the amount of scaffolding and move to more complex problem formats.

4. Inductive vs. Deductive Teaching

A not altogether new issue is whether to present the problems first or the structures first in teaching (in Chapter 6, we discussed this same issue in relation to teaching concepts—examples first, then attributes). This issue has played out in earlier incarnations as the debate over "direct instruction" versus "discovery learning" and "inquiry learning" or, now, "constructivism." Not surprisingly, there is little consensus in the research literature on the question.

Van Merrienboer (1997) suggests that an "inductive expository" approach is the most effective: first present the problems; then teach the structure, approaches to generating heuristics, and reflection. He also suggests teaching the needed declarative knowledge in a deductive mode just in time during the problem-solving training.

A final note on this debate: We believe that teaching ill-structured problem-solving procedures using the principles described here, while necessary, is also apparently time-consuming enough that most trainers will choose to favor the familiar and apparently efficient direct instruction of declarative knowledge and well-structured procedures. Whether this is desirable depends on a complex set of tradeoffs between the need for far transfer, the size of the curriculum, the prior knowledge of the learners, and the capabilities of learning environment, including the instructors.

ISSUES IN TEACHING TROUBLESHOOTING

We used to think that troubleshooting was always well-structured problem solving. But there are at least five limitations to treating troubleshooting in this way. First, well-structured problem solving doesn't transfer well, so teaching troubleshooting that way requires the learner to recall (or retrieve from a job aid) every individual troubleshooting procedure. Second, when details of the procedures change (as when a new model of the equipment comes out), new procedures are needed—and often they require costly retraining. Third, if the learner has to troubleshoot a number of devices and models, each requires its own procedure and corresponding training. Fourth, if the learner encounters a fault for which there is no procedure, there's a good chance he or she will not be able to fix it.

The fifth limitation is perhaps the most important: Well-structured problem solving has turned out not to be an accurate description of the way experts do many troubleshooting tasks. Research in the 1970s and 1980s on expert troubleshooters, ranging from electronics technicians to programmers to physicians, showed that their actual troubleshooting processes often treat the troubleshooting task as a special kind of ill-structured problem solving. The goal state is clear, but the means of getting there are invented by the expert problem solver on the spot. To differentiate this from ill-structured problem solving (where both goals and means are undefined), we call this *moderately structured* problem solving.

There are some ways in which moderately structured problem solving is more efficient. Researchers found that expert troubleshooters who had this skill could easily adapt to new equipment of the same general type, without constant retraining when new models came out. Therefore, total training and retraining requirements were lower than with training in well-structured problem solving, even though it takes more time to teach moderately structured problem solving than to teach (or look up) a well-structured procedure.

Thus, when you train learners to do troubleshooting, you have a choice of teaching them well-structured or moderately structured problem-solving skills. You know you need to teach troubleshooting as moderately structured problem solving if:

- You can't anticipate all the possible faults the learner will have to fix.
- The problem is not so ambiguous that the learners will have to figure out whether there's a problem and what kind of problem it is.
- The number of possible faults is known, but too large to train for all of them.
- The systems the learner must work on change constantly.
- A significant goal is generalization (to other similar systems or new versions or models) with only minimal retraining.

On the other hand, well-structured troubleshooting is much easier to teach and faster to learn. If you can give the learner a job aid with a troubleshooting procedure, once the learner can follow the job aid, you're finished with training.

Moderately structured troubleshooting is a complex skill. We mentioned above that expert troubleshooters know:

Declarative Knowledge
- How the system works when it is working correctly.
- The ways each component or subsystem in the system can fail.
- How the system (mis)behaves when each of these faults occurs.
- The probabilities of each type of failure.
- The time, cost, and risk involved in fixing each component or subsystem.
- The time, cost, and risk of each test used to isolate the fault.

Procedural Knowledge

- How to use this information to decide how to approach finding out what the problem is.

These are all the elements our learners must know in order to become efficient troubleshooters (Anderson, 1985; Bonner, 1988; Foshay, 1988; Newell & Simon, 1972). Note also that, as with other kinds of problem solving, most of the knowledge used to troubleshoot is context-specific. The abstract knowledge, such as general troubleshooting strategies, is an important but fairly minor part of the training task.

The instructional design issues surrounding teaching moderately structured problem solving such as troubleshooting are basically the same as those for ill-structured problem solving, except that the goal is a given: You need to make the system work (or work again). If you are repairing a system, then you also know something important about the system structure: It used to work, so the system structure is basically complete and properly structured, so you can concentrate on finding components that are malfunctioning or have been removed. We have illustrated how these differences apply in the discussion in Chapter 10.

SUMMARY

The cognitive view of problem solving is quite a bit different from the representations on which a typical general problem-solving course are built. You have seen how well- and ill-structured problem solving differ, in terms of the way in which the problem space is constructed, the types of declarative and procedural knowledge needed, and the way expert and novice problem solvers work. You also should appreciate why we say that problem solving is mostly a context-bound skill. We also mentioned current thinking on problem-solving types, with an extended discussion of the special characteristics of troubleshooting expertise.

It should be clear that, while well-structured problem-solving procedures can be simply memorized (or looked up on a job aid) and followed, ill-structured problem-solving procedures have to be taught using sophisticated inductive strategies.

We discussed the importance of using authentic problems—and ways of scaffolding them to reduce cognitive load for novices. Finally, we encouraged you to think about times in which the apparent inefficiency of ill-structured problem-solving instruction is worth it. If a goal is far transfer (to new or unpredictable problems) or reduction of repetitive training and retraining, then you should define the training goals to include moderate- to ill-structured problem solving.

Further Reading

Anderson, J.R. (1985, 1990, 1993, 1995a). *Cognitive psychology and its implications* (2nd, 3rd, 4th, & 5th eds.). New York: W.H. Freeman.

Anderson, J.R. (1995b). *Learning and memory.* New York: John Wiley & Sons.

Ausubel, D. (1968). *Educational psychology: A cognitive view.* New York: Holt, Rinehart and Winston.

Best, J. (1989). *Cognitive psychology* (2nd ed.). St. Paul, MN: West.

Bonner, J. (1988). Implications of cognitive theory for instructional design: Revisited. *Educational Communications & Technology Journal, 36*(1), 3–14.

Clark, R.C. (1998). *Building expertise.* Washington, DC: ISPI.

Clark, R.C. (1999). *Developing technical training: A structured approach for the development of classroom and computer-based instructional materials.* Washington, DC: ISPI.

Clark, R.C., & Mayer, R. (2002). *e-Learning and the science of instruction: Proven guidelines for consumers and designers of multimedia training.* San Francisco, CA: Jossey-Bass.

Dick, W., & Carey, L. (2001). *The systematic design of instruction* (5th ed.). New York: HarperCollinsCollege.

DiVesta, F., & Rieber, L. (1987). Characteristics of cognitive engineering: The next generation of instructional systems. *Educational Communications & Technology Journal, 35*(4), 213–230.

Elstein, A.S., Shulman, L.S., et al. (1978). *Medical problem solving: An analysis of clinical reasoning.* Cambridge, MA: Harvard University Press.

Ertmer, P.A., & Newby, T.J. (1993). Behaviorism, cognitivism, constructivism: Comparing critical features from an instructional design perspective. *Performance Improvement Quarterly, 6*(4), 50–72.

Fleming, M., & Bednar, A. (1993). Concept-learning principles. In M. Fleming & H. Levie, *Instructional message design* (2nd ed.). Englewood Cliffs, NJ: Educational Technology Publications.

Foshay, W.R. (1986). *ASI instructional design standards.* Arlington Heights, IL: ASI.

Foshay, W.R. (1991, May). Sharpen up your schemata. *Data Training,* pp. 18–25.

Foshay, W.R., & Gibbons, A. (2001). *Teaching and designing problem solving: An assessment.* Bloomington, MN: PLATO Learning.

Foshay, W.R., & Kirkley, J. (1998). *Principles for teaching problem solving.* Bloomington, MN: PLATO Learning.

Gagne, R.M. (1985). *Conditions of learning* (4th ed.). New York: Holt, Rinehart and Winston.

Gagne, R.M., Briggs, L.J., & Wager, W.W. (1992). *Principles of instructional design* (4th ed.). New York: Holt, Rinehart and Winston.

Hannafin, M., & Hooper, S. (1993). Learning principles. In M. Fleming & H. Levie, *Instructional message design* (2nd ed.). Englewood Cliffs, NJ: Educational Technology Publications.

Hartley, J. (1978). *Designing instructional text.* New York: Nichols.

Horn, R. (1976). *How to write information mapping.* Lexington, MA: Information Resources.

Jonassen, D. (1982, 1985). *The technology of text, volumes 1 and 2.* Englewood Cliffs, NJ: Educational Technology Publications.

Jonassen, J.H. (1997). Instructional design models for well-structured and ill-structured problem-solving learning outcomes. *Educational Technology Research and Development, 45*(1), 65–94.

Jonassen, J.H. (2000). Toward a design theory of problem-solving. *Educational Technology Research and Development, 48*(4), 63–85.

Keller, J. (1987). The systematic process of motivational design. *Performance & Instruction, 26*(8), 1–7.

Keller, J., & Burkman, E. (1993). Motivation principles. In M. Fleming & H. Levie, *Instructional message design* (2nd ed.). Englewood Cliffs, NJ: Educational Technology Publications.

Klatzky, R. (1980). *Human memory: Structure and processes* (2nd ed.). San Francisco, CA: Freeman.

Mager, R.F. (1984). *Preparing instructional objectives* (rev. ed.). Belmont, CA: Pitman Learning.

Mayer, R. (1984). Aids to text comprehension. *Educational Psychologist, 19*(1), 30–42.

Mayer, R. (1993). Problem-solving principles. In M. Fleming & H. Levie, *Instructional message design* (2nd ed.). Englewood Cliffs, NJ: Educational Technology Publications.

Merrienboer, J.J.G.(1997). *Training complex cognitive skills; A four-component instructional design model for technical training.* Englewood Cliffs, NJ: Educational Technology Publications.

Merrill, M.D. (1983). Component display theory. In C. Reigeluth (Ed.), *Instructional-design theories and models.* Hillsdale, NJ: Lawrence Erlbaum.

Merrill, M.C., Tennyson, R.D., & Posey, L.O. (1992). *Teaching concepts: An instructional design guide.* Englewood Cliffs, NJ: Educational Technology Publications.

Miller, G. (1956). The magical number seven, plus or minus two—some limits on our capacity for processing information. *Psychological Review, 63,* 81–97.

Newell, A., & Simon, S.A. (1972). *Human problem solving.* Englewood Cliffs, NJ: Prentice Hall.

Paivio, A. (1983). The empirical case for dual coding. In J. Yuille (Ed.), *Imagery, memory and cognition*. Hillsdale, NJ: Lawrence Erlbaum.

Reigeluth, C.M. (1999). *Instructional-design theories and models, vol. 2: A new paradigm of instructional theory*. Hillsdale, NJ: Lawrence Erlbaum.

Reigeluth, C., & Stein, F. (1983). The elaboration theory of instruction. In C. Reigeluth (Ed.), *Instructional-design theories and models*. Hillsdale, NJ: Lawrence Erlbaum.

Rummler, G.A., & Brache, A.P. (1995). *Improving performance* (2nd ed.). San Francisco, CA: Jossey-Bass.

Scandura, J.M. (1977). *Problem solving: A structural/process approach with instructional implications*. New York: Academic Press.

Schank, R. (1988). *The creative attitude*. New York: Macmillan.

Seels, B., & Glasgow, Z. (1998). *Making instructional design decisions*. Upper Saddle River, NJ: Merrill.

Silber, K.H. (1998). The cognitive approach to training development: A practitioner's assessment. *Educational Technology Research and Development, 46*(4), 58–72.

Silber, K., & Stelnicki, M. (1987). Writing training materials. In R. Craig (Ed.), *Training and development handbook* (3rd ed.). New York: McGraw-Hill.

Silber, K., & Stelnicki, M. (1993). Deep in the head of experts: What's there and how to get it out. *NSPI Bulletin*. Montreal: Montreal NSPI.

Smith, P.L., & Ragan, T.J. (1999). *Instructional design*. Upper Saddle River, NJ: Merrill.

Stelnicki, M., & Silber, K. (1990). *How successful performance technologists improve performance by changing trainee attitudes*. Workshop presented at the 1990 National Conference of the National Society for Performance and Instruction, Toronto, Ontario, Canada.

Stepich, D., & Newby, T. (1988). Analogizing as an instructional strategy. *Performance & Instruction, 29*(9), 21–23.

Sweller, J. (1999). Instructional design in technical areas. *Australian Education Review, 43*.

Tiemann, P.W., & Markle, S.M. (1983). *Analyzing instructional content: A guide to instruction and evaluation*. Champaign, IL: Stipes.

Tosti, D. (1990). *Feedback revisited*. Session presented at the 1990 National Conference of the National Society for Performance and Instruction, Toronto, Ontario, Canada.

Wellins, R.C., Byham, W.C., & Wilson, J.M. (1991). *Empowered teams*. San Francisco, CA: Jossey-Bass.

West, C., Farmer, J., & Wolff, P. (1991). *Instructional design: Implications from cognitive science*. Boston, MA: Allyn & Bacon.

Wlodokowski, R. (1985). *Enhancing adult motivation to learn*. San Francisco, CA: Jossey-Bass.

Zechmeister, E., & Nyberg, S. (1982). *Human memory: An introduction to research and theory*. Monterey, CA: Brooks/Cole.

Zemke, R., & Kramlinger, T. (1982). *Figuring things out*. Reading, MA: Addison-Wesley.

About the Authors

Wellesley R. Foshay is vice president for instructional design and cognitive learning for PLATO Learning, Inc., makers of the PLATO® computer-based learning resource. Dr. Foshay is responsible for PLATO's product designs, development methodology, and internal instructional design training, as well as evaluation of PLATO's instructional effectiveness. His background includes faculty positions at the high school and university levels, as well as over eighteen years' experience in corporate technology-based training. His doctorate is in instructional design from Indiana University. He has contributed over fifty major articles to research journals and books on a wide variety of topics in training, technology, and education and speaks frequently before educators and trainers worldwide. He currently serves on the editorial boards of three research journals and has served on the boards of directors of the International Society for Performance Improvement and the International Board of Standards for Training, Performance and Instruction, as well as a national committee that develops standards for training and education under the ISO 9000 system. He received an honorary Certified Performance Technologist from ISPI.

Dr. Kenneth H. Silber has been contributing to the instructional design field since its inception almost forty years ago. Dr. Silber is associate professor of educational technology research and assessment at Northern Illinois University, where he teaches human performance technology and instructional design. He is also president of Silber Performance Consulting, a performance consulting firm specializing in analysis, design, and evaluation of instructional and other performance improvement interventions (www.silberperformance.com).

Dr. Silber is a life member and past president of CISPI. He has been an external consultant with Hale Associates, an internal ID practitioner in the business sector, with Amoco, Applied Learning (ASI/Deltak), and AT&T, and has worked in academia as university professor of instructional technology at Governors' State University. He also has extensive experience in the not-for-profit sector and is a nationally recognized author and professional leader. He has co-authored three books, including IBSTPI's *Instructional Design Competencies: The Standards.* He was also series editor for ISPI's *From Training to Performance in the 21st Century* book series. Dr. Silber also started and edited the *Journal of Instructional Development.* He holds a Ph.D. and an M.A. in instructional technology, with a minor in educational psychology, from the University of Southern California. He was the thirty-first person to receive ISPI's Certified Performance Technologist designation.

Dr. Michael Stelnicki is a professor and head of the human performance and training (HPT) graduate program at Governors State University. Dr. Stelnicki co-founded the HPT program nearly thirty years ago. This business-oriented masters' program includes intensive training in instructional design, classroom-training techniques, scriptwriting for training products, and instructional message design. Dr. Stelnicki is a long-time contributor to local and international professional organizations through serving as a director of educational programs, making numerous presentations, and leading workshops at conferences and local meetings. In addition, he consults with large and small companies in the areas of instructional and message design and performance enhancement. Dr. Stelnicki earned a B.A. degree in psychology and English at DePaul University, an M.A. in radio and television from Northwestern University's School of Speech, and his doctorate in educational technology from Northern Illinois University. He has worked as a journalist, psychology instructor, instructional television producer/director, and consultant to business and industry.

Index

A

Algorithms, 214

Anderson, J. R., 196, 214

Attention: applied to beginning of lesson, 42–43; described, 24, 25, 40*fig*; sample scenario on applying, 46, 47*fig*; teaching facts using, 68

Ausubel, D., 51

AutoRent: description of, 35; organizational level of performance, 137*fig*; performance improvement interventions for, 36

AutoRent employees: assimilating new/ existing knowledge, 107, 160, 161, 162; assimilating new/existing knowledge of, 71–72; factual knowledge of, 66; objective for teaching facts to, 71; organizing procedural information for, 51, 53*fig*, 54, 59*fig*, 60–61*fig*; providing feedback to, 73; Rental Car Fact Sheet for, 70*fig*; scenario applying attention, WIIFM, YCDI to, 46–47*fig*; scenario of using lesson elements to teach facts at,

68; strengthening knowledge to memory of, 72–73, 108, 109; summarizing structure of content for, 73; teaching ill-structured problem-solving procedures to, 135–136

AutoRent training problems: described, 35, 42; involving concepts, 80; lack of troubleshooting skills, 152

AutoRent's Customer Satisfaction Course, 104*fig*

AutoRent's Problem Resolution Model, 103*fig*

Avoiding lesson redundancy, 171–172

B

Bednar, A., 196

Behavioral approach: comparing cognitive and, 195–198*fig*; described, 10–11

Behaviorism, 195

Best practice. *See* ID (instructional design) best practice

"Brain power," 217

C

Carey, L., 3, 16, 191

Chunking: described, 13; for organizing new information, 26, 54–56, 62

Clark, R. C., 34

Cognitive approach: comparing behavioral and, 195–198*fig*; on how learning occurs, 11–14; to instructional design (ID), 10–11; purpose of, 195; structure of content in, 8*fig*; turned into "best practice" techniques, 1–2. *See also* ID (instructional design); Lesson design

Cognitive coaching, 217

Cognitive load: described, 217; management of, 171; problem formats which increase, 229, 231

Cognitive Training Model: benefits of using new, 24; compared to Gagne's nine events of instruction, 30–31, 231; how to read, 28–30; how to use, 31–32; illustration of, 22*fig*; information to recall/relate to, 23; learner tasks/lesson elements, 24–28,

How to Use the CD-ROM

SYSTEM REQUIREMENTS

Windows PC

- 486 or Pentium processor-based personal computer
- Microsoft Windows 95/98/2000 or Windows NT 3.51 or later
- Minimum RAM: 16 MB for Windows 95 and NT
- Available space on hard disk: 8 MB Windows 95 and NT
- 2X speed CD-ROM drive or faster

Netscape 3.0 or higher browser or MS Internet Explorer 3.0 or higher

NOTE: This CD requires Netscape 3.0 or MS Internet Explorer 3.0 or higher. You can download these products using the links on the CD-ROM Help Page.

GETTING STARTED

Insert the CD-ROM into your drive. The CD-ROM will usually launch automatically. If it does not, click on the CD-ROM drive on your computer to launch. You will see an opening page. You can click on this page or wait for it to fade to the Copyright Page. After you click to agree to the terms of the Copyright Page, the Home Page will appear.

MOVING AROUND

Use the buttons at the left of each screen or the underlined text at the bottom of each screen to move among the menu pages. To view a document listed on one of the menu pages, simply click on the name of the document. To quit a document at any time, click the box at the upper right-hand corner of the screen.

Use the scrollbar at the right of the screen to scroll up and down each page.

To quit the CD-ROM, you can click the Quit option at the bottom of each menu page, hit Control-Q, or click the box at the upper right-hand corner of the screen.

TO DOWNLOAD DOCUMENTS

Open the document you wish to download. Under the File pulldown menu, choose Save As. Save the document onto your hard drive with a different name. It is important to use a different name, otherwise the document may remain a read-only file.

You can also click on your CD drive in Windows Explorer and select a document to copy it to your hard drive and rename it.

IN CASE OF TROUBLE

If you experience difficulty using this CD-ROM, please follow these steps:

1. Make sure your hardware and systems configurations conform to the systems requirements noted under "Systems Requirements" above.

2. Review the installation procedure for your type of hardware and operating system. It is possible to reinstall the software if necessary.

3. You may call Jossey-Bass/Pfeiffer Customer Care at (800) 956-7739 between the hours of 8 A.M. and 5 P.M. Eastern Standard Time, and ask for Jossey-Bass/Pfeiffer Technical Support. It is also possible to contact Technical Support by e-mail at *techsupport@JosseyBass.com.*

Please have the following information available:

• Type of computer and operating system

• Version of Windows being used

• Any error messages displayed

• Complete description of the problem.

(It is best if you are sitting at your computer when making the call.)